Acce**lerating**
Social Change

Impacting Our World While Transforming Ourselves

Luigi Morelli

ACCELERATING SOCIAL CHANGE
IMPACTING OUR WORLD WHILE TRANSFORMING OURSELVES

Editing: Kristine Hunt
Graphics: Jaye Marsh and Ella Lapointe

iUniverse books may be ordered through booksellers or by contacting:

iUniverse
1663 Liberty Drive
Bloomington, IN 47403
www.iuniverse.com
844-349-9409

ISBN: 978-1-6632-3096-6 (sc)
ISBN: 978-1-6632-3097-3 (e)

Print information available on the last page.

iUniverse rev. date: 10/30/2021

Contents

Introduction vii
  - Two Houses viii
  - Paradigms as Leverages for Change xi
  - Prevailing Paradigm/Future Paradigms xiv
  - How to Read This Book xvii
  - My Own Journey xviii
  - What Will This Book Address? xx

Chapter 1: One Example of Status Quo, Three Examples of Change 1
  - I. Free Market and the Food System: The Example of Corn 2
  - II. Trisector Logic in the Food System: Community Supported Agriculture 18
  - III. Multi-Stakeholder Logic in the Food System 22
  - IV. Multiscale Logic: Food Policy Councils/Networks 27
  - In Conclusion: A Quick Comparison 31

Chapter 2: Trisector Logic 35
  - Balance versus Predominance 37
  - Holistic Aspects 42
  - Sectors and Drives 45
  - Sectoral/Societal Learning in Trisector Partnerships 48
  - Trisector Partnerships: Summing up 53
  - Cultural Power 54
  - From Either/Or to Both/And Thinking 59
  - Rethinking Tripolar Society 65
  - Community Supported Agriculture 80
  - Resources 97

Chapter 3: Multi-Stakeholder Processes 103

- A Defining Moment 104
- Tapping into Collective Wisdom 105
- Extraordinary Conversations: The Universal U 106
- Going Through the U 108
- The Quintessential Process of Decision Making...........111
- Creating a New Way of Relating..............................113
- The Breadth of Social Technology 114
- Consensus Decision Making...................................115
- World Café..122
- Future Search 131
- Multi-stakeholder Logic: Summing Up 139
- Social Processes and Social Forms 140
- At the Intersection of Social Processes and Social Forms:
  Sociocracy...141
- Resources..152

Chapter 4: Multiscale Logic: Emergence and Self-Organizing ... 157

- Emergence and Complexity 159
- Spontaneous Emergence: Buurtzorg; Keep It Simple.....161
- Emergence at the Level of a Nation: Horizontalism.......169
- Allowing Emergence: Holacracy.............................178
- Socially Generative Networks 187
- The Paradigm Shift Beyond Top Down or Bottom Up.....215
- Resources..218

In Conclusion 221

- Reviewing the Whole...222
- Building a New Culture...224
- Expanding Our Horizons by Embracing the Three
  Paradigms 227
- Conjugating the Three Paradigms for More Effective
  Social Change 227
- Listening to the Future...230

Bibliography 231

Introduction

There are no cheap tickets to mastery. You have to work hard at it, whether that means rigorously analyzing a system or rigorously casting off your own paradigms and throwing yourself into the humility of not-knowing. In the end, it seems that mastery has less to do with pushing leverage points than it does with strategically, profoundly, madly, letting go.

—Donella Meadows

Construction on the new house is already well underway. The old house will fall on its own; instead of tearing it down, let's redirect our precious energy toward reinforcing the new structures. The old house can serve our transition to the new one.

—Tracy Kunkler

AMERICA, I BELIEVE, NOT SO differently from many other countries in the world, stands at a crossroads. Trump's government has enshrined denial to the level of a national policy: denials of the environmental crisis and of climate change; denial of human dignity, of the most elemental human values. Denial after denial, down to losing the sense and meaning of the word *denial*. A reality of denial, if that were possible. If it were only for these trends we would be spiraling down to destruction in an irreversible fashion.

And yet there are other forces, equally strong. I have found this reality articulated from yet other angles than that of the present work in two examples. Both of these come from as late as 2018.

Two Houses

Thomas L. Friedman asserts, "If you want to be an optimist about America, stand on your head. The country looks so much better from the bottom up."[1] In his article he follows the fate of cities trying to counter economic and civil decline without the help of state and federal interventions. He looks closely at the development of "complex adaptive coalitions" in various American cities, bringing together business leaders, philanthropists, social visionaries and innovators, nonprofit leaders, educators, and local government in order to advance common interests and counter national American polarization and paralysis. The fate of American cities, it seems, depends much more upon the possibility of finding this common will and building exceptional conditions of trust among motivated individuals than on what the initial objective economic conditions may be.

James Fallows, writing for *The Atlantic* in May 2018 conveys his experience of traveling one year through small American towns, particularly the most economically depressed.[2] He writes about contradictory and coexisting layers of reality. On one hand there is no denying the downward trends in national politics, the failures of the health system, the plight of economically depressed cities, the polarization around immigration, to name just a few.

Relying on extended first-hand experience, he reports that while Americans see little light at the end of the tunnel in national politics, their outlook is almost the reverse at the local level: at that level issues like immigration are not perceived as strongly, even in conservative cities. He notices that younger generations are consciously returning in numbers to their small towns of origin to make a difference; community colleges are

---

[1] Thomas L. Friedman, July 3, 2018, "Where American Politics Can Still Work: From the Bottom Up." https://www.openpolitics.com/links/where-american-politics-can-still-work-from-the-bottom-up/.

[2] James Fallow, "The Reinvention of America," *The Atlantic*, May 2018, https://www.theatlantic.com/magazine/archive/2018/05/reinventing-america/556856/.

focusing resources on their regional economies; downtown revitalization efforts are a growing reality; land conservation efforts are on the rise, even as the complete opposite takes place nationally; city after city in half of the country is aligned with the Paris climate goals that the Trump administration has denied; informal networks are naturally emerging toward common goals, though they may lack the full picture of what other like-minded groups are doing.

The result of his observations is confirmed by recent polls that Fallows quotes. The Pew Research Center periodically conducts polls about national problems that most concern Americans. Matters of immigration rarely emerged in the top five in the five years previous to Trump's election. Neither were things all that different six months after: two-thirds of Americans felt comfortable with the level of immigration or thought it could go up. During the 2016 primaries, a Gallup poll commissioned by *The Atlantic* and the Aspen Institute highlighted the split between local and national politics. While 64 percent of interviewees were pessimistic about where the nation is heading, two-thirds expressed satisfaction about their own financial situation; 85 percent were from somewhat to fully satisfied with where they were in their present life. Other polls over the last 6 years have highlighted that most Americans have little faith in what the nation as a whole is doing but see positively what is happening in their own communities.

The journey of this book started likewise with an injection of hope. It started when I attended a conference called Frontiers of Democracy in June 2016. The annual conference explores ways to improve our democratic discourse, or to set it on other foundations. The first proposition is the one most strongly articulated; the other is present alongside in a creative dialogue. I knew I was coming for the second one, and I quickly connected with three individuals who work on this field: Tom Atlee, whose work on *Empowering Public Wisdom* had left an imprint on my thinking; Tracy Kunkler, who has expanded to new levels the work with sociocracy and has worked with facilitation, governance, and socially generative networks; and Steve Waddell, whose books occupy an important part in this exploration.

I left the conference energized, and for 18 months I collaborated in the mapping of "socially generative networks" collaborating across two or three sectors—government, business, and civil society. My horizons enlarged, and I started to recognize a "frontier of democracy" and source of hope for the social future. This played in contrast to my views concerning the dissonance and cacophony that is our national discourse. So yes, there is a tremendously impactful discourse of denial, and on the other hand waves after waves of renewal, myriads of surprising entrepreneurs and visionaries in many places across the land who are strong voices of innovation. Each one of these in isolation may not amount to much, but all of them in unison may create a powerful concert.

One image started to guide my path: the houses that we want to inhabit. The tone for this was set by the dynamic of the dialogue at the Frontiers of Democracy. It was reinforced by reading from Tracy's work. We are at a crossroads: our old house is crumbling, and most of us know it or feel it. However, that's not all of the truth. A new house is being built alongside, and those who are building its new parts may not know each other, nor see the whole picture. While shoring up the old house is undeniably important, this book is all about building the new house, seeing the emerging reality as fully as possible and rendering it more approachable both conceptually and practically.

Armed with this inspiration, I decided to take the road and meet many of these innovations and innovators on a four-month road trip to targeted areas: New England (mostly Rhode Island and Vermont) and the Midwest (mostly Minnesota and Wisconsin) to look at innovations in the fields of the food system, and to a minor extent in the energy system and climate change field. I started with some set goals, and adapted to others. As I expected I was inspired by the variety and strengths of the initiatives I saw, though I realized that I was partly naïve in expecting to gather enough inside information about each and every one.

I nevertheless managed to test all the hypotheses I was interested in, and to generate insight that would allow me to string together ideas, people, and initiatives. The stimulating dialogue and exchange of views gave weight and nuance to the ideas I was started to formulate. I could start to see the larger patterns at work. And most of all I asked myself how this could be put together and offered to a reader.

Along the way I was offering a presentation of my growing perceptions of the paradigms of change that can counter the prevailing predicament and act as levers for change. This was an effective tool for dialogue that I would either discuss as a slide show or send out via email. On one hand it allowed me to evolve what I will present below, and on the other it made me think about the format of the book. This is how I resolved to write a primer about a large field of inquiry. As such, it is divided in three parts (chapters 2 to 4), and the reader can go through these according to her interest. Each paradigm can be read separately from the others, though they are written in a sequence that is also in itself organic. And each of the three main sections is no more than an introduction: resources may actually be the most important part of the work after the chapter itself and should allow you to have a bird's-eye view and some significant vignettes of each field.

Paradigms as Leverages for Change

Paradigms are somehow worlds in themselves, worlds in which we either live or could live in. We presently are part of one paradigm, a worldview about which we can form some judgments when we raise our perspectives toward embracing all its aspects, or as many of them as possible. By managing to gain some distance, with effort we can formulate how the paradigm operates, what are its assumptions and ground rules, whether it fulfills the goals it pursues, and so on.

This book approaches other paradigms than the prevailing ones when it comes to social change. It looks at paradigms as leverage points for social change. Why more than one paradigm? Wouldn't it be sufficient to predicate that one paradigm is the solution and the next destination? As a researcher and author, but first of all as an individual participating within my means in the creation of a new social reality, I have not set out to find paradigms. They have come my way, and naturally I did not see them at first. It is only through immersion in a paradigm that something surfaces into consciousness, and that I start to realize that I live between paradigms and can choose which one fits me best, and which one has the greatest potential to more fully embrace reality and create new, more life-fulfilling scenarios. Ultimately the validity of a paradigm lies in how faithfully it embraces and encompasses some part of our given reality. Because, ideally a paradigm is a fuller way of relating to reality around us, acting from an understanding of it offers us a powerful leverage point to more effectively effect social change.

However, there is a problem, or a challenge! A paradigm cannot be given an easy definition, nor be used in the spirit of a manifesto, a quick solution, a political platform. In fact the reverse is true. At first, and even for a long time, it is not possible to perceive the reality of a paradigm. To know a paradigm is to grow into it, to be *altered and made new* by it. When the reality of a paradigm fully penetrates our own inner world, we become aware of a before and an after, and of a gap between the two. The paradigm in which I live now—better said *predominantly live in* now—cannot be referred to in terms of what I knew before. In describing a new paradigm I enter into a collision course with the prevailing paradigm, from which I have to borrow words and usual terms of reference in order to portray what is essentially different. An alternative lies in looking for examples, analogies, and a contemplation of the results of embracing another paradigm. In essence, unless I want to take an epistemological or philosophical approach, I need to take a pragmatic approach to a larger world of ideas or experiences. This will be my choice.

Parts of what I will offer will sound self-evident to those who have lived and explored a given paradigm. Others will find that something of the paradigm is already known and/or speaks to them, either because they have been exposed to it, or because we could say they are "naturals." Other paradigms will simply not approach their horizon of experience.

So how do I propose to move into this ever-shifting territory? I will explore the lay of the land with stories, analogies, and a very basic field exploration before directing the reader to the resources that will allow her to accomplish her own paradigm shift. For the purpose of this book I will start by looking at the food system: what it looks like under the present paradigm and what new directions future-looking paradigms are mapping out. Occasionally I will offer examples from other fields as well.

All throughout the book I will compare a paradigm to an iceberg. A paradigm makes itself visible through what comes to the surface in our present culture. Much of it remains hidden as potential yet untapped. The overview I will offer will be like exploring the tip of the iceberg: what is most visible. Through some examples I will sound the depths of the iceberg in a few particular spots and direct you to the whole iceberg if you intend to explore it further.

I will start with some general considerations. We don't need to encompass and understand a paradigm to walk toward it. But we do need to practice with discipline new ways of seeing / thinking / relating / connecting / operating / being in order to make the new reality perceptible over time.

An example from my life: I took on Nonviolent Communication (NVC) with extensive training and practice especially over the first five to six years of complete immersion. NVC was already satisfying in terms of a tool/method that allowed me greater expression of self-disclosure, empathy and self-connection in my life. It allowed me and still allows me to better respond to life challenges and better meet my needs.

It could have continued to be a "method," except that every now and then some experience stood out from the routine of all other little experiences. I was seeing that at those moments the practice was allowing me to pierce behind the veil of everyday experience, as it were. When it came time to express it to myself and put it into words, I could awkwardly say that I had what amounted to a spiritual experience, no matter how faint that may be, that I pierced through a veil of everyday reality into something else. I had in fact no doubt that the new experience had led me to something more real than what I normally perceive. It became a beacon, an indicator of what is possible. What I can say for myself I have often also heard from others in very similar terms; thus I knew it wasn't just an arbitrary, subjective experience.

Over the years it became less and less important to impart to people that I practice NVC; I would actually perceive this as a stereotype. Rather I would say that I prize the consciousness for which NVC has opened the door, and that is where I want to live rather than in the practice of the NVC method alone. This is how I can put it into words. I know of many others who express this inner reality in different, though very convergent ways. They have come to similar conclusions from tools other than NVC. We know the same level of reality and we each see various facets of it, though I would dare say only some facets of it. When we all express what these facets are, we may come to a fuller articulation of the paradigm and what degree of change it creates in our lives.

In essence, to return to my example, I know that there is another way of being than what I was used to relating to that gives me deeper satisfaction and understanding of myself and other fellow human beings. I know that I have no reason to revert to the old paradigm in which I experienced separation and alienation to a high degree. Soberly speaking, I still live between the two paradigms but am more and more anchored in the new. I daresay I will never cease this dialogue and tension in my lifetime.

I encountered the reality of the paradigm through NVC, but NVC is not the paradigm. What I have achieved through NVC others have reached through a multitude of other practices. When we talk to each other we can recognize the bedrock of truth from which we can all have parallel and similar experiences. When it comes to expressing the bedrock of the paradigm, we all encounter the limitations of prevailing words, expressions, and ideas from which we try to express that which is different and new.

Prevailing Paradigm/Future Paradigms

We live in a time of great evolutionary potential as well as escalating challenges. Trailblazers are first intuiting, then offering the world new ways forward. Those who seek will hear right and left about new territory charted into the unknown, of new ways to confront seemingly intractable problems. Below are a few examples just within the food system.

In Burkina Faso, a man by the name of Yacouba Sawadogo has found ways to reclaim land from the advancing desert in the Sahel region.[3] Before his ideas took root, people thought he was crazy. The Tigrai region of northern Ethiopia is reclaiming hundreds of square miles that seemed lost to desertification. A man by the name of Aba Hawi, and many other organizations, have played a pivotal role.[4] Now the effort is spreading over the whole of Ethiopia and even beyond. Aba Hawi too was branded crazy and mistreated before his ideas and hopes gained ground. Before then the world knew of the work of Wangari Maathai in reforesting Kenya, so much so that she received a Nobel Prize. Through the Green Belt Movement, which she helped start, Kenya has been reforested on a large scale.[5] Wangari deeply embraced her own culture, but also threw it some unique challenges.

---

[3] See the documentary: *The Man Who Stopped the Desert,* directed by Mark Dodd at http://www.1080films.co.uk/Yacoubamovie/

[4] See *Ethiopia Rising: Red Terror to Green Revolution,* documentary directed by Mark Dodd at https://www.imdb.com/title/tt5089398/. It follows the story of the phenomenal transformation of a nation told through the experience of one man, Aba Hawi.

[5] For an overview of Wangari Maathai's life and the work of the Green Belt Movement see *Taking Root: the Vision of Wangari Maathai,* directed by Lisa Merton and Alan Dater at http://takingrootfilm.com/.

For a time, as a woman who loudly challenged culture and regime, she was the laughing stock of Kenyan elites and large majorities in Kenya who bought into their message. That too passed. The community of Gaviotas, in western Colombia, has found ways to reclaim the rather infertile llanos and revert them to the original tropical forest from which they came.[6] What seemed an irreversible natural process—the loss of the rain forest—can now be reversed. These are few examples among a multitude.

And yes, for all of the above, the good I mention goes hand in hand with obvious downward trends, continuing and even accelerating the destruction of the past. Who will win, there is no way to tell. Those who engage in this epochal struggle don't even ask the question. They just play their part, moved somewhere deep inside by a quiet hope that they have wrested something from the forces of destruction, within and outside of themselves.

Since the fifteenth century the European West and then North America have inaugurated the paradigm that accompanied the scientific revolution. It was marked by the empirical and deterministic approach to knowledge—a change oh so necessary, since it has emancipated the individual from all tradition, from all dogma and habits of the past, and allowed the expression of full individuality, at least potentially. All individuals who speak against this paradigm today, those like Aba Hawi, Yacouba Sawadogo, Wangari Maathai, and Allan Savory, are almost invariably those who, even while respecting them, break away from all those traditions of the past that stifle the future; who are able to stand as one person against all when necessary; who are willing to be maligned before receiving recognition, not for themselves, but for what they have to offer. They have benefited from being modern human beings, fully emancipated from tradition.

The paradigm of the past is one of separation. It can be expressed in terms of a spectator consciousness. By separating, we are able to be individuals against all odds; able to offer something different from what all the past ideas have offered to humanity. Because it is a spectator consciousness, we can so detach ourselves from nature and our fellow human beings that potentially, if we so choose, nothing matters any longer. Herein lies the possibility of destruction that we witness on so many levels and on such a large scale.

The present paradigm predicates that what is true is only that which can be apprehended through analytical thinking, through indirect

---

[6] For a story of Gaviotas see *Gaviotas: A Village to Reinvent the World* by Alan Weisman.

observation (microscope, telescope, spectro-analysis, etc.) and quantitative measurement. Quantity is the norm. Humanity has collectively lost sight of qualities and of a more synthetic/holistic way of thinking, relating, and acting. By *quality* I mean such things as what we can learn from colors and forms and what they express of plant or animal nature, gestures such as we can find them in the movements of water or in the tides, patterns of relation both in the natural world and in the social world, and so on. All of these things reach us though the senses, but unlike everything else of this nature, they are discarded from the scientific method.

We could say that the scientific revolution has set the trend for what can be characterized as dualistic thinking: black and white, right and wrong, good or bad, more or less, yes or no, 1 or 0 of binary computer language, and so forth. All of these criteria can be quantified. While this thinking emancipates, it also sows in itself the forces of isolation and destruction because it originates from a one-sided perspective, that of quantity. By excluding quality it is constantly at war with self and world. Nature all around us does not know of dualistic patterns, nor does our mind or soul. Neither one can be so simplistically explored and understood. In the final analysis, we seem to stand powerless in front of the enigmas and riddles of the human being and of nature, because so much depends on those qualities that we leave out of the equation and that mean so much in the expression of every living being.

The forces in nature cannot be understood through dualism but rather through a wholistic gymnastics of yin and yang as traditional cultures intuitively knew. In the living world growth holds the balance with decay, expansion with contraction, night with day, winter with summer, anabolism with catabolism, photosynthesis with respiration, plant with animal. Problems in nature arise when there is imbalance. The forces at work in our souls/minds are likewise forces that hold each other in balance: attraction and repulsion, love and hate, depression and mania, wakefulness and sleep, introversion and extroversion, individualistic and communal, and so on. Problems arise when one pole loses the balancing power of the other.

It has often been pointed out that science has gone awry because it has been used for selfish purposes. It can be argued that science itself has set in motion the larger, inherent limitations of exclusively dualistic thinking. But science also has in itself the capacity to overcome, to break through to a more living understanding of world and self. Ultimately we need an enlarged scientific perspective, not a return to pre-scientific worldviews. It is the lot of the modern human being of wanting to act because he understands, no longer because he has been told or he blindly believes.

The paradigms we will present here set the tone for breaking beyond dualism, while retaining the scientific mindset; they are paradigms that move away from either/or to both/and, from "thinking in twos" to "thinking in threes." This is the great watershed of our time, which is articulated in many ways.

By the same token the new paradigms are not paradigms of opposition, not even to the paradigms of the present. They seek to include and transcend. That is the greatest strength of the paradigms of social change when they are fully practiced and internalized. It is by transcending and including that what look like unsurmountable obstacles become approachable. The greatest leverage point for the problems of the present is neither inward nor outward. It is both. It is a continuous dialogue between self and world. Through what others have made their own, we can borrow the tools they have generated and see their effects in the world. Conversely, through the effects of this work we can strengthen our consciousness and better use the tools. When we start to align with powerful inner forces, we express ourselves in the world in ways that do not oppose and say no; instead they say yes and invite the new from unforeseen leverage points. They no longer oppose the world because they no longer fear it, or at least don't fear it as much.

How to Read This Book

The paradigms we will approach are powerful antidotes and exacting masters. They require our full attention and participation. We cannot quietly observe them from the outside; if we do so, we cannot understand them and let them touch us and change us. Each of the three paradigms explored here can require our life's attention; each can set us on a life-changing path to the end of our days. This obviously means that I who am presenting these paradigms could not possibly master them. In fact I know that I have differing degrees of penetration and embodiment, so to speak; for each aspect that I present I know of others who can do it far better than I. For this very reason I intend to continue walking my talk and integrating them in my life journey as best I can, and without illusions. And for this reason the book will be nothing more than a primer.

In the first part of the book we will look at prevailing paradigm(s) of the present and where they lead us. Then I will offer a vista in three different directions with succinct examples (chapters 2 to 4). For this purpose I will utilize the food system as a yardstick of contrast/comparison. In keeping with the analogy offered earlier on, the examples are only the tip of the iceberg. They are meant to offer food for thought. In fact I invite the reader at the end of the exploration to gage her own reactions to each of the paradigms. Ask yourselves: Which one speaks the most to me? To which one do I relate more from experience, from character and temperament? To which other one do I feel attracted? To which one do I feel antipathy and resistance?

In each of the three chapters I will explore the larger expression of the paradigm, but still as it were only probing at depth in only some points of the iceberg. Through examples I will try to round off an exploration that lends weight to the inner coherence of the paradigm. From there I will direct the reader to resources that explore the paradigm in depth; an invitation for a course of study and practice that can take each one of us on a long journey.

Finally I will explore the open territory of what it means to practice the three paradigms, collectively rather than separately, and bring them to cross-pollinate and fructify efforts for social change.

My Own Journey

If paradigms are whole worlds in themselves and if they take time to assimilate and internalize, how could one person possibly be guiding you into such vast territories? The answer lies at two levels. First of all I am guiding you to only a few areas of the icebergs, and for that I have enough of a field overview. Second, I want to qualify my answer and explain my connection with each field of experience.

I have already offered an important piece of my journey with the deepening of the practice of Nonviolent Communication. But the first paradigm came under my field of scrutiny already thirty-five years ago. It met me under the name of "social threefolding" and the ideas of Rudolf Steiner. I delved into it wholeheartedly, but my strong political persuasions at the time prevented me from fully entering it. Somehow I was holding to the past and the usual and could not make room for the new because it required a leap and a discontinuity. I had read about these ideas, in fact read as much as I could. My enthusiasm did not allow me to break through at the speed I wished.

Why this delay, you may wonder? I know of other people who could take these ideas in much more straightforward fashion. Well, after some seven or eight years I approached anew the thoughts of this great thinker and first of all those most accessible to the public. This time I could let them touch me more deeply. Ever since then they have been organically growing, until I can say I have made them my own to a good degree. In the intervening years I have also seen how these lively and living ideas sprout right and left, so to speak, independently from the one who articulated them first, and for each thinker or practitioner independently from the other thinkers or schools of thought. And I have only inquired about them in this continent, mind you! It seems that these ideas are organic and they sort of impregnate the air we breathe.

The second paradigm entered my life wholeheartedly from very early on. It met me first in my mid-twenties when I entered the practice of men's groups and support groups, practices like Jungian dream work and interpretation, the Destiny Learning of Coenraad van Houten first and Nonviolent Communication later. I had embraced the work of Bert Hellinger in between and what came through Hospice. I called this the field of *experiential spirituality*.[7] In between I also took a mastery in Technology of Participation, dabbled into Future Search and World Café, Dynamic Facilitation and Conversation Cafes and Consensus Decision-Making. It was only through the work of Otto Scharmer, as it is formulated in Theory U, that I realized together with other people in the field that I was dealing with a paradigm. Here even though all of the methodology had come naturally to me and I could not get enough of it, it was only much later that I could give a name to the paradigm that I most often recognize and operate from.

Finally, the third paradigm I will refer to came to me from various horizons and more fully in the last three years, through an in-depth immersion. First I timidly met the ideas coming from Argentina's Horizontalism some eleven or twelve years ago, then the ideas about self-organizing expressed in some of

---

[7] Luigi Morelli, *A Revolution of Hope*, see chapter 6.

the chapters explored by Frederic Laloux's *Reinventing Organizations*. I was deeply immersed in learning about sociocracy, aka dynamic governance, and in rendering it operational at the community level when this new aspect lit up at the Boston conference that I mentioned.

At first the field itself eluded my grasp. I was not sure I was doing what I was meant to do. The idea itself of what we called "multi-sector, multi-stakeholder, multi-scale networks" was hard to encompass in my thinking or level of experience. When it finally hit me after trial and error, I realized it was a new goldmine. I absorbed everything I could from people with more experience, and I avidly read the few books on the topic that are available at present. The more I read, the more I got inspired. So much so that I launched on a four-month road trip to explore it further. Only toward the end of the journey could I start to realize what united all the various threads I had met previously. In retrospect the idea that got me going may have seemed naïve to many, myself included. The results, however, started to trickle in, and I could test the hypotheses I wanted to firm up in my mind. Thus, of all the paradigms this is the newest one, and also the one that is biographically fresher. It is the one about which I remain most actively curious.

What Will This Book Address?

The breakdown of societal safety nets, the inability of national governments to take care of the commons, the sheer complexity of multilayered issues such as climate change, and how these affect all other endeavors mean that most of the important issues we need to confront at present are so complex that they defy our understanding, or the understanding of any single group of stakeholders. The first step in this exploration is to realize the dimension of problems that we want to tackle. It is useful to place the situation within a visual context (Figure 1). We can distinguish these:

- "Simple" realities are those that we can sense, categorize, and respond to with best practices.
- The "complicated" level of reality can be thoroughly analyzed, as in the case of some piece of sophisticated machinery, and addressed with sets of strategies.

- In the "complex" systems we cannot predict how parts will interact with each other, and interactions are non-linear. It is not possible to discern root causes or act from single control mechanisms.
- Finally, "chaotic" situations (e.g., emerging after natural or manmade disasters) can be approached through the parts that respond as complicated systems, then resort to the approach of complex systems, outlined above.

The last two levels introduce us to a qualitative shift, a discontinuity from the previous two levels. At present more and more of our challenges come from here, but we still want to address and act upon them as if they were complicated at most.

How can we address complex or chaotic situations and bring at the same time deep change? We can characterize progressive stages of change as:

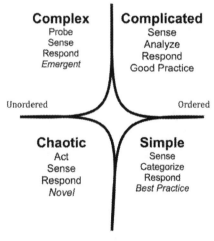

Figure 1: four types of systems and strategies
(source: Steve Waddell, *Change for the Audacious*, 21)

- incremental change (variations within a given context)
- reform (breakthroughs obtained through activism and political action)
- transformation that requires what Otto Scharmer calls "listening to the future that wants to emerge."

Incremental changes will be effective with simple systems. Reform will work with complicated systems once they have been fully understood. To enter transformational pathways, we need to operate away from the control and command paradigm to one of "sense and respond": by foregoing the illusion of predictability, creating multitudes of paths and alternatives that we can explore and with which we can experiment, and associating the experiences with rapid cycles of learning that allow to map out further steps. Most of all we need to engage in out-of-the-ordinary approaches.

This book follows only the challenge of complex systems and consequently the path of transformation: a both/and that encompasses political reform but does not take its departure from it. In the next chapter we will give examples of the problem and the alternatives. We will start with one major example in our national food system and contrast it with three short, succinct examples of possible alternatives. Welcome to the collective effort of building our new house alongside the old one.

Chapter 1

One Example of Status Quo, Three Examples of Change

Addiction is finding a quick and dirty solution to the symptom of the problem, which prevents or distracts one from the harder and longer-term task of solving the real problem.

—*Donella H. Meadows*

No one can define or measure justice, democracy, security, freedom, truth, or love. No one can define or measure any value. But if no one speaks up for them, if systems aren't designed to produce them, if we don't speak about them and point toward their presence or absence, they will cease to exist.

—*Donella H. Meadows*

LET'S TAKE A QUICK DIVE into new/emerging levels of social reality. Since these are the object of this book, here we will simply attempt to offer thumbnail sketches of a whole that cannot be subdivided in a simplistic way. Nevertheless, it is possible to offer significant vignettes and highlight the differences in a first attempt, before returning to the whole and its parts in more depth.

In the examples that follow we will use the food system as a yardstick, and see how it can be affected from various angles and perspectives. We will look at how to change the food system from a multisector, a multistakeholder, and a multiscale perspective in this order. But first let's have an extensive look at our current paradigm with an example that pervades our lives as Americans: corn. We will look at the present paradigm, then present the three tools that can accelerate social change and introduce new paradigms.

I. Free Market and the Food System: The Example of Corn

Modern economies live by and large under the aegis, or yoke, of neoliberalism. It is a paradigm that has overrun its course and obscured and defamed the original meaning the word *liberalism* had in Europe at its inception.

Classical Liberalism

In the nineteenth century the call for democracy and the emancipation of the individual from the state found its voice in liberalism, and two different nuances in German and English liberalism. It is also around the end of the nineteenth century that the newly coined expression "world economy" reflected something that already had taken root in the world. The two aspects of liberalism—the emancipation of the individual and the rise of the global dimension of the economy—were reflected in the two views of liberalism.

German liberalism came to the fore early in the nineteenth century and found its death knell in 1848 with the end of the liberal revolution and the rise of the authoritarian, paternalistic brand of the welfare state under Bismarck. What German Romanticism completed in the political realm was a view of the balance between the role of the state and the newly affirmed place of the individual. A seminal work that influenced a whole epoch was Wilhelm von Humboldt's *The Spheres and Duties of Government*. Here what is predicated is a role of government such that no hindrances are posed to the free unfolding of the individual; in other words, the necessary force that government needs to use to protect its citizens should not be used at the expense of the free expression of individual aspirations. Something similar had been articulated by Schiller in his *Letters on the Aesthetic Education of Man*, in which the author held the role of the politician as the highest expression of art in its balancing of freedom and necessity in working with living reality on a large scale.

British liberalism, as it was expressed by someone like Stuart Mill, still claimed continuity with Von Humboldt's ideas. However, the accent fell on the emancipation of economic activity from the sphere of government. And this finds its crowning in the one who is considered the father of capitalism, Adam Smith, who wrote the famous *The Wealth of Nations*.

A world economy in which precious resources, particularly those crucial to industry and manufacturing, can be extracted for the benefit of all is crucial at present to national economies. It is a reality of modern economic life that national economies are dependent on foreign resources and raw materials, which can be extracted or produced where their costs are lowest. With the division of labor that is the hallmark of global economy, resources can be exploited with the most effective use of labor and energy, potentially for the benefit of all. Conversely, isolationism at present can only lower living standards; economic warfare to protect national economies, with the corollary of unintended consequences and disruptions, becomes the sure avenue for military warfare. This is for the positive side of the ledger. Let us continue looking at the whole and where the problems arise.

Adam Smith and *The Wealth of Nations*

What limited Smith's perspective and consequently that of capitalism, and now neoliberalism, is the perspective of individual interest and profit as the engine for progress and wealth. We are now at the place in time in which we need to take a larger view of the economy, one that includes the earth as a living organism; and a larger view of economic interest, no longer that of the individual alone, but of stakeholders, communities, and nations. And all of this has to be done in a way that is mutual, fair, and completely inclusive and transparent. All interests need to sit at the table, included the interests of planet earth itself.

What was true of an incipient economy with individual players is no longer true in the midst of impersonal players or forces whose logic trespasses upon individual freedom and state sovereignty. Suffice to think of such powers as transnational corporations, with their budding and sprawling cartels and monopolies, financial holding companies, or information technology and artificial intelligence. Such is the force, presence, and impact of these agents as to render individual freedom and national sovereignty no more than empty slogans. And moreover, there are inherent contradictions when we look at Adam Smith's ideas as the foundational predicament of neoliberalism. This is what we want to explore at present, no longer classical liberalism. In fact, neoliberalism is no more than a tragic caricature of it.

Free Market Contradictions and Limitations

Free market theory holds that in perfectly and equally accessible market conditions—de facto hardly attainable—the price of a product or service will adjust itself in relation to its supply and demand. An abundant supply will bring down prices. Conversely, a low supply, causing high prices, will act as a motivation for higher competition and new supply on the market that will adjust the price downward. The forces of the market will reestablish balance. The optimal theory implies a perfect and equal access to market and to information on all sides.

Balance in the market that Adam Smith envisioned, and that neoliberalism still upholds, is reached by individuals pursuing their self-interest and consequently through competition. Governments ideally play the role of umpires in guaranteeing a level field for all competitors in the economy. A simple look at the facts of the matter articulates why this is hardly possible, first from a theoretical standpoint, then in the practice.

If we look at the market with its four main roles—producers of goods and services, financial institutions providing credit, traders and middlemen, consumers—each of them stands in relation to the others with different sets of expectations (see Figure 2).

The + and − signs in the graph indicate the expectations of each players: at the bottom of the figure, the producers expect to get more from their product; the middlemen want to bring the prices of products down; the producers want cheaper financial services; the bankers or financial institutions want higher returns on these, etc.[8]

---

[8] Nicanor Perlas, *Associative Economics: Responding to the Challenge of Elite Globalization* (Quezon City, Philippines: Center for Alternative Development Initiatives, 1997), 17.

Considering that self-interest is the number one motivator of the free market, there are no reasons for the individual players not to promote exactly their self-interest against the interest of others. In the agricultural market, agribusiness can acquire a competitive edge through massive investment in land and capital, forming monopolies and cartels. Through their combined market share they can dump their product on the market by selling at prices below the margin of profitability of small producers, drive them out of the market, and eventually buy their competitors off when they can only sell at rock bottom price. The traders, on the other hand, especially in developing countries, can bully and intimidate the small producers to sell at low prices and themselves sell back at high margins of profit. Small producers rarely have the means of knowing the market or of acting in concert against financial powers greater than theirs.

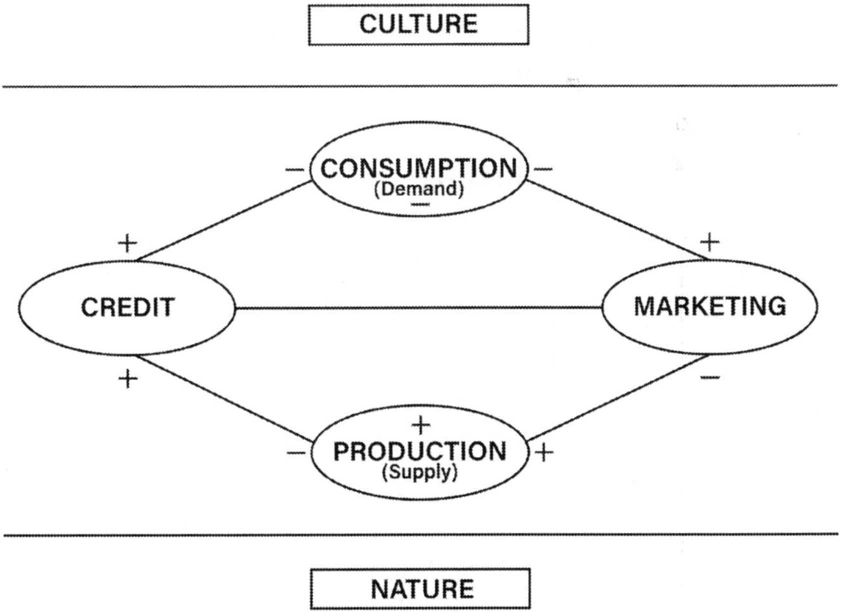

Figure 2: Market role expectations
(Source: Perlas, *Associative Economics*, 17).

Since the market does not factor in anything but short-term variables, the longer-term costs of doing business, such as the impact on environment, labor, health, or local culture, are externalized and de facto borne by nature and the larger community. These are constant, hidden subsidies to those who need them the least.

At the other end of the social ladder, small producers, operating with no safety nets and often indebted, have no other choice than working for the short term. Many land erosion problems worldwide derive from sheer necessity to survive, to sacrifice long-term subsistence for a short-term relief. The same farmers may even end up borrowing from those who are their creditors and traders, often under the condition that they sell the harvest back to the trader with all but very predictable consequences. What year after year, decade after decade, are described as the side effects of a system that can and should be perfected, are in effect systemic and ingrained mechanisms that assure continuation of the status quo. They are the logical consequence of the culture and implicit negative spiritual values of self-interest, competition, and race to the bottom.

An example of this plays a large role in the American food system and even beyond our borders. It illustrates how far we are from an idealized level field.

The American Food System and King Corn

Corn is native to this continent and is a truly amazing crop in terms of its biology and adaptability to a great range of climatic conditions. It was the staple upon which the Maya accomplished their cultural revolution.

Corn has come to dominate the American food system in ways hardly fully known to the average American. And part of this domination happens for good reasons. Corn is an amazing crop in terms of the amount of use one can get from the whole plant, its yield, the ease with which it can be stored or transformed, and lastly the variety of products its transformation can yield. It has been prized most of all for the ease with which it responds to mineral fertilization, that it hybridizes, that it adapts through genetic modification to culture with herbicides, and how its seed can be patented. It has long been the number one US crop, but not without a good amount of external help.

When we trace the path of corn into our bodies, Americans eat more of it in all its forms and derived products than their Mexican neighbors. Mexicans absorb corn in 40 percent of the calories in their food, mostly in the form of tortillas. Although Americans eat only 11 pounds of corn flour per year, based on carbon-13 measurements on hair or flesh we know that they actually consume more corn than their neighbors, both directly and indirectly through what makes its way into the livestock and from all other industrial corn-derived food products.[9] Much of what will be related here comes from the ground-breaking work of Michael Pollan, in his *The Omnivore's Dilemma*.

From corn we derive for our diets the following: high fructose corn syrup (HFCS), glucose syrup and maltodextrin, starch and modified starch, crystalline fructose, dextrose, ascorbic acid, lactic acid, lysine, maltose, MSG, polyols, xanthan gum, and more. These corn products in various combinations are thus present in sodas (almost 100 percent) coffee whitener, frozen yogurt, soups and snacks, cake mixes, frostings and gravy, ketchup, mayonnaise and mustard, hot dogs, margarine, bologna, shortening, salad dressings, twinkies, vitamins . . . more than a quarter of 45,000 items in an average supermarket contain corn-derived products.[10] The presence of corn products also extends to nonfood items: it is present in toothpastes and cosmetics, trash bags, cleaners, and coating on cardboard, among others.

Corn's Industrial Revolution

Corn has presided over a massive change of our landscapes. An average farm in Iowa in 1920 comprised horses, cattle, chickens, corn, hogs, apples, hay, oats, potatoes, cherries, wheat, plums, grapes, and pears; it was basically a closed and self-supporting system. With the introduction of chemical fertilizers in the 1950s and corn hybrids, all of this was gradually displaced in favor of a corn/soybean rotation. Corn is planted much more thickly than all other crops in a field and makes a high demand from the soil. For that reason, it is followed by soybeans, which naturally fix nitrogen. But due to illnesses in soy, in practice often corn often follows corn. Corn is considered the most efficient way for producing calories/energy, soy for producing protein. For good measure, fat in the form of oil can come from either crop.

Great parts of all the states of the Midwest and beyond, where the soil sustained a great diversified agriculture, have now become monotone landscapes of corn and soybean, and are to all practical extent what we can

---

[9] Michael Pollan, *The Omnivore's Dilemma: A Natural History of Four Meals* (New York: Penguin, 2006), 19.

[10] Pollan, *The Omnivore's Dilemma*, 19.

call food deserts. As an example, Iowa presently imports about 80 percent of its food.

What the above means for farming and the environment is a great separation of the manmade cycle of food from all ecological cycles: water, nutrients, and animal-plant integration, among others. Conservative estimates indicate that every bushel of corn requires the equivalent of 1/3 to 1/4 of a gallon of gas, or some 50 gallons of oil per acre of corn, in majority dedicated to tractor operations, fertilizing, harvesting, drying, and transportation. In the space of 60–70 years we have gone from more than 2 calories generated for calorie of energy invested in the 1920s to the 1940s to more than 1 calorie of energy invested for calorie of corn generated.[11] Moreover, what used to be a closed system, with the livestock generating the fertilizers to support the growth of the crops, has now turned into two growing problems.

Great amounts of synthetic fertilizers, often overused, evaporate, aggravating acid rain and entering the water streams and water table causing eutrophication of the waters, promoting growth of algae and choking out fish. On the other hand, we find pollution due to accumulation of manure from industrial livestock operations that farmers do not want to use due to all added chemicals. This has become a real problem on one hand, accompanied on the other with the growing use of fertilizers with diminishing returns on corn.

Corn's Extended "Ecosystem"

With corn become the king of crops, and with streams of production surpassing every possible immediate need, brand new outlets had to be engineered in the decades following the 1950s. Government programs were originally designed to limit corn production and support prices, thus also the farmers, during the New Deal. At present, ever more so since the Nixon administration that promoted subsidies, we have practically the reverse, growing production and lower prices.

Under the New Deal loans to the farmer were repaid relatively quickly, and they adjusted corn production downward. With what are now subsidies, the United States has practically removed any constraints from corn

---

[11] Pollan, *The Omnivore's Dilemma*, 45–46.

production. Maize was subsidized at the tune of $5 billion per year in the early 2000s, hardly for the benefit of the farmer but rather for the rest of the supply chain: livestock operations, agribusiness corporations, ethanol industry, etc. The trend hasn't stopped or changed.

Where the farmer stands is easy to see. Farm income has been declining from the early 1970s; millions of farmers have gone into debt or bankruptcy. In 2005–2006 the price per bushel of corn stood at $1.00 below cost of production. As an example, it cost $2.50 to grow a bushel of corn in Iowa; the farmers received $1.45 at the grain elevators. The target price having been fixed at $1.87 (loan rate), the government sends the famer $0.42 in "deficiency payments," which is still short of the costs incurred by the farmers. This leaves the farmers with the incentives to grow more to make up for their shortfall, at the risk of increasing fertilizer use, degrading the best land, and/or planting on marginal land. However, because of policies that decouple the market from human needs, this further depresses corn prices. The net result of these policies: we have gone from 4 billion bushels in 1970, when the Nixon policies took their start, to 10 billion in 2005.[12]

Farm Policies and the Farmers

The two figures below illustrate what the free market has meant for US farmers over the space of a century. The dark line in figure 3 indicates the evolution of income (cash receipts) for farmers since 1910. This is closely mirrored by the brown line showing the evolution of production expenses in the same lapse of time. The red line subtracts the brown from the orange to produce net cash income, giving a nearly stationary result in spite of great increase in productivity. At the end of the plotted period (2016–2018) net cash income hovered around zero.[13]

Figure 3 does not take into account the effects of inflation over a century's time. When we consider that a dollar of today corresponds to $25 in 1910, we obtain the modified figure 4.

---

[12] Pollan, *The Omnivore's Dilemma*, 62.
[13] Ken Meter and Megan Phillips Goldenberg, "Commodity System Creates Persistent Losses," *Organic Broadcaster* 27, no. 2 (March/April 2019), 1. https://mosesorganic. org/wp-content/uploads/2019/03/MOSES-Broadcaster27.2-for-web.pdf.

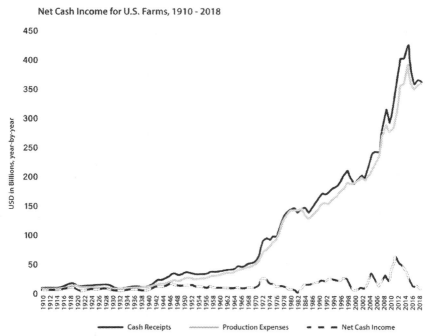

Net Cash Income for U.S. Farms, 1910 - 2018

Figure 3: Net cash income for US farms, 1910–2018
(Source: USDA Economic Research Service Farm Income Balance
Sheet data in Meter and Phillips Goldenberg, "Commodity System," 1)

The result of these data, adjusted to correspond more closely to reality,
show a downward trend, with the lows of 1983, 2000, and 2018 greater than
those of the Great Depression. The data show that in 1960 farming families
earned $20,000 per year from farm sources; as of 2018 this was $24,000
per household despite the fact that productivity has more than doubled.[14]

Corn and Meat Production

Americans only eat 11 pounds of corn and corn flour per year. Most of it
comes from minor varieties: sweet corn or white corn for the great majority.
It is consumed as corn on the cob, corn flakes, tortilla or chips, popcorn
and in muffins. And yet we consume about a ton of corn per year, all forms
considered. So where does the rest of the corn we produce go? And how do
we end up consuming more of it than Mexicans?

---

[14] Meter and Phillips Goldenberg, "Commodity System Creates Persistent Losses," 8.

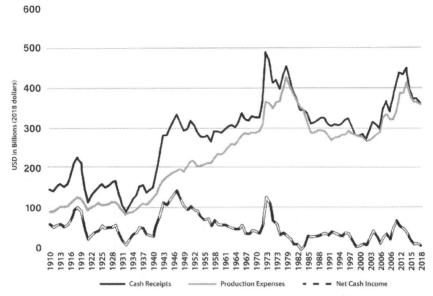

Figure 4: Adjusted net cash income for U. S. farms, 1910–2018 (Source USDA Economic Research Service Farm Income Balance Sheet data in Meter and Phillips Goldenberg, "Commodity System," 8)

Not counting what leaves the country, the lion's share, 60 percent of corn production, goes to feeding livestock, and mostly to feed cattle. Some 20 percent of it enters the human body (part also goes to other industrial uses) after an industrial transformation. This diversion of the corn cycle causes considerable duress on livestock and humans alike. Let us look at the two streams in succession.

The excess of corn calories had to be transformed, and this gave rise to a whole new, manmade ecosystem. It required the rise of the factory farm, a true modern animal metropolis. And this flow of corn is controlled by very few players; the Cargill and ADM corporations garner 1/3 of the corn operations in the United States. And they lobby hard on all agricultural policies. Cargill itself is the largest private corporation in the world. At the other end, once the corn has been metabolized, the United States counts four giant meatpacking companies: Tyson subsidiary IBP, Cargill subsidiary Excel, Swift and Company, and National. Their activity totals 80 percent of the national market.[15]

---

[15] Pollan, *The Omnivore's Dilemma*, 63.

Leaving aside pork and poultry, we can have a look at beef production, to which most of corn is diverted. The advent of cheap corn has completely altered the cow's lifestyle and diet. After being fed on grass on ranches for some six months, the cows go to a feedlot. The new large-scale operations have been called concentrated animal feeding operations (CAFO). It is not possible for the farmer to compete with these with his corn production, because, as we have seen it, it costs more for him to produce it than what it does for Cargill and ADM to buy it. Corn is thus presently fed to cows, who used to eat very little of it (and even to salmon, who had no interaction with it at all). Indeed cows have evolved to digest grass, not energy-packed foods like corn.

Raising cows on corn has allowed ranchers to shorten their fattening from 2 to 3 years in the 1950s to 14 to 16 months at present. Over that time a cow's weight will go from 80 to 1,100 pounds. And corn plays the most important role in this apparent miracle. The other typical ingredients of the diet are protein sources (like alfalfa and in addition molasses and synthetic urea), silage (for roughage), and fat supplements (beef tallow is often used). Just like beef tallow, blood products, feather meal and chicken litter, and chicken, fish, and pig meal are accepted in beef production—all elements that an herbivore never knew in his diet. To complete the cocktail are a number of drugs and additives, including liquid vitamins, synthetic estrogen, and antibiotics—mostly Rumensin and Tylosin. The corn is flaked for easier assimilation, and the whole is blended and poured out.

Grass that was grown by the sun has been replaced with corn produced with great input of fossil fuels. The resulting meat contains more saturated fat and less omega-3 fatty acids than grass-fed beef.

Virtually all cows undergoing this diet have fragile health and can only survive through added medicine. When they eat corn, naturally foreign to their diet, the fermentation in the rumen produces gas and causes what is commonly known as bloat. Too much corn also commonly causes acidosis, with resulting diarrhea, ulcers, rumenitis, and liver disease. Indeed, under this regime the cows could hardly last beyond their fourteenth to sixteenth month without a lot of "help." The lowering of the immune system resistance also opens the doors to pneumonia, coccidiosis, enterotoxemia, and feedlot polio, which need recourse to large doses of antibiotics. Rumensin buffers rumen acidity, while Tylosin lowers the rate of liver infections.

In addition to the above, because pathogens can accumulate in the feces, such as the lethal *Escherichia coli* O157:H7, the manure is often irradiated to prevent the bacteria from accumulating on the animal's hides and in their guts.

It has been calculated that 1/5 of America's oil consumption is used in producing and transporting food. Beef plays an important part in this picture: the energy input for a beef cow to reach optimal weight is as high as 35 gallons of oil.[16]

The Industrial Transformations of Corn

The United States has known an exponential growth of what are known as "wet mills," mills other than those that produce cornmeal from corn. Once more we find the presence of two giants: Cargill and ADM process most of America's maize through physical pressure, acids, and enzymes. In the first step the grain is generally left for thirty-six hours in water with small doses of sulphur dioxide. Here takes place the ominous transformation, described by Michael Pollan: "What the wet mill does to a bushel of corn is to turn it into the building blocks from which companies like General Mills, McDonald's, and Coca Cola assemble our processed food."[17] From the corn three parts are processed, the most important one being the last one:

- Skin (fiber) for vitamins and nutritional supplements
- Germ (embryo) for oil
- Endosperm, containing a great variety of substances, mostly complex carbohydrates that can be broken down and rearranged into acids, sugars, starches, and alcohols. Among these we count: starches and modified starches, citric and lactic acid, glucose, fructose, maltodextrin, ethanol (for alcoholic beverages and fuel), sorbitol, mannitol, xanthan gum, dextrins, cyclo-dextrins, maltose, MSG, and more. The endosperm also contains gluten, often used in animal feed. Other related products from the endosperm are stabilizers, gels, thickeners, adhesives, coatings, and plastics.

---

[16] Pollan, *The Omnivore's Dilemma*, 83–84.
[17] Pollan, *The Omnivore's Dilemma*, 86.

In the 1970s a process was discovered and perfected for extracting a 55 percent fructose–45 percent glucose or high fructose corn sweetener (HFCS) blend, in perfect synchronicity with the cheap corn policies. In addition, corn was used to replace butter with margarine, to produce juice drinks and sodas instead of fruit juices, or even juice-free drinks, cheese substitute Cheez Whiz, and Cool Whip substitute whipped cream.

In the above processes, corn, which has been produced at great expense of fossil fuels, undergoes another transformation in order to reenter the food system. The process of the wet mills burns an estimated average of 10 fossil fuel calories per 1 calorie produced.[18]

Reentering the Food System

America now fashions most of its processed foods from many of the products of corn, some soybean, plus some coloring and sources of flavoring, vitamins, and minerals. This is a food supply driven by an industrial advertising machine.

Lab analysis requested by Michael Pollan detected in decreasing order the following content of corn (direct and indirect): sodas (100 percent), milk shakes (78 percent), salad dressings (65 percent), chicken nuggets (56 percent), cheeseburgers (52 percent), and French fries (23 percent because of the oil).[19]

As a result of its food policies and the industrial transformation of corn, America's intake of calories has increased by 10 percent between 1977 and 2005. Since that time farmers produced some 500 extra calories per person per day, on top of the 3,300 previously produced.

As of 2005 America was producing 17.5 billion pounds of HFCS from 530 million bushels of corn. And from 1985 to 2005 HFCS individual consumption has risen from 45 to 66 pounds per year, while at the same time sugar consumption itself increased slightly by 5 pounds per individual per year. When all sugar intake is measured (adding honey, maple syrup, and glucose), we register a sharp rise, from 128 to 158 pound per person per year.[20] One easy way to understand the spike is to see into how many foods HFCS has found its way. Besides the obvious soft drinks and snack foods, we find it in ketchup, mustard, relishes, breads, crackers, cereals, hot dogs, hams, salad

---

[18] Pollan, *The Omnivore's Dilemma*, 88.

[19] Pollan, *The Omnivore's Dilemma*, 117.

[20] Pollan, *The Omnivore's Dilemma*, 103.

dressings, sauces, and so on. Most of all we consume it in our soft drinks, considering that in 1984 Coke and Pepsi completely switched to it from sugar. And from around that time companies dropped the price per unit and started offering super-sized portions. The impacts on human health are not a mystery.

Corn and Human Health

We can now trace the consequences of the prominence of corn in human diet. Obesity has risen since the 1970s according to most researchers, indicating the very likely link to the farm policies that changed under Nixon—cheap food and most of all cheap corn (see figure 5). Consider in addition that one in three children in the United States now eats fast food every single day. And 19 percent of meals are eaten in the car.[21]

Three in five Americans are overweight; one in five is obese. And one in three, (even two in five among African Americans) runs the risk of diabetes. The estimated costs to the health system reached around $90 billion in 2005.[22] Type II diabetes, which has been on the rise, occurs when the body's mechanism for dealing with sugars wears down from too much of the substance. What aggravates the problem is that, especially for those with limited income, it is much more efficient financially to resupply the body with calories from processed food than it would be with vegetables, fruits, legumes, and whole foods, often by a factor 5.

A look at one iconic fast food item will speak volumes. A chicken nugget contains 38 ingredients, among which are those directly derived from corn on top of corn-fed chicken: corn starch and modified corn starch; yellow corn flour; mono-, tri-, and diglycerides (emulsifiers); dextrose; lecithin; vegetable shortening; corn oil; and citric acid. As we have seen previously, chicken nuggets are 56 percent corn or corn-derived products. To the above, outside of the realm of corn, are added antioxidants like sodium aluminum phosphate, monocalcium phosphate, sodium acid pyrophosphate, calcium lactate, and tertiary buthylhydroquinone (a form of butane) for preservation; and agents like dimethylpolysiloxane for preventing foaming during the cooking of the mixture.[23] Consider that the nugget has become so popular as to replace beef, being much cheaper to produce.

---

[21] Pollan, *The Omnivore's Dilemma*, 109–110.

[22] Pollan, *The Omnivore's Dilemma*, 102.

[23] Pollan, *The Omnivore's Dilemma*, 113.

Overweight U.S. Youth; Percentage by Age

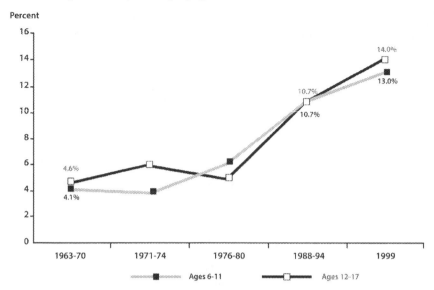

Figure 5: Overweight US youth, percent by age
(Source National Center for Health Statistics National
Health and Nutrition Examination Survey 1999 in Meter
and Phillips Goldenberg, "Commodity System," 8)

Free Market and Neoliberal Utopias

As we have seen from the premises to this exploration (Figure 2, p. 5), all the players in the market are often at odds with each other. Resolving this divergence in a competitive economy means setting up the basis for perpetuating a state of conflict of interests leading to power inequalities. Since Adam Smith did not predicate transparency and collaboration as values counterbalancing self-interest in the free markets, the results are to be expected. To his credit, the economy at the time of Adam Smith was simpler and more genuinely competitive.

At present those who have access to money, or power, will inevitably create a situation of imbalance. Add to this that self-interest most often only looks at the short term and sacrifices sustainability when the lure of profits are the only motivator. Not surprisingly, the system continues to make sense financially but not under any other lens of reference. It may fulfill the needs of some, but at the expense of the needs of everybody else, plus the environment and our future.

To summarize, the free market is based on core values of self-interest and competition, to some degree creativity and inventiveness, which is assumed to be healthy in and of itself. This is the pole of unchecked individual initiative linked to the pursuit of wealth and power, which naturally gives rise to cycles of booms and busts that are painful to the underdogs but end up strengthening the powerful, with a continuous reinforcing of the same dynamics.

Neoliberalism tends to evolve towards the formation of monopolies and extreme wealth disparity. From the original free market naturally arises neoliberalism, which denies the hopes of the free market. Sober and pragmatic as the free market sounds in theory, it is in reality an unattainable utopia. A destructive neoliberalism is the sober permanent reality of free market capitalism, only tempered by the checks and balances of the welfare state in times of abundance.

We can say that neoliberalism arises from distorted spiritual values, from a sort of spiritual vacuum, an illness of civilization. A corollary to these tendencies is the blurring of the boundaries between the public sphere and the economy. The economy, most of all in the form of transnational corporations, buys off the political elites. It is a sorry spectacle of American "democracy" to witness how individuals pursue their interests first in business or in the lobbying industry, then in government, to eventually return to the private sector.

The disastrous consequences of neoliberalism amount to a complete alienation from the environment and from local cultures, and ultimately induce a complete alienation from self. The life-negating values shoring up neoliberalism will only be countered when life-affirming values have sufficiently taken hold of society as a whole, or in large enough pockets of it. These culture-forming attempts are the object of the present work.

Profit-driven economy—neoliberalism—stands at the antipode of examples of more collaborative economy that we will offer below. The umbrella term "collaborative economy" used below indicates the shift from profit-driven economy to one that is needs based. The satisfaction of needs is not limited to economic agents but extends to all stakeholders or parties affected by the economic activity. While a collaborative economy is a generous and distant ideal, it is interesting to compare its goals with satisfaction of needs in a profit-driven economy. The unique needs endlessly upheld are those of the shareholders, not as individuals but as generators of usable capital. In last resort they represent the need of money to make money and give shareholders the capacity to increase revenue solely because they have available capital.

Finally, more specifically in relation to our example, the free market as a paradigm scarcely works in farming; demand for food isn't elastic. People will not eat that much more corn because it is cheaper, unless they are induced through the detour of advertising to use food by-products to optimize the industrial corn cycle. On the other hand, reducing supply isn't simple; you can't force people to let their land go fallow, especially when economic pressure increases. The existing infrastructure (in our example, grain elevators and wet mills) dictates the direction of the market for years and decades to come. There is little elasticity in terms of adaptation and access to the market for new crops as a pure free market would predicate.

It is time to turn the page and look at what a food system would look like that would satisfy the needs of all stakeholders. We present here three vignettes:

- Trisector logic: community supported agriculture
- Multi-stakeholder logic: Sustainable Food Lab
- Multiscale logic: food policy networks

We will return to these more fully in chapters 2, 3, and 4.

II. Trisector Logic in the Food System: Community Supported Agriculture

Community supported agriculture (CSA) started in Europe and Japan in the 1970s; in Europe the CSA movement was fostered by biodynamic farming. In Japan *Teikei* (meaning Partnership or Collaboration) was started in 1971 by a group of women concerned about the destructive trends they were seeing in farming.

Land Is Not a Commodity; A Farm Is Not a Factory

The ground for the emergence of the CSA phenomenon has its origin in some simple commonsense realizations.

Land and farming are not just economic variables like all others, say, manufactured goods. The land is the prerequisite for all life on earth and for all economic activity. Land cannot be produced and can scarcely be equated to a commodity. And farming is not a business like others, because, unlike all other businesses, it can, if skillfully devised, produce out of the relationships between soil, plant, and animal organisms, with little external input, unlike a factory.

CSAs want to fulfill three basic functions:

- producing healthy food,
- fostering a healthy self-preserving environment for present and future generations, and
- serving as a basis for culture and education.

At present we are caught between the two examples, of the surviving traditional small farm on one hand, and of the agribusiness model on the other. The latter's destructive effects at ecological, social, and cultural levels have been so amply documented, and the example of corn in the United States is a significant one. The traditional small farm model is hardly viable and places the farmer in a constant struggle against the forces of the market.

So what do CSAs do differently from a regular organic farm? Essentially they predicate that farm operations have to be taken away from market logic and that the farmers who operate them are the ones who can best see the needs and productive potential of a piece of land. They have to be rendered free to fully observe and understand the land and its components with a view to fulfilling the three functions expressed above.

Ideally, a CSA farm is owned by a land trust or, if individually owned, a land trust owns an easement on it regulating its use and development. Again, ideally the budget is established by the farmers, based on their individual/family needs and on what the land will need in order to operate and produce what its members want in the coming year. The budget is then adjusted with the input of the shareholders. When agreement is reached, the budget is divided among the number of shareholders to determine the cost of a share. In this lies the shift from market logic—paying for the produce—toward a needs-based approach to economics—supporting the objective needs of the farm and its stewards.

Practical Advantages of CSAs

CSAs at their best maximize the interests of farmers, shareholders, environment, and community:

-   They offer unique levels of freshness and quality. Consumers know where the food comes from and can offer immediate feedback, thereby improving quality.
-   Consumers and farmers bypass the middleman and obtain savings. CSAs bypass the intermediary costs of transportation, packaging, processing, storage, and marketing, which comprise up to 75 percent of the average food price.
-   There is little waste; even "unaesthetic" produce can readily be used. All of the surplus will not be destroyed to satisfy market demands but can be made available to those in need (e.g., food pantries).
-   The land can build increasing fertility and sustain a very diverse ecosystem with benefits accruing to environment and community.
-   The farmers can be assured a set income since the whole community shoulders the risk. They can have an easier work schedule and be better stewards by carefully observing their land and their crops and improving the land and its productivity.
-   Farmers don't have to market during the growing season, their busiest time of the year. They can alleviate the temptation to overproduce due to economic pressure.
-   Farms can be places to bring people together around a variety of common concerns, chiefly recreational and educational.

Note that all the advantages contribute to the development of a true economy from all perspectives: reducing costs and waste, linking most efficiently producers to consumers with the greatest amount of feedback loops.

Cultural, Social, and Economic Goals

CSAs address three sets of overlapping goals: the cultural, the social, and the economic:

Cultural: for the land to be managed in optimal conditions, and to preserve/ improve its potential for future generations. For this aim the separation of land, property, and farm operations is essential. To understand this aspect, we must envision the CSA as an ideally enclosed entity that plays a part in the whole surroundings like a cell or organ plays in the human body. Farms can also play an educational role for schools, or for particular segments of the population: children, individuals with special needs, homeless people, underprivileged people, and so on.

Social: healthy food, wood, and fiber can be optimally made available to all regardless of economic background. A whole new array of social relationships comes into being that varies according to the CSA's legal organizational structure: between farmers and members/shareholders, among people who share in the risk of the operations, between any given CSA and other CSAs or farm associations.

Economic: where CSAs really present new, wide horizons for the future is in their offering a completely new economic model. In fact, we could say that they are truly economic, whereas the present model of agribusiness, profitable as it may be, stands as the antithesis of true economy.

AGRI-BUSINESS	COMMUNITY SUPPORTED AGRICULTURE	STATE SUPPORTED OR RUN FARMING OPERATION
LAND AS A COMMODITY	Land as a resource for present and future generations.	Land as a common good.
PROFIT MOTIVE: FARMING AS BUSINESS	Land as a living organism: Supporting soil, farmers, and community	Justice motive: Farming as a place of equal opportunity

Table 6: CSA in relation to other farming models

CSAs truly create an alternative to capitalistic or socialistic thinking. Capitalism only looks at the freedom of the individual and believes in the abstract force of the market that tempers it. The farm becomes a business. Purely socialistic farm models, as those of surviving communist regimes, all but kill the freedom of the individual in the name of equality. The farm will tend to resemble an institution. In the CSA ideal, the farmer is selected to function in the interests of the land itself and of the community. The farmer is freed to pursue the development of his individuality and his entrepreneurial spirit in accord with the needs of the land.

Ideally the hand of the market is removed from the equation and the farmer can increase his stewardship skills. The land trust or nonprofit that ensures the future uses of the land for benefit of environment and community has no resemblance whatsoever to a government agency. The entrepreneurial motive of capitalism and the equalitarian concerns of socialism are reconciled at a higher level with the maxim "To each according to his needs." The objective place of individual human needs replaces the working of the market, or the seemingly generous but abstract notion of the state providing for individual needs. We will return to this example in more depth in Chapter 2.

III. Multi-Stakeholder Logic in the Food System

The multi-stakeholder approach to change lies in facilitating the collaboration of diverse, often mutually alienated, stakeholder groups through meeting the whole person in out-of-the-ordinary conversations.

Meeting the whole person in generative dialogue can be done through the stages of the so-called U (see figure 7) made popular by Otto Scharmer.[24] We will here refer to the U as a universal pattern referring to many approaches (e. g., Appreciative Inquiry, Open Space, World Café, Future Search, Technology of Participation), rather than the specific methodology followed by Otto Scharmer.

Open Mind, Open Heart, Open Will

- Open Mind: complete sharing of and access to the data
- Open Heart: disclosure about what lives in the realm of feelings, fears, projections, stereotypes, concerns, objections that would otherwise block, delay, or diminish collaboration

[24] Otto Scharmer, *Theory U: Leading from the Emerging Future; The Social Technology of Presencing* (Cambridge, MA: Society for Organizational Learning, 2007).

- Open Will: a laying out of all options with a collective endeavor to manifest fresh, new ones. These are rendered possible because of the previous access to the Open Mind and Open Heart.
- Presencing: the above conditions create the grounds for situations of collective breakthroughs, generating new insights and solutions that have the buy-in of all parties

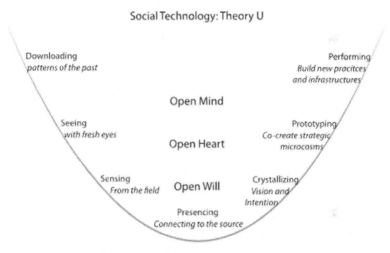

Social Technology: Theory U

Downloading
patterns of the past

Performing
Build new pracitces
and infrastructures

Open Mind

Seeing
with fresh eyes

Prototyping
Co-create strategic
microcosms

Open Heart

Sensing
From the field

Open Will

Crystallizing
Vision and
Intention

Presencing
Connecting to the source

Figure 7: Theory U: Open Mind, Open Heart, Open Will
(modified from Scharmer, *Theory U*)

The above is made possible by skillfully designed processes and facilitation. With any of the above-mentioned approaches, securing the best possible results means inviting a variety of stakeholders from one, two, or three of the sectors (business, government, and civil society). In the sustainable food system these can be any of the above in any possible combinations: farmers at any scale of operation, artisanal and/or industrial makers producing added value, distributors, food hubs, incubator kitchens, wholesalers, retailers, government agencies, restaurateurs, food banks, food-related nonprofits, consumers, and so forth. For the sake of simplicity, we will mostly look at the left side of the U, up to presencing, and return to fuller examples in Chapter 3.

Open Mind: Leading to "Seeing"

In a first stage of the process, we need to overcome the silos mentality that sees the challenges from a limited, institutional perspective. Bringing stakeholders together can allow us to generate a larger tapestry of information that highlights the interconnections of all the elements of a situation (systems thinking). The assembled stakeholders will go through the Open Mind by collectively enriching and rounding off everybody's perspective.

Open Heart Leading to "Sensing"

Withholding from forming judgments and criticisms is what allows a shift toward the stage of the Open Heart. From the jungle of facts, new relationships, patterns, and themes emerge. Stakeholder groups will realize that this was only possible by breaking the boundaries of the silos. In a build-up of trustful relationships, individuals and groups start to see the part they play in a complex and challenging situation, take responsibility for their own part, and better understand other perspectives.

Open Will Leading to "Presencing"

When all previous ideas, perceptions, and assumptions are loosened, it is easier to imagine an open field of inquiry. All processes using the U will guide participants to a clear understanding of a common ground from which it is possible to operate.

The stakeholders will typically brainstorm loosely ideas for action, from which will be selected those that all stakeholders see suitable, most immediately reachable, most efficient in terms of the investment of time and energy that they require, most strategic, and so on. Success is manifested when a scenario is formulated that brings satisfaction to everybody and that no stakeholder could have reached on her own. This feeling of something that is more than the sum of the parts manifests in what has been called *presencing* (from presence and sensing).

Presencing

Presencing is an all-encompassing experience of which any given individual can only apprehend a facet. Experienced practitioners provide us with examples. Betty Sue Flowers indicates: "When I am part of a social field that crosses the threshold at the bottom of the U, it feels as if I am participating in the birth of a new world. It's a profound, quieting experience in that I feel as if I've been touched by eternal beauty. There is a deep opening of my higher Self." For Joseph Jaworski, "moving through the bottom of the U is becoming aware of the incredible beauty of life itself, of becoming re-enchanted with the world.... When the sort of commitment you are talking about happens, you feel as if you're fulfilling your destiny, but you also feel as if you're freer than you've ever been in your life. It's a huge paradox."[25]

From these two quotes we can fathom why presencing is a turning point of the whole experience and why it is necessary in order to achieve lasting results. Through presencing the letting go of the past makes room for allowing the new; in Otto Scharmer's words "letting come."

Crystallizing, Prototyping, Performing

On the left of the side of the U we place everything that leads to collective decision making, the setting up of balloon tests that can be replicated, all the way to the establishment of a new organizational culture that can produce these changes on a continuous basis.

Sustainable Food Lab

How is this done in practice? Let's have a look at Sustainable Food Lab and a concrete situation that integrates Theory U with approaches from the Society for Organizational Learning.[26] In such scenarios the participants to the project may do any of the following:

- Pledge a sizeable amount of their time over two years.
- Look at their collective part of the food system with a systems thinking approach.
- Go through in-depth interviews.
- Go on learning journeys to places of great diversity and great potential.
- Commit to a generative dialogue which is the basis for generating Open Mind, Open Heart, and Open Will.

---

[25] Peter Senge, C. Otto Scharmer, Joseph Jaworski, and Betty Sue Flowers, *Presence: Exploring Profound Change in People, Organizations and Society* (New York: Crown Business, 2004), 111, 113.

[26] See https://www.solonline.org/organizational-learning-2/.

- Collaboratively envision how to change the system in a way that works for all as a result of all of the above.

U.S. Organic Grain Collaboration (convened in 2014)[27]

This is a project that works with farmers and other stakeholders in the food chain in Aroostook County, Maine, and in the Northern Great Plains.

Project Goals: addressing key challenges in expanding the supply of organic grain in the United States by:

- improving profitability and market access
- improving resiliency

Project Partners: Annie's Organic, Ardent Mills, Clif Bar, General Mills, King Arthur Flour, Pipeline Foods, Stonyfield Organics, Organic Valley, Sustainable Food Lab.

The study found that the challenges of entering and staying in organic grain production are

- the high cost of transition and market guarantee at the end of the transition period,
- soil fertility and weed suppression, and
- suboptimal farm management resources.

After going through generative dialogue, the project partners determined the industry solutions needed:

- provide long-term forward contracts,
- coordinate and develop markets for noncash crops that increase soil fertility and suppress weeds, and

---

[27] Elizabeth Reaves, Carol Healy, and Jedediah L Beach, *US Organic Grain: How to Keep It Growing*, U.S. Organic Grain Collaboration, February 2019. https://ota.com/sites/default/files/indexed_files/US Organic Grain_How to Keep it Growing_Organic Trade Association.pdf.

- develop new models of knowledge delivery: support farmers to learn and innovate together around solutions and research adapted for regional conditions.

IV. Multiscale Logic: Food Policy Councils/Networks

There are many kinds of food policy councils (FPCs) or networks. We will look here only at those that work from a systems-thinking logic and that operate as "socially generative networks."

Socially generative networks rely on a loose, though clearly articulated, coordination of efforts and high degree of local autonomy through self-organization. They generate results at a variety of scales simultaneously, from the very local up to their larger level of operation (city, state, regional, national).

Central to a generative network is a whole systems approach, which means the consciousness and desire to see the whole system in its complexity by convening key players from two if not three of the sectors concerned (public, private, nonprofit) and all the concerned stakeholders within a given sector. The goals of this approach are the following:

- See the web of relationships and feedback loops existing between all players and steps in a system. If this were the food system, it would mean mapping the whole from production to distribution and consumption, and tracing all the variety of relationships among the participants.
- Detect the positive and negative feedback loops with all their intended and unintended consequences over the system.
- Discover the leverage points upon which change can more easily occur through coordination of efforts and resources.
- Monitor the system on a continuous basis in order to revise and adapt strategies.

Network Evolution

Networks operate through one or two levels of membership. At the core are those who will comply with a larger set of requirements, and they often have voting rights. At the periphery are those with lower levels of requirements, which often are not as deeply aligned with and affected by the network's mission as are the members at the core.

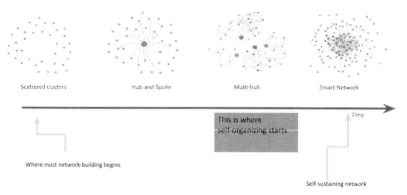

Figure 8: Stages of development of socially generative networks
(courtesy June Holley)

Figure 8 represents the stages of evolution of a network. These will go from a very sparse landscape of players with very few connections (links) and very limited nodes (centers of coordinated activity). Of particular interest are stages 2 and 4. When the situation corresponds to stage 1, it is the task of a network weaver to create new links among the nodes interested in similar work. The network weaver will act as the central node with the greatest levels of links, becoming in fact the hub of the network (stage 2). But all along he will be training others to acquire the same skills of interconnectivity. When the time comes the network weaving can be transmitted to a new individual, or more likely to a "backbone organization." This is the stage that can correspond to what is known as "Collective Impact," and which can be seen as a final destination, or a step along the way. We will look at this stage first and at stages 3 and 4 later.

Entering a Collective Impact scenario engages a group of important stakeholder groups from different sectors to a common agenda for solving a specific social challenge. Network weaving takes time. It's only through extensive connection efforts that the members will align on a common agenda and then create the desired impact. The common agenda, most often reached through consensus will lead to:

- the establishment of set goals (often corresponding to the leverage points of the system);
- coordinating through continuous communication the use of resources, energy, and competencies in such a way as to avoid competition, duplication, or gaps;

- ensuring progress through mutually reinforcing activities toward any of the established goals;
- continuously monitoring through measurements relative to the desired outcomes; and
- forming of a "backbone organization." The individuals at its center do not do any work on behalf of the network other than ensuring and fostering growing collaboration. They can best be characterized as stewards, rather than leaders.

An example: VT Farm to Plate (F2P)

VT F2P was established in 2009 through the Vermont legislature. Through stakeholder input it delineated a set of 25 goals to be achieved in the food system. The collective impact model is composed of 5 working circles, according to the phases of the food system (Farmland Access and Stewardship, Aggregation and Distribution, Production and Processing, Education and Workforce Development, Consumer Education and Marketing) and 6 cross-cutting circles, which influence the system at all stages of its development (food access, soil, labor, energy, financing, research). At the center sits the backbone organization, here indicated as the steering committee. From 2009 to 2014[28] the work of the Farm to Plate network:

- added some 2,162 jobs and 199 establishments;
- decreased food insecurity in the state for the first time since the Great Recession;
- expanded number of food hubs/incubators in the state;
- thanks to the work of F2P's Meat Processing Task Force, launched in 2011, opened five new slaughterhouses and two new processing-only facilities;[29]
- provided financing and access to solar, wind energy, methane digestors, and biomass heaters to farms in VT; and[30]

---

[28] Vermont Farm to Plate 2016 Annual Report: https://www.vtfarmtoplate.com/uploads/Farm to Plate 2016 Annual Report FINAL.pdf.

[29] Carrie Abels, *Gathering the Herd: A Vermont Meat Processing Case Study*, 2017: https://www.vtfarmtoplate.com/assets/activities/files/F2P Meat Processing Case Study FINAL 6.20.17-1.pdf.

[30] VT Farm to Plate Energy Success Stories: https://www.vtfarmtoplate.com/assets/resource/files/Energy Success Stories Feb-2015.pdf.

- expanded the palette of loans and financing options to new food-related initiatives.[31]

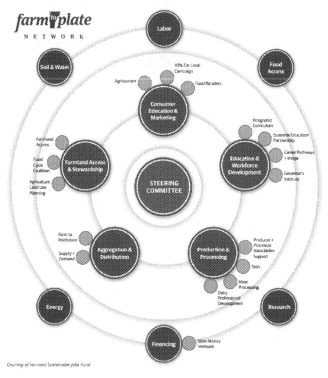

Figure 9: Organizational structure of VT Farm to Plate network (Source: Institute for Sustainable Communities, *Case Study: Vermont Farm to Plate Network*, 6. See https://www.vtfarmtoplate.com/uploads/Case Study - Vermont Farm to Plate Network.pdf)

---

[31] See https://www.vtfarmtoplate.com/network/financing/activity/60. VT Farm to Plate's Financing Cross-cutting Team convened encounters to gather results and highlight financing options across the food system. Some of these alternatives have been summarized in short articles: See Carrie Abels, *Cookie Royalty: How Liz Lovely Used Royalty Financing to Grow a Pace That Made Sense*, 2015: https://www.vtfarmtoplate.com/assets/resource/files/Financing Case Studies Liz Lovely June 2015.pdf; Carrie Abels, *Complex Dough: How Bread and Butter Farm Worked with a Patchwork Quilt of Funding Sources to Keep Land Conserved for Agriculture*, 2015: https://www.vtfarmtoplate.com/assets/resource/files/Financing Case Studies Bread and Butter Farm FEB 2015.pdf; Carrie Abels, *Seeding the Future with Convertible Debt: How High Mowing Organic Seeds Used Convertible Debt to Plan Wisely for Its Future and Keep Fueling Its Growth*, 2014: https://www.vtfarmtoplate.com/assets/resource/files/Financing Case Studies High Mowing Organic Seeds Sep 2014.pdf.

After 5 years, members report:

- For 75 percent of them, the network helps advance their goals.
- 75 percent are building new relationships.
- 80 percent are strengthening existing relationships.[32]

System Shifting Networks

At a later stage of network development, we find the "core/periphery" or "system shifting" phase. After promoting the activity of a multitude of hubs (stage 3) rather than one alone, a network acquires great resiliency. Over time it can form links with other networks in its environment (stage 4).

At stage 4 a sort of symbiotic relationship arises between core and periphery. From the edges flow to the center information and ideas new to the network. The core is where the greatest potential lies for coordinated action. The periphery allows the core to sense what lives in its larger environment. Too great of a density at the center without a living relationship to the margins carries the risk of both work overload and lack of flexibility.

In Conclusion: A Quick Comparison

Notice that the three examples vastly differ both conceptually and in size, though this is not meant to say that this is the inescapable logic of the three paradigms for any example given. In other instances, the differences could take different forms, though great contrasts would still remain.

CSA is a thoroughly thought-out change at the micro scale, in fact the smallest possible scale: the individual farm. Mostly producers meet with consumers, with minimal need for intermediaries; the interaction can be very intimate. In the choice of the model, great attention has been given to understanding the logic of farming, the pressures of the market, and the needs of the land, the farmers, and the consumers.

Sustainable Food Lab operates at a medium or large scale, and a discontinuous one; parties involved are not contiguous geographically, even less so culturally. What is unique about this approach is the involvement

---

[32] VT Farm to Plate 2016 Annual Report: https://www.vtfarmtoplate.com/uploads/ Farm to Plate 2016 Annual Report FINAL.pdf.

of the greatest variety of stakeholders—the greatest differences to be bridged—whereas the operating system in which we live is modified only very gradually. What is greatly changed is the logic of human relationships.

The VT Farm to Plate network operates at a macro scale, the size of a state; it is also the one involving the widest variety of players, though the goals it addresses can be at first very minimal, given the variety of interests. There may be no immediate need to engage a thorough understanding of stakeholder logic. The network relies on a systems-thinking view of the food system and moves according to emerging possibilities; quite the contrary of the CSA model, which involves a thorough conceptual understanding and acting upon a single piece of the food system. What is central to this approach is the totally novel social structure and the decentralization of initiative.

We will now revisit the three examples in greater depth and within a much larger context.

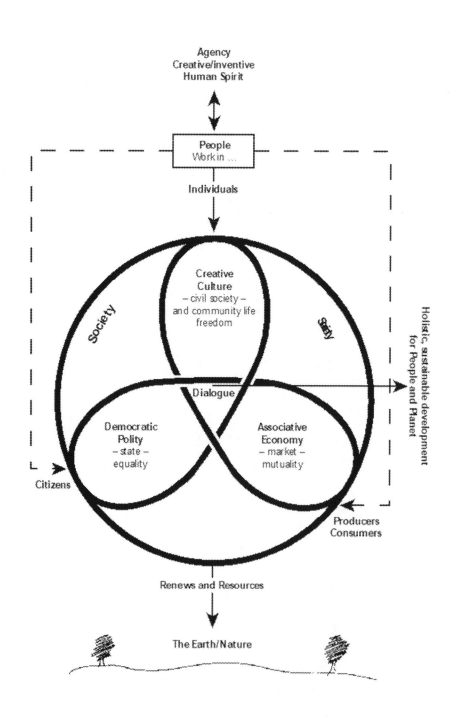

Chapter 2
Trisector Logic

The Civil Society [tripolar society] is radically self-organizing and predominantly cooperative in the manner of healthy living systems, and seeks to maximize the opportunity for each individual to fully and freely develop their creative potential in service to the whole of life. Thus Civil Society differs in every dimension from the capitalist economy in which we currently live.

—David Korten

Rarely do we find men who willingly engage in hard, solid thinking. There is an almost universal quest for easy answers and half-baked solutions. Nothing pains some people more than having to think.

—Martin Luther King, Jr.

IN THIS CHAPTER:

SEEING SOCIETY HOLISTICALLY
- Government, the economy and civil society
- From predominance to balance
- From opposition to dialogue

FUNCTIONAL TRISECTOR LOGIC
- Trisector partnerships
- The work of the Institute for Cultural Affairs
- Involving the Three Sectors
- Growth at all levels: individual, organizational, societal
- Sectoral and societal Learning

IDEAL TRISECTOR LOGIC
- From thinking in twos to thinking in threes
- What can we learn from MLK the thinker?
- What is the role of culture in social change?
- Cultural activism
- Sectoral checks and balances
- Collaborative economy; An example in agriculture: CSAs

THAT SOCIETY AS A WHOLE is better thought of in three sectors rather than in the traditional two—government and the economy—is an idea that has been growing in the United States since the 1970s. It is the addition of civil society as a player at the table that makes this possible. This means that there can be a new way of looking at social change; a departure from the ideologies of the past, which favored either of the two traditional sectors. And a way forward exists beyond the alternatives of capitalism and socialism, one no longer based on ideology, but upon a closer understanding of social reality.

We will look at the various ways in which this has presented itself since the 1970s and integrate the elements that add to each other to outline a larger understanding of the three-sector paradigm. This will add up to a way of freeing our minds in understanding social issues: a new paradigm of both/and, beyond the present paradigm of either/or.

Balance versus Predominance

We will now look at three authors who approach the question of the three sectors of society from different and complementary angles. The first one is the result of the collective work of the Institute of Cultural Affairs. The other two are Henry Mintzberg and Steve Waddell. Independently from each other, they build complementary facets of a new way of seeing the social question.

Cultural Commonality and the Birth of ICA

Started as an effort for church renewal and community development, the Ecumenical Institute spread worldwide at the end of the 1960s. It took on the name of Institute for Cultural Affairs (ICA) in 1973, to distance itself from the fading ecumenical element and to acknowledge its global, cultural dimension. The decision to change its name was a direct result of an effort undertaken two years earlier, in conjunction with the birth of the "Social Process Triangles." The so-called Corporate Reading Research Project was conducted through a comprehensive literature review involving the institute's offices throughout the world. These conversations were made possible through new deliberate, collectively created practices of Focused Conversation and Consensus Workshop. These are processes that favor the generation of new insights.

The research project took one year and covered the study of 1,500 seminal books that explored all aspects of the social question. The work was narrowed down by a core group of about 30 people meeting every weekend during the winter and spring of 1970–71. It then culminated in the summer of 1971 with a gathering of 1,500 people coming to Chicago with the aim of understanding how to look at the issues engaging global society.

The major insight emerging from the study was that social questions were usually framed in reference to either economic or political dimensions, and additionally some other aspects like health and education services. The discovery of the team effort was that culture could be added as a third category to politics and the economy, encompassing health and education services, but also much more. The social question could thus be articulated through the contribution of the economic, political, and cultural "commonalities." The understanding of the underrated role of culture was

LUIGI MORELLI

affirmed in the later choice of a name for the renewed organization: the Institute of Cultural Affairs.

The data, sifted from the books, was used to create the so-called model of the Social Process Triangles, of which we look at more below. The interrelationship of the three commonalities was conceived in this way:

> The ideal (rarely found) is a balanced tension between the economic, the political and the cultural. When this happens, society is in a healthy state. When these three processes of society are not held in balance, society gets sick. When we are deprived of the means of adequate livelihood, political chaos and rioting can result. When we are deprived of participation in the political process, our livelihood is likely to suffer while masters grow rich on the resources denied us. When our culture is taken away from us, we easily become political and economic victims, or find our lives devoid of meaning.[33]

And further:

> To be a social human being is to be inexorably involved in issues of sustenance and survival (economic); of ordering and organizing society to overcome chaos (political); and of education, family and community, and the celebration of life and death (cultural). These three, together with all the particular processes that make them up, create the whole system that we call society, or the social process. Because the social process is systemic, any malfunction in any one part will reverberate through the whole system. The same goes for the good things going on in any one part. In addition, if there is not some kind of basic balance

---

[33] Brian Stanfield, *The Courage to Lead: Transform Self, Transform Society* (Toronto, ON: Canadian Institute of Cultural Affairs, 2000), 151.

between the three major processes, the whole social process suffers.[34]

Among key learnings to be drawn from the work of the Institute of Cultural Affairs is the idea of the prominence of the cultural commonality, its central role in the present and coming future. This is what explains the placement of the cultural commonality at the top of the triangle with economic and political commonalities at the bottom, as we will see shortly. (See Figure 3.)

Plural Sector or Social Sector?

Some forty years after ICA, similar views to the ones above have been developed by Henry Mintzberg from independent sources. He prefaces his work by underlining that centuries of debate have crystallized the idea that there are only the public and the private sectors. And that there is only capitalism and socialism to choose from. Both capitalism and socialism are fatally flawed, and both have relentlessly undermined what Mintzberg calls "the plural sector." An example: China, like all communist regimes, fears independent associations undermining the role of the party, such as Falun Gong in the 1990s, just as much as capitalism fears losing control over its mass media apparatus and advertising machine.

Henry Mintzberg is a Canadian professor of management studies at McGill University, Montreal, and author on themes of business and management. In his book *Rebalancing Society* he looks at the growth of what has been called "not-for-profit sector," "third sector," and "civil society," which he dubs the "plural sector," for in it we find a great variety of players. Among those who represent this sector, he lists foundations, places of worship, religious orders, unions, cooperatives, organizations that take care of the environment (e.g., Greenpeace), social movements and initiatives, hospitals, and universities. And he notices that the plural sector is the one in which most of us are constantly engaged and represented, more so than in the other two.

The dynamics of right and left politics, argues Mintzberg, leaves us in a black or white kind of thinking. The electoral body is split 50/50 and people in the middle determine the winner. The winning party serves the

---

[34] Jon C. Jenkins and Maureen R. Jenkins, *The Social Process Triangles* (Groningen, The Netherlands: Imaginal Training, 1997), 8.

majority while ignoring the minority. And we end up in pendulum politics with a mutual canceling of initiatives, and with micro solutions for macro problems. To the left lies the danger of state despotism; to the right, predatory capitalism. But neither is the plural sector immune from any danger: it can favor one cultural sector at the expense of another (exclusive populism) as we can see in the case of fundamentalist regimes in Muslim countries.

Not unlike the Institute of Cultural Affairs, Mintzberg gives the plural sector the role of leading the process of rebalancing society that we so desperately require.[35] He gives examples of manifestations of imbalance: "Governments can be crude; markets can be crass; and communities can be closed."[36] This is why each sector needs the other two to be kept in check and in balance.

Capitalism and socialism have tried to balance society from one end alone, from one sector. A balanced society would sit on a stool with three sturdy legs:

- A public sector of political forces rooted in respected governments
- a private sector of economic forces based on responsible businesses
- a plural sector of social forces manifested in robust communities."[37]

It is most interesting that Mintzberg's thinking comes from a wholly different quarter than that of ICA; there is no direct relationship between what he is advancing and what ICA championed. In fact, there are differences; he calls civil society the "plural sector," giving it a community, not an objectively cultural role, and including among its members co-ops, which ICA would have included in the economic commonality. Still he sees the need of balance between the sectors and gives the plural sector an important part in initiating the movement to rebalance society.

Mintzberg sees the role of the plural sector, with its social movements and initiatives in promoting renewal, in some of the following possibilities:

- immediate reversals of destructive practices

---

[35] Henry Mintzberg, *Rebalancing Society: Radical Renewal Beyond Left, Right and Center* (Oakland, CA: Berrett-Koehler, 2015), 29.

[36] Mintzberg, *Rebalancing Society*, 40.

[37] Mintzberg, *Rebalancing Society*, 27.

- widespread regeneration through introduction of better practices (These can start with a single new idea, coupled with grassroots education. They can also be produced through two-sector or three-sector partnerships in which relationships are balanced. From single initiatives coalitions need to be created.)
- reforms, such as the separation of state and corporation[38]

Steve Waddell espouses views very similar to the above, though he calls the third sector the "Social System" (figure 10). Waddell defines the Social System as a group of organizations that are "a domain parallel to, but separate from, the state—a realm where citizens associate according to their own interests and wishes."[39] The interest of the social sector is the "achievement of community justice." In a larger sense CBOs (community-based organizations) also include unions and churches.

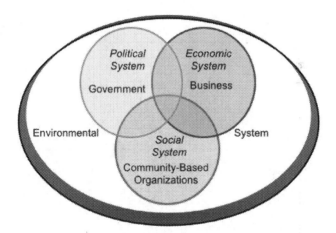

Figure 10: Political, economic, and social systems
(Courtesy of Steve Waddell)

The work of Waddell expands from the view of the three sectors into what he sees as the practice of trisector partnerships and the resulting "societal learning," to which we will return shortly.

---

[38] Mintzberg, *Rebalancing Society*, 51–58.

[39] Steve Waddell, *Societal Learning and Change: How Governments, Business and Civil Society are Creating Solutions to Complex Multi-Stakeholder Problems* (Abingdon, UK: Routledge, 2017), 11.

Holistic Aspects

Of great interest for our further explorations is the work of ICA. Among the tools developed by the institute for community and economic development were the so-called social processes triangles, practical diagnostic tools for social change based on the understanding of the three sectors. These triangles can be applied at every level of social reality for transformational purposes. The first-level triangle (Figure 11) quite simply introduces the reality of the three commonalities, but it also brings out something more than the obvious.

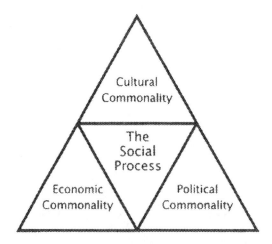

Figure 11: Social process triangles, first level
(Source: Stanfield, *The Courage to Lead*, 149)

In this triangle we can see the relationships of three parts, which are respectively:

- Foundational (bottom left): the economy. Without the economy the other two poles cannot go on.
- Ordering or organizational function (bottom right): politics, "the communal pole, which pertains to the relationship of power and decision-making in the midst of any social group. . . . [it] counteracts people's fundamental tendency to destroy each other by creating a social contract."

- Sustaining, meaning-giver (top): culture. "This is the dynamic which dramatizes the uniquely human in the triangle; it is the spirit which makes participation in the social process worthwhile. This is the arena of the symbols, style, and stories which give significance to the whole."[40]

Placing the cultural pole at the top of the triangle is a statement attesting to the determining place it occupies in relation to the other two areas, at least in this present time in world history. It is not surprising that ICA also offered one of the earliest global conferences on the emergence of civil society, in 1996 in Cairo.

Something else emerges from the triangles. Each of the three processes limits, sustains, and creates the other two. Each of the three processes can be broken into its components at deeper levels, and there one would find again the tension between a foundational process (economic component) at the bottom left, a connecting/ordering process (political component) at the bottom right, and an informing process (cultural component) at the top.

Let us see what a triangle looks like at the second level. The second level (Figure 12) shows how each pole of the triangle repeats the threefold ordering present at the first level. In the economy we have resources (economic component), production (political component), and distribution/consumption (the cultural component). At least in a naturally evolving system, it is consumer demand (cultural) that drives supply and production. Massive advertising is an attempt to condition the system from the supply side, to create new needs.

At the level of the political commonality we meet corporate order (capacity to enforce the law, providing security for a functional culture), corporate justice (upholding individual rights, ensuring equitable structures, providing links between bureaucratic structures and the grassroots), and corporate welfare (assuring that rights and responsibilities serve all citizens, and providing motivation for cooperation). We can look further at just one example of the third-level triangle. At the third level of the political commonality, in what corresponds to the US federal government, we have executive (economic component), legislative (political component), and judicial (cultural component).

---

[40] Jenkins and Jenkins, *Social Process Triangles*, 24.

The triangles allow us to place any of the smaller processes in society into a comprehensive context, showing how they are connected to the other areas of the social organism, enabling one to assess the health or imbalance of any given social unit. They can serve to visualize what patterns are at play in any given situation, thus throwing light on where the leverage points are. If action were taken at these points, positive effects would ripple throughout the system.

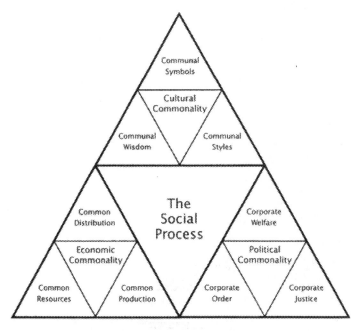

Figure 12: Social process triangles, second level
(Source: Stanfield, *The Courage to Lead*, 149)

Besides helping us look at society in a more organic way, the social process triangles were eminently practical. After 1975 ICA started some 300 projects in 25 nations, bringing together all stakeholders of the community, voluntary consultants from the public and private sector, and ICA staff, and designing a comprehensive four-year plan of local development. The triangles were used in highlighting and acting upon critical leverage points that would produce best or fastest results.

The above underlines the holistic dimension of the tri-articulation of society. There is something foundational about these three aspects. So much so that we can find it at any given place within the smaller units of social reality. It is therefore not surprising that various authors see correspondences between the sectors and the human make-up; between the outer and the inner, as we will see next.

Sectors and Drives

Underlying the forces at work in the social field, the work of ICA defined three human drives.

> The three major processes of society—economic, political, and cultural—are based on three basic drives found in all humans and in all societies. The first is the *drive for survival, for resources, livelihood, and money*—the economic dimension of life—the "that-without-which" there can be no decision-making and no consciousness. . . . The second is the *drive for order*, for the organization of society through law-making, and law-enforcing bodies so that there is security and justice for all—the political dimension of society. . . . Third is the *drive for meaning*, that bleeds significance into both the economic and political dimensions of society. This is the cultural dimension.[41]

Similar correspondences are reported from the literature that Steve Waddell quotes. A number of studies have shown correspondences between sectors and individual learning styles.[42]

- Political systems, corresponding to the mentally centered type of individuals
- Economic systems, corresponding to the physically centered
- Social systems, corresponding to the emotionally centered

---

[41] Jenkins and Jenkins, *Social Process Triangles*, 9.

[42] Jenkins and Jenkins, *Social Process Triangles*, 88–90; Sandra Seagal and David Horne, *Human Dynamics: A New Framework for Understanding People and Realizing the Potential in Our Organizations* (Waltham, MA: Pegasus Communications, 1997).

Tables 13 and 14 analyze the learning styles and their relationships to the three sectors.

In the three types of individuals—the emotionally, physically, and mentally oriented—Seagal sees parameters that go deeper than age, race, culture, and gender. She calls them "principles". According to her studies 99.9 percent of individuals operate from one predominant principle to which they associate a second one. She concludes, "The competences are organizational manifestations of the basic types of human beings. That is to say, we have produced these three basic types of systems in response to the three basic principles guiding our make-up as humans."[43]

	Mental	Physical	Emotional
Emphases	Concepts, structures, ideas	Actions, operations	Relationships, organization
Process	Linear, logical, sequential	Systemic (by a comprehensive process of gathering, linking and seeing the interconnections among relevant data)	Lateral (by emotional association rather than logical connection)
Functions	· Thinking · Envisioning · Planning · Focusing · Directing · Creating structure · Seeing the overview · Establishing values, principles · Maintaining objectivity · Analyzing	· Doing · Making · Producing · Concretizing · Detailing · Making operational · Utilizing · Ensuring practicality · Cooperating · Synthesizing · Systematizing	· Feeling · Connecting · Communicating · Relating · Personalizing · Empathizing · Organizing · Harmonizing · Processing · Imagining

Table 13: Individual archetypes
(Source: Steve Waddell, *Societal Learning and Change*, 89)

---

[43] Waddell, *Societal Learning and Change*, 90, paraphrasing Seagal.

Mental	State		Physical	Market		Emotional	Civil Society
Establishing values, principles	Rules-focused activity		Doing	Efficiency-focused activity		Feeling	Human impact-focused activity
Creating structure	Creating level playing field		Actualizing	Profit generation		Relating	Community thrust
Seeing the overview	Redistribution of benefits		Making	Delivery of goods and services to medium and upper income		Empathizing	Support of the marginalized
Directing	Administering		Producing	Managing		Processing	Developing
Creating structure	Standardized production		System	Commercial production		Creative imagination	Artistic production

Table 14: Individual functions and sectoral competences
(Source: Steve Waddell, *Societal Learning and Change*, 89)

This approach sees individual development integrally connected to social development. Waddell concludes:

> Therefore the SLC [societal learning and change] challenge at the individual level is to develop the ability of individuals to understand the world from the vantage point of distinct logics and work together well. . . . often this requires that individuals move to a higher individual "development stage." The types of people having reached a higher integration are the "strategist" and "magician" level of development according to one description, in contrast to "opportunists," "diplomats" and "technicians," who can only see the world from their own viewpoint.[44]

---

[44] Waddell, *Societal Learning and Change*, 90.

Sectoral/Societal Learning in Trisector Partnerships

We are coming here to a last aspect of the importance of the articulation of society in three sectors. If it is true that society is like a stool supported by three legs rather than two, then to the old dynamic of dualistic opposition we can replace one of vigorous dialogue and collaboration.

Talking about the new idea of societal learning and change (SLC) Waddell comments, "We can call SLC the change needed because it requires that all parties accept responsibility for changing themselves and their own actions to address the focal issue."[45] Among the targets of this approach, the book *Societal Learning and Change* explores eight examples worldwide, addressing the areas of community-level concerns, industries and products, public infrastructure, and global change strategies.

SLC approaches imply a shift from perception of problems from the present paradigm to that of opportunities asking for new behaviors. They require collective capacity building. They also require two kinds of learning:

- Experience-based, which draws from the past, resulting in such things as methodical reviews.
- Future-oriented processes that connect aspirations and work, along the lines of what Otto Scharmer articulates in his book *Theory U*, which we will approach in the next chapter. For now, suffice to say that these are processes in which the new can be discovered and operated upon with processes that allow individuals to meet in head, heart, and will and unleash the greatest potential for common action.

Organizational Sectors and Their Dynamics: Rationale for Cross-sector Collaboration

At the heart of the societal learning that can be fostered through trisector partnerships lie the changes that can derive from each sector learning to play new roles. Table 15 offers an overview of the logic from which each sector operates, which societal learning tries to modify and expand.[46]

---

[45] Waddell, *Societal Learning and Change*, 14.
[46] Waddell, *Societal Learning and Change*, 93.

	State Sector	Market Sector	Civil Society Sector
Primary concern	Political systems	Economic systems	Social systems
Control unit	Voters/rulers	Owners	Members
Primary power from	Laws, police, fines	Money	Traditions, values
Primary goals	Societal order	Wealth creation	Healthy communities
Assessment frame	Legality	Profitability	Justice
Goods produced	Public	Private	Group
Dominant organizational form	Governmental	For-profit	Non-profit
Operating frame	Administrative	Managerial	Developmental
Relationships basis	Rules	Transactions	Values
Temporal framework	Election cycles	Profit-reporting/ business cycles	Sustainability/ regeneration cycles

Table 15: operational parameters of the sectors
(Source: Steve Waddell, *Societal Learning and Change*, page 83)

We are presently at a point in time in which each of the three sectors is facing challenges and opportunities. Government forces are presently under pressure from two sides:

- globalization (global economic interaction and information technology among others), which destabilizes local economies and undermines national and local sovereignty
- citizens' pressure to tackle issues that government can no longer address alone (e.g. global commons), in reaction to the above

Business is balanced between the pressures of globalized markets and the competition they generate and the opportunities provided by technological innovation. Additional pressure comes from:

- the power of consumers to act according to their values (e.g., boycotts)
- the needs to address sustainability for sheer survival reasons: e.g., scarcity of water or other limited resources

Civil society can unleash its potential through a variety of new opportunities:

- new and sophisticated processes of dialogue and deliberation (See chapter 3)
- large systems interventions, e. g., forming of socially generative networks (see Chapter 4)

Initiatives that bring the three sectors at the table as equals are complex and time consuming. One of the key changes lies in

- bringing about unusual connections;
- embracing a whole systems approach, a both/and paradigm;
- realigning the relationships between the three core systems toward more equal power; and
- shift of focus among sectoral agents, where each sector operates within its inherent but one-sided logic. Collaboration forces them to expand their roles and capacities. The motivation for change can be crisis and/or hope for better outcomes that only collaboration can provide.[47]

What is advanced here can be rendered concrete with an example of trisector partnership.

The Pittsburgh Example: Community Bank Innovation[48]

Inner cities throughout the United States face the challenge of poor access to capital and adequate financial services, and consequent inability to foster economic development. Pittsburgh, as an old industrial capital, is one of many. Steve Waddell's case study follows what evolved in the city from an intentional trisector partnership.

The major players in the partnership were Integra Bank and Pittsburgh Community Reinvestment Group. The Pittsburgh trisector collaboration

---

[47] Peter Senge, Bryan Smith, Nina Kruschwitz, Joe Laur, and Sara Schley, *The Necessary Revolution: Working Together to Create a Sustainable World* (New York: Broadway Books, 2010); see chapters 6 and 7 for collaborations between industry and nonprofits to address sustainability.

[48] Waddell, *Societal Learning and Change*, 126–27.

was an experiment in which a bank collaborated with local community-based organizations while federal and local governments played an important support role. The result made possible the development and delivery of banking products and services to people who traditionally lack access to them. What made the situation unique were innovations from civil society and from government.

The opportunity arose, oddly enough, through the merger of two Pittsburgh banks and the resulting creation of Integra Bank. Stanley Lowe, a local community activist and head of the Pittsburgh Community Reinvestment Group (PCRG), saw in this an opportunity for establishing new working relationships, resulting in broader collaboration.

After federal regulators gathered community input, PCRG wrote a letter of demands. Though the situation was tense, Gayland Cook, the would-be president of Integra, saw value in what the community was arguing for, and was instrumental in the drafting of a memorandum of understanding that ushered in a new bank-community type of collaboration.

As in most American cities, there has been in Pittsburgh a migration of residents from the inner city to the suburbs. The inner city was left deprived of access to mortgages and other forms of financial services, thus compounding its economic decline. Federal regulators rated the banks on how they served the community and offered residents input in public hearings, especially in case of mergers. To the benefit of community activists, they also obliged the banks to offer public access to data on their volume of business according to geography and business type.

Over the years thirty neighborhood organizations joined in forming the PCRG, whose mission was to "promote neighborhood reinvestment by financial institutions." The local government acted as a broker by creating the Urban Redevelopment Authority (URA) in which both PCRG and the banks were members. And the URA formed Community Development Advisory Groups (CDAGs) with each bank. See figure 16 for a summary of the whole.

Through the help of the CDAGs arose the first memorandum of understanding, which was renegotiated at regular intervals. The result was that Integra collaborated directly with the community organizations in developing new bank products tailored to the needs of the inner city. The collaboration process has implied a shift in roles and responsibilities of the partners.

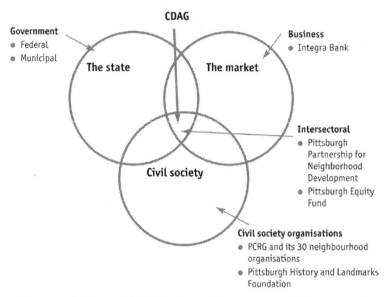

Figure 16: (Steve Waddell, *Societal Learning and Change*, 127)

The community organizations have put in place a system similar to a peer lending model, which offers education about the banking products and support in meeting loan repayments for defaulters, eliminating the bank's need for expensive legal steps to exact payments. The collaboration is beneficial to Integra, who has pledged a $55,000 annual commitment to PCRG. The government plays an additional role through lending programs to low-income communities, made possible through the collaboration of a variety of institutions: Integra, PCRG, the Pittsburgh History and Landmark Foundation, the Pittsburgh Equity Fund, the Pittsburgh Partnership for Neighborhood Development, and two other nonprofits.

From the above, we can see that the goal of inner city economic development has brought benefits to the three sectors: civil society's goals of furthering community development and offering access to nondiscriminatory financial services; the government's goal of improved and beneficial bank-community relationships; and the business goals of maintaining profitability where it was previously jeopardized, expanding the types of services offered, and operating sustainably in a supportive environment.

After six years of operation, Integra's clients count 60 percent of city residents, and the bank has significantly increased both the community's access to financial services and the percentage of those assigned to minority- and female-owned small businesses. Integra has discovered that markets traditionally considered marginal and risky can be served with mutual benefit through newly designed products, delivery structures, and ways to ensure loan repayments. In this new type of collaboration, the three sectors have each played new roles.

The CDAG, sponsored by the city but mostly formed by Integra and PCRG, has greatly accelerated the experiment by its regular monthly meetings, allowing greater alignment of interests. The government can use the incentives of its large buying power in promoting new behaviors since it can direct where its hospitals and schools turn for their business. The PCRG shifted from pure advocacy to a crucial intermediary role in reshaping business services and products for the benefit of the community.

From the above we can see that each sector can expand its roles and capacities. The government can move from regulating to supporting, and from being arbitrators to facilitators; businesses from acting solely for profit to incorporating sustainability goals or tailor their products for underprivileged populations (often with the help of NGOs); and NGOs from being advocates and watchdogs to drafting new alliances and promoting larger collaboration according to community values. This example offers meaning to what could sound rather abstract under the name of societal learning and change.

Trisector Partnerships: Summing up

So far we have been looking at various aspects of the tri-articulation of society and what these mean from a purely pragmatic perspective. We have recognized the central role of civil society, whether this be called cultural, social, or plural. We have discerned a shift in social interventions from enforcing one of the perspectives (political or economic) to seeking balance between the three. This is a momentous change of focus in social interventions.

We have recognized an inherent holistic dimension of this division of society in three sectors. ICA brings it to the surface in how the threefold membering of society reappears at any level of social reality that can be considered. The rebalancing is something that can be done through discerning the leverage points at larger or smaller levels of social reality. This analysis has gone further into the holistic aspects of the three sectors. It appears in how the three sectors embody basic human drives (ICA) and how they each correspond to different kinds of personality types and learning styles.

Finally, moving into the practical work carried out in societal learning and change, we can see what this balancing can mean in trisector partnerships. We took the example of Pittsburgh and the effort to bring financial services to the inner city. The result of that collaboration implied a rebalancing of the activity of the three sectors through the learning and new capacities that each developed in order to bring about a new state of equilibrium.

What has been treated in this chapter will be continued in the next. Trisector partnerships blend two elements: a new vision of society articulated around three poles, rather than the two traditional ones, coming from a pragmatic perspective; and a new way of bringing stakeholders at the table, which will be the subject of the next chapter, multi-stakeholder logic.

So far we have looked at trisector reality from an empirical/practical perspective alone. We have not weighed in on which of the three approaches corresponds more closely to social reality: cultural, social, or plural. Nor have we looked at how we can completely modify the way we think about social issues. For this we will first turn to additional considerations.

Cultural Power

In a way that is reminiscent of both ICA and Mintzberg, Nicanor Perlas converges with Mintzberg and ICA in his assessment of balance and imbalance in what he calls "threefolding": "We live in a healthy society if the three social poles mutually recognize and support each other and develop their initiatives with awareness of their potential impacts on other realms. We live in an unhealthy society if one realm dominates and tries to subjugate the others."[49]

---

[49] Nicanor Perlas, *Shaping Globalization: Civil Society, Cultural Power and Threefolding* (Forest Row, UK: Temple Lodge, 2019), 4.

What Perlas adds to the equation is a fuller view of the role of civil society: "Through its emergence, civil society also gives birth, consciously or not, to cultural life as an autonomous realm within larger society."[50] Among the institutions of civil society, Perlas includes NGOs, people's organizations, youth and women's groups, media, religious groups, foundations, voluntary organizations, professional groups, academe, "and others whose direct and dominant activity *does not involve business or government operations*" (emphasis added).[51] Under civil society he thus includes education and the media. The latter's cultural role is hard to recognize, at least in our country, given its close connection to political or corporate interests. This simply means that its role has been corrupted.

Cultural power, for Perlas much as for ICA, rests not on political voice or weight, but through issues connected with meaning, identity, morality, and authenticity. He concludes: "In short, culture is the well-spring that determines and sustains human behavior. Loss of meaning results in a cluster of aberrant and destructive behaviors. Discovery of meaning brings greater creativity, compassion and productivity."[52] Understanding of the nature and essence of this power will allow us to alter our social behavior.

The majority of civil society organizations (CSOs) do not impact the economy with activities such as production, distribution, or consumption of goods and services. Cultural activity does not generate economy; on the contrary, it has to rely on excess money generated in other fields, typically gift money generated from economic activity and administered by foundations and philanthropic institutions. And the more it can show that it has an impact in altering our common assumptions and in attaining the social good, the more it is attractive to foundations and donors.

On the other hand, even though CSOs often intervene in matters of human rights, protection of the environment, social justice, and rights of minorities, they enter the field because the government is not doing what it should do, as it is the government's task to actively uphold everyone's rights. However, CSOs do not campaign for office, and civil society does not operate in society through political parties or groupings. Thus civil society

---

[50] Perlas, *Shaping Globalization*, 3.

[51] Perlas, *Shaping Globalization*, 20.

[52] Perlas, *Shaping Globalization*, 38.

is involved neither in economic activity nor in direct political activity. By fully coming to this recognition, it can clarify and champion its cultural role.

Many institutions that are presently a conglomerate of economic and cultural interests are really part of the cultural arena, the media and the whole of education for one. It is clear that the corporate media has understood by default what it means to shape culture. It spends billions of dollars to purvey a culture shackled to political and economic interests. Neoliberalism knows how important it is to have an almost complete predominance over the minds and hearts of its citizens, and thus preserve what it is its culture, or lack thereof. The same is true of the political regimes that depend on exclusive political hegemony, though they will do it differently.

A confusion arises and will persist as long as we do not fully realize the kinds of power that each sector has. The state has coercing power, used at its best in ensuring the respect of all human rights. The economy has the power to generate wealth and address the needs of all, used at its worst to buy political favor and influence.

Cultural power cannot compel. Cultural power is much less immediate than political power, but much more long-lasting. Cultural revolutions take years to prepare before they become societal norms, as we will illustrate with a couple of examples. It is also more subtle and hard to recognize. By the time cultural change has become the norm, people have forgotten what it took to generate it.

That transnational corporations are vulnerable through consumer education and changed values around products that the consumer purchases is an example of cultural power. This is the whole point of the enormous role played by advertising. Consumer boycotts play this role in reverse, when people subjugate their behaviors to newly found values, replacing those generated by the advertising machine. There are numerous examples of this: Pepsi Co. had to withdraw from Burma due to boycotts; the 1994 anti-pesticide campaign caused a $2 billion decrease in sales; the ban on genetically modified crops in Europe pushed supermarkets, fast food restaurants, and food producers to align themselves with the newly expressed cultural values.[53]

---

[53] Perlas, *Shaping Globalization*, 147.

Examples of Cultural Power

It is hard to think of a movement that has had more shaping power over America's minds and hearts than the Twelve Steps of Alcoholics Anonymous (AA). It is not an NGO, does not have a significant national budget, operates purely voluntarily, and is practically everywhere around us.

Bill Wilson's effort had its impetus from one important spiritual experience that shaped his recovery and the remainder of his life. When that happened in 1934, Wilson was a changed man, so much so that he came back from the brink of irreversible alcoholism. After a small number of failed attempts, and specially thanks to his collaboration with Bob Smith, he hit upon a way to replicate the essence of his experience for other alcoholics. Thus we can say that AA was an inspiration from the spirit through a modern individual. It was also a manifestation of that universal spirit that can touch anyone who is in a place of dire need. The spirit in words such as "the higher power as I understand him" is a formulation that leaves anybody free to relate to it in his or her own individual fashion. And more than the words, the power lies in the process of the Twelve Steps that anyone can try for themselves.

Ultimately, the proof of AA and other Twelve Step processes lies in the results. Hundreds of thousands, if not millions, worldwide have been touched and healed, who before the 1930s were simply deemed incurable— all of it through the power of individuals being held in circles of support without the help of any paid staff. In this lies another example of cultural power. Twelve Steps has altered the perception of what it means to be addicted to a substance or behavior; it has spread out tolerance; it has rayed out hope. And it is an irreversible shaper of values for our culture.

Another example: When in 1973 Elisabeth Kübler-Ross did her famous interview with Eva, the word *death*, or the idea of discussing death publicly, was a deeply entrenched taboo. Kübler-Ross was fired and ostracized for taking this courageous stance. With the success of *On Death and Dying*, she alerted the American and worldwide public that there is another way of looking at death, one more imbued with value and meaning, and that the dying can depart with dignity surrounded by the presence of their loved ones. Her work went hand in hand with that of the early Hospice, which had its start in the United Kingdom through Cecily Saunders.

At present death and dying has become the subject of endless debates, books, and initiatives. It is so commonplace that it is easy to forget that it took much of its impetus in the United States from an individual and that that individual had various spiritual experiences that shaped her life.[54]

The fact that the above two individuals mentioned had spiritual experiences is very significant, though it is not a qualifying factor in a cultural contribution. Other individuals in the United States have made equally significant contributions to American culture without the need of spiritual experiences; they nevertheless have a firm grounding in the reality of culture, or in deep inner sources of meaning and identity.

To close I want to show how the cultural perspective embraces the plural or social ones.

Social, Plural, or Cultural?

What is the name that reflects the reality of the third sector more than any other? The problem lies in characterizing a new paradigm while operating from the old one. How we live in the old paradigm colors the way we see the new. And the old is mostly the political perspective, through which we often still see and try to define a reality larger than the political. How do you pull yourself away from that which you are part of in order to see that which lies above?

When we look at all the NGOs, nonprofits, community-based organizations, and movements that are inspired traditionally from the Left, we find at their center advocacy and action in social matters, whether they are concerned with justice, poverty alleviation, fighting social injustice, the environment, collective crises, and so on. The change that is sought is social. However, there is another change that goes hand in hand with the first and that may be less noticeable.

The focus of a conservative perspective often lies in the strengthening of individual values, with the belief, hope, and assumption that society is changed by those. Among those who seek purely individual change, we could find churches and movements that have few direct political or

---

[54] For more on Elisabeth Kübler-Ross see Luigi Morelli, *A Revolution of Hope: Spirituality, Cultural Renewal and Social Change* (Victoria, BC: Trafford, 2009), chapter 6.

social goals. And some among these cross political affiliations or the larger conservative/progressive divide. An excellent example of the above, often broadly overlooked, is the whole of Twelve Steps or Hospice, another set of independent but interrelated organizations with a large presence in the social arena. Their focus, however, is primarily on the individual.

Twelve Steps does not pronounce itself on political matters; it does not advocate social change. Bill Wilson was politically speaking a conservative, but his personal choices did not color Twelve Steps. If that had happened, it would have been the end of such a movement. It worked precisely because it had a great impact on American and worldwide society by painting another image of what it means to be human—a purely cultural pursuit, not a political one.

The same discourse would apply to much of the Christian evangelical movement, whether we personally like it or not. Such a movement does not predicate social change; it only subordinates it to individual change. Traditionally most, but not all, of it falls on the conservative side of the political spectrum, once it comes to voting.

What appears as a conundrum of opposition of values in the political arena (the old paradigm)—the stress on individual or social values— presents no problems of integration when we move to a higher perspective, precisely the cultural perspective presented by ICA or Nicanor Perlas. The new paradigm will be built at the intersection of individual values that define a new way of seeing the human condition, and social values that predicate interconnectedness of issues and stakeholders and the need to act upon these. The words of a great spiritual authority and quintessential cultural figure—"Be the change you want to see in the world" (Mahatma Gandhi)— encompass both sides of the spectrum, individual and social responsibilities, and give either a greater meaning. In the final analysis, this book is all about paradigms that can birth a new culture.

From Either/Or to Both/And Thinking

Capitalism sees culture as something that adds pleasure to life and mostly comes from the past. It then turns culture into another area to exploit for commercial aims, certainly not into the creator of meaning for a new worldview.

Marx on the other hand turned Hegelian dialectic upside down, and devalued the role of culture. Hegel postulated the supremacy of ideas in determining the course of history. He saw meaningful action inspired by the spirit of the age. Marx adopted a completely materialistic dialectic. In his views of society, culture is a superstructure that reflects, rather than conditions or influences, a certain social reality. The new culture of socialism is one that erects socialism to the status of culture, just as capitalism erects its own ideology and calls that culture. In other words, in socialist thinking culture is whatever a dominating group establishes as the justification for its role and power.

Ultimately culture cannot be enlivened by those ideologies that want to deny its independence (socialism) or want to strive in every possible way it to subjugate it to its economic aims (capitalism). So far we have shown pragmatically how the addition of civil society to the other two sectors modifies the dynamics of social change. In going a step further, we can go beyond the utopias of the past and the stranglehold they have upon modern thinking and social imagination. To do that we have to qualitatively change our thinking. We have to be able to think both/and rather than either/or: thinking in threes rather than in twos is the beginning of it. We will offer one example of what this thinking looks like in one famous individual and then show how a new thinking can transcend models of the past in agriculture.

Observation and Science

If society is no longer the arena of the confrontation between the forces of the economy and those of government but the place of interplay between three, we have a new status of equilibrium that can continue to take the form of opposition between each two terms within the three (economy against state, state against civil society, civil society against the economy) or give rise to a new possibility, the opportunity of constructive collaboration between the three. What interests us here is the latter possibility as a move toward deeper social transformation.

What emerges from this chapter is a thread that works its way out throughout the book. It is the first instance that illustrates the shift from either/or to both/and thinking, from thinking in twos—as terms that oppose each other—to thinking in threes in the forming of new syntheses. With thinking in threes we refer to the possibility that each term of a dichotomy (capitalism and socialism are the ultimate in social terms) can only oppose the other in a sterile way (thinking in twos) or be resolved at a higher level of synthesis in which what lives in either term of the opposition appears in essence, not in actual form, and is *transcended and included* at a higher level. In practical terms, a society integrating the impulses of economy, state, and social/cultural arena, will neither be capitalistic nor socialistic, neither anticapitalistic nor antisocialist, but will carry the fundamental essence of both within something much larger and comprehensive.

We will approach this thinking shortly, then look at how it finds expression in one famous individual and offer an example of what it can lead us to in farming and the food system.

When we think in twos, or either/or terms, all of our field of reality is arrayed in terms of opposition. We arrange reality in sides and favor one against the other. Inevitably this means elevating one to the state of good, quite regardless of our personally stated convictions, whether religious or secular, on the matter of good or evil. Sooner or later we will feel obliged to throw our weight on one side, the good one, and against the other, the bad one.

It is in fact the unchecked tendency of the pure intellect to see everything in dualities, and most of our education at present favors the intellect in a way that leads us to this inner separation from the whole in favor of one part, and outwardly to all degrees of opposition and polarization.

Modern science separates and analyzes to understand. It takes an organ out of the body, the tissue out of the organ, the cell out of the tissue. To the extent to which this is actually necessary, it is not compensated by an ability to reassemble the whole in order to perceive its higher unity.

Of course we must have recourse to the intellect, but we can also refine it with a more artistic side, which we may call the right-side brain or intuition, which allows us to let objects speak to us and offer us insights about their essence and nature out of the wealth of their physical manifestations, not from beyond these in any transcendental fashion. By balancing these two modes of cognition, analytical and intuitive, we can re-create a higher unity in knowledge. Out of the two a third arises that reconciles any two terms that intellect alone perceives but cannot unite.

All order of reality is more akin to the yin and yang, which intermixes the one into the other. Night and day, growth and decay, light and darkness, order and chaos, self-interest and altruism, contraction and expansion are forces that complement each other, and without which a higher order is not possible. Each of the two terms left unchecked creates unbalance. The two together create a dynamic tension, which is something higher than a simple sum or average.

We can also discover these realities through a simple look at ourselves. Human courage can be seen as the opposite of cowardice, but looking closer we can discern a third state of mind that is not fearlessness but foolhardiness. Courage needs both fear and presence of mind; it is not the absence of either or both. It is found between the two extremes. Male and female, masculine and feminine, form a sterile average in neuter. Otherwise they are the principles with which we can create a higher synthesis in physical, psychological, and spiritual terms.

In social matters we are more and more forced to take a firm stand in an ever-growing movement of polarization, in which each side genuinely believes the other to be wrong or evil. It takes courage to genuinely listen and suspend judgment, to see what has value on either side of the divide, not in order to borrow from each, but to create something higher than both. This is what we can recognize to a high degree in Martin Luther King Jr's way of thinking.

MLK the Thinker

We are turning now to that part of Martin Luther King Jr seldom fully appreciated: the man and his thinking. MLK is a truly revered moral leader, though in my opinion his greatness is not fully apprehended. What is brought forth here is explored in depth elsewhere.[55]

Before becoming the celebrated mastermind and strategist of the civil rights movement, King was faced with a choice; on both sides of it he could have succeeded. He could go into the ministry and into a hands-on approach to the matters of racial justice, for which he opted, or pursue an academic career in which he would have excelled. MLK was just as brilliant in his intellect as he was in practical social pursuits; in fact, strong in one because strong in the other. What made him such?

---

[55] For more on MLK see Luigi Morelli, *Legends and Stories for a Compassionate America* (Bloomington, IN: iUniverse, 2014), chapter 5: "Martin Luther King Jr.: Moral and Cultural Leader."

MLK saw life's contradictions with great interest, and had the uncanny ability to withhold judgment, whether this be on practical or theoretical questions. Matters of the spirit interested him greatly, and in his studies he absorbed a great deal of philosophy from Aristotle and Plato to modern philosophers and thinkers. Ideas had a truly formative power in his soul. He went at great length and pains to understand them and make them his own. One of these, which remained a lifelong leitmotif, was Hegel's idealistic dialectic. From that moment onward this "include and transcend" approach of Hegel formed the bedrock of King's thinking and strategic approach to his social work by his own admission.

Hegel's dialectic posits that each one term of a cognitive, scientific, social, or historic matter—a thesis—can be countered by an opposite one— an antithesis. By living in one and the other, the mind can resolve what appears as a contradiction, and finally unite thesis and antithesis at a higher level than either—the synthesis. A few examples from King's life will suffice.

King was as critical of capitalism as he was of socialism. His position in regards to capitalism is well known: he saw in it a tremendous waste in terms of environmental, social, and human capital. Of socialism he could not accept the "ends justifies the means" methodology of social change with its justification of violence, nor its purely materialistic outlook. But neither could he simply discard and condemn socialism. On the contrary a question arose in him: "If this is so, how come people of faith do not have the drive and passion for social justice that Marxist people have?" He was asking himself how that spirit could be brought into his own faith. Overall, however, he laid the foundation for questioning both ends of the spectrum, but could not find a synthesis. And for a good reason; this is probably the most daring enterprise of the mind. This whole chapter takes a stab in this direction, resting on the shoulders of giants.

Matters of faith interested King a great deal. One could wonder why he spent so much of his time in this direction. Conservative Christianity showed him a facet of the whole: it showed him the inherent limitations of the individual. You may call it the pessimistic view of human nature. MLK knew firsthand of those personal flaws that he felt powerless to change in himself. But he also saw from other parts of himself what is best and greatest in human nature and how it can bring us closer to the divine. With that he could relate to much of liberal Christianity. You could call this the optimistic pole. He summed up this contrast by saying that there is "a Mr. Hyde and a Dr. Jekyll in us," and that "I am a sinner like all God's children."[56] This was said in relation to his sexual infidelities.

King could do the same he did above in bridging the gap between transcendent Christian views pitted against immanent ones. The former place the divine where the human being cannot fathom its fullness. The latter see the divine in the expressions of daily life and not beyond. It is interesting to note that the two aspects of this relationship to the divine manifested in King's own life with three spiritual experiences. In these what is transcendent and beyond words is also made deeply personal, thus immanent.

Never could King discard one side of the equation in favor of the other. On the contrary his curiosity was sharpened because he knew he could learn from both sides and beyond either. For him, as for Hegel, one represented the thesis, the other the antithesis. In succeeding to formulate a synthesis, he would see the justification of one and the other, but also find the resolution of the contrast at a level higher than either—the synthesis.

What would seem just a simple intellectual game has implications that have not been fully measured in the social realm. Nonviolence had been applied before MLK in the United States, notably by Bayard Rustin. And yet people practically do not remember others than MLK when it comes to that. The reason for it is that King elevated nonviolence from mere utilitarian strategy to world outlook. To start with King was highly skeptical of pacifism and could not join ranks with it. He thought it was just a naïve opposition to war, or a term of a foundational dualism. But he was obviously loath to violence. In nonviolence he saw a synthesis that was perfectly in line with his faith. In *Stride Toward Freedom* King wrote, "Like the synthesis in Hegelian philosophy, the principle of nonviolent resistance seeks to reconcile the truths of two opposites—acquiescence and violence—while avoiding the extremes and immoralities of both."[57]

---

[56] Stephen B. Oates, *Let the Trumpet Sound: A Life of Martin Luther King* (New York: Harper & Row, 1982), 282.

[57] See http://www.openculture.com/2015/02/how-martin-luther-king-jr-used-hegel-to-overturn-segregation-in-america.html.

The above was not just an intellectual game. In King, Hegelian dialectics had acquired force of inner habit. They had completely changed the human being; he had imbibed the new paradigm.

Seen from the above perspective, another characteristic of King's work stands out with force: MLK never endorsed political power. Even though he interfaced with JFK and Lyndon Johnson, his strategies did not impel him to compromise his goals with political ones. Though he had a positive relationship with both presidents, he opted for his movement to exert pressure on the political apparatus and bring it to change, rather than offering the whole of the movement as an appendix of the political machines. In this way he brought forth much more than had he been their political ally. King truly exerted cultural power and created a cultural movement.

With hindsight we could say that the civil rights movement was quintessentially cultural, rather than just political. In this lay its success; conversely we can say that very little of this nature has been achieved since, precisely because deeper change has been sought mostly in the political arena.

Before moving to practical illustrations of the fruitfulness of a new way of thinking in social terms, let us look at everything that this chapter has uncovered so far, in Table 17.

Rethinking Tripolar Society

Having looked at what it means to affirm the cultural dimension of civil society and shown how a more encompassing way of thinking can be achieved in the social field, as in the example of MLK, we will now look at what it means to rethink the whole of society. In so doing we will essentially move from thinking in terms of either/or to thinking in both/and.

Capitalism and socialism, in their purest forms, as well as in their transition aspects, see society around the poles of the public sector or of the private sector. Capitalism stresses the role of free enterprise in the economy and subordinates the state to this goal. Socialism exalts the role of the state and subordinates the economy to it. Neither one of them articulates or fully apprehends the role of civil society. A tripolar society sees public and private sectors as equally important, but also gives equal value to the cultural sector.

Thinking in 2s	Thinking in 3s
Either or	Both and
Antagonism of thesis and antithesis; choice of either term; no resolution	Thesis / antithesis / synthesis Polarity (yin/yang) in which both terms contribute
Oppose	Include and transcend
Final goal	Evolutionary approach
Starts from the premise that it knows where it needs to arrive; holds a plan	Seeks the new; the path is not much more than a blueprint
Recognizes economic and political sectors; cultural sector mostly subsumed within either of the two	Distinguishes economic, political and cultural sectors. Gives primacy to the cultural as the source of values and meaning
Sets some societal needs against other needs (e.g., social versus individual responsibility)	Sees all societal needs as equally important
Solutions mostly framed from within a certain ideological perspective	Seeks completely new solutions from a new way of thinking, not an ideology
Whole can be understood from the sum of the parts	Whole is more than the sum of the parts
Set fully within the materialistic perspective	Makes room for a more holistic perspective

Table 17: From thinking in 2s to thinking in 3s

As long as we privilege one of two sectors, dualistic thinking is sufficient, even if it does not uphold reality in its fullness or fully promote the social good. When we articulate a reality of three equal partners, we enter by necessity in a way of thinking that requires much more effort, and the ideas that it generates cannot be applied in the same spirit as can a party platform. The organic thinking we are advancing is one that only applies to reality within a given context. A tripolar society will be different in Europe than in the United States, or in an African country; within the United States it will have to find a nuanced expression in Vermont, another one in Hawaii or Oklahoma, and so on.

A great part of the arguments and debates about social change are grounded in a form of thinking that takes much of current reality for granted and does not challenge common assumptions. Most energy is geared toward generating desired outcomes while agreeing on a large amount of unquestioned existing conditions, which are taken for self-evident wisdom. But are they?

What follows will unearth how much of these are just assumptions of a spectator consciousness that has rightly challenged all wisdom of the past, but in the process has lost much of the common sense of traditional cultures. In doing so I do not advocate a return to the past but rather a broadening of perspectives that moves away from the black or white political platforms and their anchoring in the great utopias of the twentieth century. It is a lens of perception and thinking that offers guidelines that can only be approached in a living and flexible way. We must live into them to alter the very way we perceive and think about social reality. What is offered here are only very general, introductory concepts and some examples. For more I refer the reader to the resources at the end of the chapter.

Balancing the Three Sectors

The present paradigm is one in which cultural/spiritual values are seldom present, or implied in the background. It is one in which the marriage of political and economic interests renders democracy a pale image of its greatest potential and leads to an erosion of political rights, a constant and growing economic disparity, accompanied with growing signs of social pathology. In the United States alone, the growing economic disparity can only be logically maintained at the expense of one of the highest per capita rates of incarceration worldwide.

To subvert this state of general cultural vacuum, it is imperative to foster a new culture, and this is the role that civil society alone can fulfill, indeed is already attempting to fulfill with various degrees of success. To understand what a new paradigm would entail, let us review some of the basics.

The three sectors encompass different realities, operate according to different logics, and exert unique kinds of power. They need to operate within clear boundaries and engage consciously where their areas of operation overlap.

The economic sector (private sector) is that which supports all our physical/existential needs through goods and services; its prime institution is business at all levels, from a single proprietorship business to a large corporation. The public sector represents all its citizens as equal; it protects the individual from the encroachments of other individuals, the country from other countries. It is represented by government, from the level of a village to that of single nations or associations of nations, and even global institutions. Civil society, or the cultural sector, is that which affirms the unique value of the individual, and the communities and cultures he or she belongs to. It is best represented by nonprofits, many of whom are known as NGOs (nongovernment organizations), or CBOs (community-based organizations), two variously overlapping terms. Here too their sphere of action ranges from the local to the global. Think of Oxfam, the Red Cross, or CARE International.

We could say that the economic sector operates at its best within a logic of sustainability and mutuality; it has to provide fairly to the needs of all, and can do so only in an atmosphere of goodwill and interdependence. The political sector's main emphasis is that of equality under the law; all citizens deserve equal protection for their rights, no matter what their economic or cultural status. The cultural sector is that which honors the individual's differences and unique potential, that which assures her highest degree of freedom of expression.

Each of the sectors and its representative institutions relies on different kinds of power. Businesses have economic and material/resource power; governments have legal and coercive power; NGOs and CBOs have normative or culturally assertive power (think of boycotts).

Each of the three sectors acts according to different drives, or primary values. The primary economic driver is efficiency, or the best use of resources, labor, and energy to satisfy human needs. Left in freedom to interfere with the other sectors, this efficiency becomes the ruthlessness that is familiar to most Americans and the driver of social inequality. The political driver is uniformity. Bureaucracy has a place in government, where we all need to be treated as equals. Bureaucracy, left to itself, can turn into stultifying absurdity that tends to preserve itself and disregard the context of its actions. The chief cultural value is that of diversity of expression. Left to itself, civil society can either splinter in lack of cohesion in all directions, especially if it does not reach awareness of its role, or eliminate diversity in the name of a reigning racial, cultural, or religious prejudice.

Each of these three systems exists in a state of balance when it does not overwhelm the other two. Left to itself, the economic system becomes a plutocracy in which the few have most of the resources and subjugate the rest of the population to their needs. When it overwhelms the other two sectors, government can pave the way to dictatorship. When a certain section of society imposes its cultural values upon the rest, we have exacerbated prevalence of a nationality/ethnicity or of a religious/cultural group over all the others, a sort of fundamentalist outlook. In most of the above cases one sector will join forces with a second one and exclude the third one.

Two objections could arise at this point. First, isn't this a view of society that artificially compartmentalizes the whole? To this we can answer that what unites the whole is the individual who partakes of the activities of the sectors. We are each, at turns, part of each sector, and when that happens, we can honor the logic that assures its best functioning.

And second, what of interactions and boundaries? Aren't the sectors continuously interacting with each other? This is something that we are actually partly familiar with in the area of government itself, especially in the United States. We know how important it is to have an executive clearly defined in its powers in relation to the equally well defined legislative and judicial. This system of checks and balances doesn't put undue obstacles to their collaboration. It only adds safeguards and improvements.

In the case of the American government we can see how the three branches keep each other in balance, though this state of equilibrium can be disturbed in various ways at different times in history by each one of the branches. The executive has been vying for expanded war powers and de facto declaring war while bypassing Congress. The Supreme Court has been stepping into disguised legislative action at various times in our history. In the *Dred Scott v. Sandford* case of 1857, Chief Justice Roger Taney attempted to rewrite the Constitution in the interest of vastly expanding slavery. In the 2010 *Citizens United v. Federal Election Commission*, the Supreme Court rewrote the law of the land, giving unusual rights and unfair advantages to corporations, which in turn vastly increased their power and influence over Congress. The legislative branch on its end can unduly influence the selection of the president through voter suppression in key swing states. These are but some of the examples of the necessity of checks and balances and how the equilibrium can be altered for the worse when we lose sight of the importance of these mechanisms in a healthy democracy.

We know how important was the separation between church and state espoused by the Founders: it shows that they were conscious that the sphere of government should not be intruded upon by sectional cultural concerns, that the national aspirations could not be fulfilled by and equated to this or that religion or denomination. By the same token, we know that we desperately need to separate government from corporations, that the power corporations hold over government at present is extremely unhealthy for our democracy.

What a tripolar view of society offers to the bipolar options of the twentieth century is a dose of both/and outlook. Tripolar society, as we will see below, predicates many things that traditional cultures have held as self-evident truths for millennia. The ideas espoused may resemble old traditions, but they are inserted within a modern reality of much higher complexity. No return to the past is advocated.

On the other hand, the logic of a tripolar society pushes us to espouse views that can be seen as liberal, and others that can be seen as conservative. In reality they are neither of the two, because they are articulated in newer contexts that do not strictly compare with the old paradigms. This is another seeming conundrum of both/and paradigms.

Let us now look at each sector and the overlapping areas. In doing so we will only offer general indications and offer some examples among a multitude that is possible. The general considerations brought forth here do not call for standard responses; they can be addressed with a variety of existing tools, but many more approaches can and should emerge in the future.

Political Sector

One of the major departures from bipolar society lies in the place of government. On one hand much that is now given to the state does not really belong to it. And more importantly, the reverse: much that actually belongs to it, is left outside of its area of influence. By starting from government, we can more easily visualize the boundaries between the three sectors.

Government does not successfully intervene in the running of the economy or of culture, simply because these are not the goals it can pursue best. Government is not equipped to understand the multitude of variables that enter production, distribution, and consumption. In fact only economic operators deeply involved in the economy can do it, and only when they unite with each other. Such is the complexity of world economy under the division of labor, that only larger organizations can apprehend it, not individuals.

Likewise the autonomy of culture needs to be assured because political logic does not apply to the optimal development of individual capacities, only to that which is common to all. The political sector renders everything uniform; indeed, it is its role. Only an independent cultural arena can assure not just the preservation but the vibrancy of culture.

We can argue that by intervening in these two realms, government has had palliative effects mixed with unintended consequences, without addressing the root causes. It can have much more direct effects at the root of many matters and set the boundaries of action in the economic and cultural sectors.

Some examples: much of what are considered economic matters have never been considered from this angle before we entered modern consciousness, even more so after the Industrial Revolution. Such are the examples of land, labor, or means of production, or access to health care. All of these are presently equated to goods to be produced by the economy, when they are clearly not. Land does not accrue in value like a product in which human ingenuity has truly brought a transformation. At present land could accrue in value even when it has actually degraded in its productive capacity. On the other hand, land is the foundation upon which rests a measure of individual survival. We all need access to at least some land upon which to have a dwelling, an indispensable human right. Assuring this right is something to which the resources of the state and its powers should be turned.

Labor does not lawfully belong to the market; rightly seen it is what entitles the individual to live out his needs while assuring the needs of others. The assurance of these needs for survival should be within the purview of the state. Human remuneration, hours and length of work, and all other labor regulations belong outside of the realm of the economy. Left to economic considerations, labor remuneration engages us in a struggle for survival and becomes a tool for social control. Labor matters are questions that should be decided within legal parameters; each nation, state, or region may come to different assessments on these. Corporations are not the best authorities in terms of administering social justice, much less so the impersonal forces of the market.

We can here appreciate what it means to think in three. On one hand we have the idea that great differences of income are justified in light of the ingenuity of the entrepreneur and different skillsets that each bring to the job market; on the other we can argue that we should split the pie somewhere in the middle and all should get the same, or a similar share. Both ideas place the matter of remuneration within the market logic alone. A new way of thinking lies in going to the basis of what labor is and recognizing it as a matter of rights, not as a market concern. An idea that is going into that direction is the so-called citizen basic income or universal basic income that has been experimented with in various countries, or parts thereof.[58] This idea goes a step further than living wage, and moves deeper toward honoring the reality of labor.

The means of production have accrued through the ingenuity of dozens or hundreds of individuals and the exertion of their labor. They have resulted from ideas and innovations brought forward through education over many generations. Traditionally, we have heard that the means of production belong to the one who has exerted ingenuity and therefore can reap most of the benefits. This idea is immediately contradicted by the rights of inheritance, which indicate that nothing else than being born in the right place at the right time constitutes a criterion of merit. On the other hand, we can devolve authority over the means of production to the state or to a local government.

Here too a third way can be found that honors both social ends and individual talent. Imagine placing the means of production in the hands of a local legal association, whose goal is to serve the needs of the community. The association is then in a position to look for those individuals who will

---

[58] For an exploration of citizen basic income see Martin Large, *Common Wealth for a Free, Equal, Mutual and Sustainable Society* (Stroud, UK: Hawthorne, 2010), chapter 9: "Citizen's Income: Social Inclusion and Common Wealth for All."

best serve the needs of the community because of skills, competencies, and recognized integrity, and only for as long as they serve the community's needs. No one owns the association in their personal name, nor is it a government agency or similar entity. When the designated persons die or leave, the process of finding the right substitutes starts anew, bypassing the problem of inheritance. Such an idea may seem a far distant horizon. We already have its forerunner in the experiments of land trusts, which attempt to remove land from the market with the aim of preservation, or with the goal of rendering housing more affordable.[59] In the United States we can appreciate how such an example of land trust has renewed economic development in Boston's inner city neighborhood of Dudley.[60] We will see another example of it shortly in the very widespread but not fully understood idea of community supported agriculture.

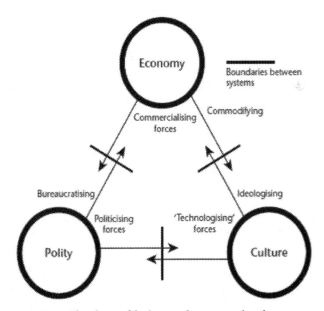

Figure 18: Checks and balances between the three sectors
(Source: Large, *Common Wealth*, 61)

[59] See Large, *Common Wealth*, chapter 10: "Land for People, Homes and Communities."
[60] See https://www.dudleyneighbors.org/ for general information; https://www.yesmagazine.org/economy/2015/09/17/land-trusts-offer-houses-low-income-people-can-afford-and-a-stepping-stone-to-lasting-wealth/; for a case study see Lee Allen Dwyer, "Mapping Impact: An Analysis of the Dudley Street Neighborhood Initiative Land Trust," https://www.dsni.org/s/Dwyer_Thesis_FINAL_compressed.pdf.

If we look at the larger picture that an organic view of tripolar society paints, we can discern that at present, the state does not intervene to secure rights "upstream." By this I mean it does not open up a conversation for a more organic perception of the reality of fundamental human rights and for breaking the deadlock of ideological thinking. It would be much more efficient to take measures upstream—defining, codifying, and assuring the basic rights—to favor an emancipation of labor from the market or promote a different relationship to the means of production or right to health care among others. It would certainly be a difficult task that would require great efforts of education and legislation, but more efficient in the long run than intervening downstream with corrective measures when, one could say, the damage is done, and little can be done to bring remedy, especially in times of economic downturns.

How each sector can serve to hold in check and balance the other two is illustrated in figure 18.

Cultural Sector / Civil Society

It is from civil society and its work that we derive and are able to satisfy our need to contribute to the betterment of society. It is culture, particularly through education, that hones our faculties of judgment and supports our ethical individualism, the balance between what we feel appropriate for our own development and being respectful of the needs of others. Individuals who affirm their inherent value and develop self-assurance will naturally contribute to the commonwealth; they will not be willing cogs in a society that wants to usurp their rights.

From this alone we should see the importance of a culture that stands on its own. Government cannot be the guarantor of a culture that should itself question when the political sector transgresses its boundaries, since it has coercive power that it can exert when left to itself. Witness of it are the extreme positions of absolutist powers; they will go to any length to squash cultural independence at its first signs of emergence. Civil society is alone in the position of being able to preserve and protect culture, not to mention promote new values and paradigms. It can only do it if is given its own sphere of action.

In reviewing the boundaries between the political and the cultural, we can distinguish, broadly speaking, two areas concerning education. On one hand education would be considered a right in most societies and nations. And, as a right, the state is best habilitated to ensure equal access to education for all its citizens. On the other hand, the striving of education is to bring out the full potential of each individual. This would seem the calling of the cultural sector.

The topic of education has become very polarized and polarizing within a dualistic perspective. On one hand there is the view that education should be a public matter and be more or less the same across the United States. This is challenged by the perspective that would like to expand mostly private and/or profit-based charter schools in which the private sector is eagerly seeking new avenues for growth.

Presenting this view within these two terms alone, as is often done, is actually shortsighted because it ignores another large and growing reality: the numbers of home-schoolers, who do not want or cannot afford private schools, and want to explore other avenues than those predicated in public schools, or those who are promoting not-for-profit charter schools. Within this field we can find all sorts of cultural directions and approaches in healthy competition with each other. Could the two terms of opposition be leading us once more into a dead end, and a false dilemma?

It is worth exploring as an alternative of thinking in both/and terms that another solution is possible that grants both equality of access and diversity of approaches, a solution to which home-schooling is already pointing. Consider that education doesn't just entail a fair, unhindered, and equal access to comparably funded schools, but also the right to choose the education that best mirrors your values and those that you would like to impart to your children. What would be more natural, after all? This scenario would mean freedom of choice in education. The right to a free education can only be granted by the state; the content of this education is better left to the lively competition of ideas that is the natural realm of action of civil society.

Promising initiatives are rendering educational choice more accessible. In 1997 Arizona passed an education tax credit law that gives individuals the choice of contributing up to $500/year ($1,000 for couples) through scholarship-granting organizations and receive a full tax credit, not deduction. The contributions can go to either public or private schools. In Pennsylvania corporations can receive up to 90 percent credit for as much as $200,000 in donations per year.[61]

The cultural sector has additional tasks within a modern world of increasing complexity. It can offer us motivation in our professional lives and can determine the directions for sustainable and ethical social economic development.

The division of labor is an established and permanent feature of our economic landscape. A little-considered advantage of this reality is the ability to assure the needs of others while being supported in countless aspects by others who do the same. It inscribes mutuality and interdependence in the fabric of human life. This comes at a price of alienation from our work, especially when labor is commodified and remuneration becomes the sole ersatz motivator for vocation. It is in the sphere of culture that are born the new paradigms that we describe here and others as well, that can provide the individual with meaning and motivation.

The omnipresence of the economic imperative and the commodification of practically all aspects of our commons lets us forget that the choice of which economic development we want for our communities, cities, regions, and nations is certainly not of an economic nature alone. More and more communities, cities, and states are struggling to wrest these choices from corporations left free to do most of what can be justified by returns to the shareholders. The choice of which development we want to allow and which one we want to curtail is an eminently cultural choice. It reflects the conscious setting of values in which a community recognizes its goals. Untold numbers of NGOs and CBOs are part of the puzzle of determining which society we desire to promote. In the coming chapters we will in fact look at how new ways of integrating and coordinating stakeholders' input converge in this direction.

Communities at every geographic level are naturally evolving toward taking in their hands the determination of at what end land and capital should be put to use, what kind of development they find desirable and

---

[61] Gary Lamb, *Wellsprings of the Spirit; Free Human Beings as the Source of Social Renewal* (Fair Oaks, CA: AWSNA, 2007); see chapter 25: "The Funding of Education from a Threefold Perspective: From Denial and Rejection to New Opportunities."

sustainable, and therefore under which criteria business of all sizes can or cannot operate.

This determination would naturally be different from region to region, country to country, and reflect of prevailing cultural norms and values.

Economic Sector

It is true that the economy needs to be based on the logic of profit, or the simple terms of the best use of material, energy, and labor, once everything pertaining to the realm of rights is administered by the political sector. But this profit motive cannot be left in the hands of single individuals if the economy is to truly serve the needs of the whole.

As more and more alternatives way of looking at the economy recognize, it is only through highly developed associations of producers, distributors, and consumers that we can create economic organs capable not only of bringing together all stakeholders but also of being truly able to recognize and integrate all variables. Neither an economist nor a politician can expect to recognize the reality of an integrated national economy, moreover integrated on a global scale. Much of what a government can do downstream in the economy has unintended consequences. Once more, complex systems cannot be approached through reform; their complexity requires the transformation that can be achieved only when all stakeholders can offer their input. In the past political economic protectionism has been an equivalent of constant, simmering conflict leading to war; we see the rocking effects of it in economic nationalism at present.

Economic protectionism is countered on the other side by the race to the bottom of what has been called "elite globalization" that has signed NAFTA and CAFTA into law and has tried to force upon the American public the highly secretive agenda of the Trans-Pacific Partnership. All advantages are stacked on the side of multinational corporations, with scant or no protections given to labor, the environment, or even national sovereignty. In this view of affairs, government becomes docile henchmen for a global economy of plunder.

A tripolar society can offer new grounds for an economy truly independent from the government, an economy that needs not derive benefits from political complicity. The collaborative associations we will explore form the grounds for a collaborative economy, or what has been called the "gift economy." Many of these initiatives are taking shape in the present, as we will see here and in the next chapters.

What we call economic associations can act as organs of perception and awareness, raising the individual members to an understanding of the whole, rendering an incredibly complex field more perceptible to all stakeholders, and offering increasing agency. Such associations rest solely upon economic grounds, not humanitarian ones.

The profit motive can only be altered and improved if some other economic entity than the individual entrepreneur can acquire a better understanding of the whole field, what initiatives should be supported, how each step of the process could be improved, and how labor could be used to the greatest benefit of all. An example could be associations bringing together all actors within the food system: producers, distributors, and consumers. Such associations have in effect emerged over the last decades, and have taken the name of "value-based food supply chains" or, in short, value chains. We will return to these below.

Only the confluence of all stakeholders within the food system will enable a perception of any given part of the economy. Consider that even this will be one-sided because it will need to be balanced out by all other sectors of the economy in order to create a more complete picture. Very quickly it will appear that higher-level structures will be needed in order to integrate all aspects of the economy and acquire a larger view of reality.

The goals of mutuality and sustainability truly depend on the coming together of all stakeholders in unprecedented processes of integration. Here we can appreciate that the new organic thinking of collaborative economy is no return to the past, nor is it simple. It would honor the complexity of the economy with correspondingly complex structures. But these would be truly representative of all stakeholders, transparent, and efficient.

Economic and Cultural Interdependence

From the very general considerations we have articulated so far, we can conclude with an important consideration. Tripolar society is truly based on checks and balances. It can also be viewed as a cycle in which the three actors become integrated and interdependent. Such is the case of the economic and cultural sectors.

There is a true organic interdependence between culture and the economy. It is through all interrelated cultural activities that the ingenuity required for a highly complex economy emerges. Scientific and technological discoveries, the higher education of countless individuals involved in the economy, the nonprofits that freely exchange and disseminate this new information, plus the infrastructure that has been placed at the disposal of the community by the government are the prerequisites of a vibrant economy. The debt that economic output owes to the formation of culture, and to the body politic, is something very important in closing the circle. It places us in front of two diverging paradigms: one of pervasive, insidious, and omnipresent destruction; another one truly life-affirming.

The economy is continuously producing surpluses. In the present view of things, a great part of these are used in the economy itself. But this can only truly happen at increasingly staggering costs. On one hand the surpluses can pile up in the hands of the few, at the expense of a true democracy. They can be used to destroy in various ways—such as in the production of armaments or products that hurt the environment—or be used to replace existing products at faster and faster rates through lower quality and accelerated obsolescence, and the inability or unwillingness to plan for reuse and recycling. In this way the economy becomes at present a parasite of the social body.

Government can levy what it needs from the economy because it has coercive power. Civil society cannot produce its own financial resources, while the economy itself cannot produce the innovations that lead to its own improvements. It is in the interest of the economy itself to close the circle with civil society, to return its surpluses to foster the creativity of the human spirit through education, arts, scientific and technological research, and social development, so that surpluses will not create burdens on the environment and social body. Incentives will have to be developed for capital to flow back into civil society in a way that preserves cultural independence. Ultimately it is from the fountainhead of the vibrancy of the individual spirit that society regenerates itself and is able to work in truly homeostatic ways.

An example has been brought up in relation to tax credits to educational choice through scholarship-granting organizations. In this instance money flows from taxpayers and from the private sector into the cultural sector, rather than through the government. The difference is not irrelevant.

The option of government-funded voucher programs to parents comes with strings attached. As is to be expected in anything that flows from the government—and rightly so—accepting government funding allows the state to regulate and therefore limit and standardize education. Contributions from the private sector, especially when mediated through granting organizations, cannot regulate recipient schools.

All of the above leads to the inescapable logic that many may refuse to see. Thinking from a clearer perspective of the integration of the three sectors truly allows to discern the leverage points of greatest power, as the Institute of Cultural Affairs recognized in the 1970s. We will have to forego preset ideological solutions in favor of what works in any given situation when we can more fully perceive social reality at its foundation. We will now turn to an economic alternative, which is also a powerful cultural innovation: community supported agriculture, or CSA.

Community Supported Agriculture

We turn now, or rather return, to an example of what it means to think in a both/and way in relation to farming and the food system, and the economy in general. We will be looking at a form of economy that transcends the tenets of free market laissez-faire or measures of state intervention in the economy—a both/and approach to farming.

Value-Based Food Supply Chains and Community Supported Agriculture

The compounded problems of agribusiness could be summarized in one word: *degrading*. Degrading of the farmer who meets his needs less and less; degrading of the land, plants, and animals; and the environment treated as commodities. The dictates of an economy based not on meeting needs (not just human but of land, plants, animals, and all future generations), but on return on the dollar lies primarily on not paying for real costs. Many alternatives have sprung up, which we could place under the heading of "value-based food supply chains" (value chains, in short). In simplest terms these are consciously established food supply chains in which economics is rendered transparent and profits equitably distributed along the chain.

Value chains are established in order to differentiate food according to added values such as local, sustainable, or organic; grass fed beef; fair wages, and so on, in order to garner higher revenue in exchange for better produce for consumers and environment alike.

In staying with the both/and kind of thinking we have entertained thus far, value chains do not depend on a capitalistic laissez-faire view of things, nor do they require state interventions in the economy. They are new economic models that try to promote a transparent and collaborative economy, and a departure from all past models.

Value chains can achieve two results. First, a fairer share of profits all along the food supply chain, which means most of all greater margins for the farmers, those who presently suffer the most from the workings of the free market as we saw in the example of US corn. Second, a determination of prices that reflects what it really costs to produce, especially in farming; in other words, a shift from a money-based economy to a needs-based economy. A fair price for farm produce is that which allows the farmer to operate in ways that cover all his needs as a human being, and enables him to continue to operate in balance with nature. It is a radical proposition whose implications have not been fully grasped and sought on a larger scale.

At its best, when a value chain extends all the way from the producer/ farmer to the consumer, the food chain can acquire some degree of independence from the market; prices can reflect true costs and cover all parties' needs. There is a great variety of value chains, but most of them stop at the level of wholesale or retail, not yet consciously at the level of the consumer.

Among all the examples of value chains we could look at, below are some examples that have been documented in the United States.

Classical Value Chains:
-   to *wholesale*: Shepherd's Grain[62]

---

[62] Larry Lev and G. W. Stevenson, *Values-Based Grain Supply Chains: Shepherd's Grain*, 2013, https://cias.wisc.edu/wp-content/uploads/2013/04/shepherdsgrain final050713.pdf.

- to *retail*: Good Natured Family Farms, an alliance of some 40 farmers with a retail chain;[63] Organic Valley;[64] Red Tomato[65]
- to *consumers*
  - Corbin Hill, including nonprofits and CSAs[66]
  - Farmers to You[67]
  - Good Earth Farms (internet sales from 5 farms)[68]

Food Hubs
- Farm Fresh RI[69]
- Intervale Food Hub: combining the CSA model[70]

Multi-stakeholder Co-ops
- Fifth Season Cooperative, Viroqua, WI[71]

---

[63] Shonna Dreier and Minoo Taheri, *Innovative Models: Small Grower and Retailer Collaborations: Good Natured Family Farms and Balls Food Stores*, 2008, http://ngfn.org/resources/research-1/innovative-models/Good Natured Family Farms Innovative Model.pdf.

[64] G. W. Stevenson, *Values-Based Food Supply Chains: Organic Valley*, April 2013, https://www.cias.wisc.edu/wp-content/uploads/2013/04/organicvalleyfinal071613.pdf.

[65] G. W. Stevenson, *Values-Based Food Supply Chains: Red Tomato*, 2013, https://www.cias.wisc.edu/wp-content/uploads/2013/08/redtomatofinal082213.pdf.

[66] Nevin Cohen and Dennis Derryck, *Corbin Hill Road Farm Share: A Hybrid Food Value Chain in Practice*, 2011, https://nonprofitquarterly.org/corbin-hill-road-farm-share-a-hybrid-food-value-chain-in-practice/.

[67] https://farmerstoyou.com/.

[68] G. W. Stevenson, *Values-Based Food Supply Chains: Good Earth Farms*, 2013, https://cias.wisc.edu/wp-content/uploads/2013/04/goodearthfarmsfinal061313.pdf.

[69] Nathaniel Brooks, *Farm Processors Community of Practice Case Study: Youth Builds Job Skills through Local Food Processing*, 2017; see https://www.farmfreshri.org/wp-content/uploads/2017/12/HK-2017FINEcasestudy.pdf.

[70] Michele C. Schmidt, Jane M. Kolodinsky, Thomas P. DeSisto, and Faye C. Conte, "Collaborative Aggregation, Marketing, and Distribution Strategy Increasing Farm Income and Local Food Access: A Case Study of a Collaborative Aggregation, Marketing, and Distribution Strategy That Links Farmers to Markets," *Journal of Agriculture, Food Systems, and Community Development* 1, no. 4 (2011): 157–75. https://doi.org/10.5304/jafscd.2011.014.017.

[71] "The History of Fifth Season Cooperative," https://foodservice.gbaps.org/UserFiles/Servers/Server_484711/File/Our District/Departments/Food Service/Farm To School/Farmer Biographies/Fifth Season Cooperative.pdf. See also Margaret

CSA Coalitions
- Fair Share, eastern WI[72]

Single Farm CSAs

At present I will just turn my attention to the simplest possible example of value chain—community supported agriculture, or CSA—for the simple reason that this is the most concrete, elegant, small-scale achievement of a whole new way of rethinking the farming economic model. It stands as an illustration for more complex elaborations of the idea of a collaborative economy. It is in fact hardly ever called a value chain; it is the example at the end of the spectrum because it links directly farmers and consumers without the intermediaries, which are common members of a value chain.

In many farms CSA is used as the sole economic model. When that is the case, the farmer gets the full value of the food dollar for all his production. Those who come closest to the CSA model—sometimes even incorporating aspects of CSA—are so-called food hubs, which aggregate and distribute a mix of organic and local produce, working collaboratively with the farmers. It has been estimated that food hubs can give back to the farmer 75 to 85 percent of wholesale revenues to the farmers.[73] This does not mean that the farmer is able to sell all his produce through the food hub; it most often remains one of his strategies. For this reason too, a farm operating solely as a CSA offers an ideal model to explore.

CSA stands under our eyes as a matter-of-fact phenomenon, though we most often fail to see what a departure it can be from anything of the past. This is because CSA can be seen and set up either as a functional

---

Lund, *Solidarity as a Business Model: A Multi-Stakeholder Cooperatives Manual*, 40–43, https://community-wealth.org/content/solidarity-business-model-multi-stakeholder-cooperatives-manual.

[72] See https://www.csacoalition.org/. Originally formed in 1992, it was called Madison Area Community Supported Agriculture Coalition; see Trauger Groh and Steven McFadden, *Farms of Tomorrow Revisited: Community Supported Farms— Farm Supported Communities* (Kimberton, PA: Biodynamic Farming and Gardening Association, 2000), 87–90.

[73] Jason Jay, Hal Hamilton, Chris Landry, Daniella Malin, Don Seville, Susan Sweitzer, Peter Senge, and Andrew Murphy, eds., *Innovations for Healthy Value Chains: Cases, Tools & Methods*, Sustainable Food Lab, May 2008, http://web.mit.edu/~jjay/Public/papers/InnovationsForHealthyValueChainsv15.pdf.

system with its pros and cons, or as a radical departure from the past of traditional farming. It all depends on where we want to stop. For the purpose of this exploration we will turn not just to CSAs in general but to those formulations of CSA that form an ideal in moving away from market logic. For the purpose of this chapter, we are interested most of all in following the radical and complete departure of thinking possible in the model.

CSA History

CSAs started in Europe and Japan in the 1970s; in Europe the CSA movement was fostered by biodynamic farming. In Japan Teikei (meaning "partnership" or "collaboration") was started in 1971 by a group of women concerned about the destructive trends they were seeing in farming all around them. CSAs were introduced in the United States in the mid-1980s. The two very first CSAs in the United States were Indian Line Farm in Massachusetts and Temple-Wilton CSA in New Hampshire, in 1986 through Robyn Van En and Trauger Groh respectively.

The 2007 estimate was of some 1,700 CSAs with around 100,000 members. These vary in size from operations with 3 to 2,100 shares. The larger clusters are formed around the Northeast; the Twin Cities; Madison, Wisconsin; and the Bay Area, California.[74]

From a functional perspective community supported agriculture presents many attractive elements: the fact that the farmer knows ahead of the growing season who will support him and what he can count upon; the capital made available by the high proportion of people who will pay their full share ahead of the month or of the season; not having to worry about marketing at the peak of the season when farmers face so many demands; the direct relationships with customers and the possibility of immediate feedback... enough reasons to stop there. They are similar to the reasons for stopping at functional trisector social thinking, without proceeding further to ideal threefolding into which we have presently moved. That there is more is obvious when we just look at how CSA was birthed in Germany.

---

[74] Elizabeth Henderson and Robyn Van En, *Sharing the Harvest: A Citizen's Guide to Community Supported Agriculture* (White River Junction, VT: Chelsea Green Publishing Co., 2007), xv, 6.

What we presently know as CSA saw its beginning at Buschberg farm (near Hamburg, Germany) when a group of biodynamic farmers realized the growing constraints faced by organic and biodynamic farms in the 1960s.[75] In order to make ends meet, most farms had to rely on low-paid foreign workers, and even so their work only generated low returns. The farmers wanted to get out of this vicious cycle. They wanted to create what they called "solidarity farms" in which the responsibility and weight of farming was distributed between farmers and community members. Beyond that they wanted to change the traditional relationships of farming to land and of farmers to wages.

Through a cooperative arrangement, the land was held in trust and a risk-sharing agreement was designed in partnership with the Co-operative Bank in Bochum. The nonfarmer members were given access to a line of credit of 3,000 Deutsche Mark, which they could turn to the farmers as farm capital for establishing a working budget. Members shared in profit or losses. If a profit was generated, it would be divided among the members; if a loss, the community members agreed to make up for the difference. We can see from this what a radical departure CSA presented from a farm running like a farm business operating in the open market.

Thinking Beyond the Market

There is in fact a deeper thinking behind the scheme that turned out to be the CSA. It has its ground in some common sense observations that laymen and farmers alike have made over the centuries.

We have already seen in the previous chapter how little free market logic applies to farming. As we have seen, ideally land needs to be addressed from a perspective other than that of the market, one that does not equate it to a commodity. The same is true for farming, which cannot be equated with any other businesses. When farming operates like other businesses, it has lost its uniqueness, that of being able to work as a closed system, with subsystems that support each other in a closed system, particularly the integration of field crops and animal husbandry that produces organic fertilizers. Unlike other businesses, the land can be so managed as to become

---

[75] Information that follows is taken from http://buschberghof.de/wirtschaftsgemeinschaft/solidarische-landwirtschaft/.

almost completely self-supporting and need very limited to no external input.

To these basic matters of fact we can add that land has many more than one value, as authors Groh and McFadden bring out in their book *Farms of Tomorrow*. Among these functions are:

- producing healthy food
- fostering a healthy self-preserving environment for present and future generations, one that can even be improved
- serving as a basis for culture and education and therefore needing to be a resource accessible to all

CSAs can transcend the boundaries of the market, or at least take great strides in this direction. Knowing that there are varieties of legal property arrangements for CSAs, we will here look at an optimal situation, not necessarily the most common: a CSA where the land has been bought back and removed from the market, being held by an ad hoc land trust or nonprofit corporation, very much in line with what Bushberg Farm tried to give birth to. We do this to illustrate the highest potential that can be achieved through CSA.

Thinking Beyond the Past

CSAs are not placed in the choice between a return to the past or a continuation of present trends into the future. They predicate something totally novel. Through a different relationship to market forces, CSA farmers and members can acquire a new relationship both to land and to the social community that lives around it and/or depends on it.

So what do CSAs do differently from a regular organic farm? Essentially they predicate that farm operations have to be taken away from the market logic and market forces and that the farmers who operate it are the ones who can best see the needs and productive potential of that piece of land. Farmers are the ones who can cater to the needs of the land by producing healthy food, preserving/improving the environment, and rendering the land accessible to those who live in its proximity or contribute to its well-being.

With this goal in mind, Groh and McFadden recognize three sets of overlapping goals; the spiritual/cultural, the social, and the economic.

- Cultural: for future human beings to live in healthy bodies most likely to develop their full potential; for the land to be managed in optimal conditions, to preserve/improve its potential for future generations. For this the separation of land, property, and farm operations is essential. To better understand this aspect of CSA, we must envision the CSA as an ideally enclosed entity which has a being of its own, which plays a part in the whole like a cell or organ plays it in the human body. It is for this reason that we will refer to a *farm organism* to contrast the farm as a living being to a farm as a business.

- As part of their cultural role, farms can play an educational role for schools and/or for particular segments of the population; individuals with special needs, homeless, underprivileged, youth at risk, and so forth.

- Social: equal access for all to healthy food, optimally regardless of economic background. A whole new array of social relationships come into being, varying with the CSA's legal and organizational structure: between farmers and members/shareholders, among people who share in the risk of the operations, and possibly between other CSAs or farm associations. A rich new social tissue is added to the physical basis of the land.

- Economic: farms can become more self-sufficient, diversified, and run more economically, not just profitably, therefore with fewer external inputs of substances and energy. A farm should be able to maintain high fertility without external inputs, generate a surplus of food for the community, and generate its own seeds.

Let us look at each of these aspects in sequence. The cultural dimension relates the CSA to an understanding of nature, the farm organism and the larger tissue it is part of. It looks at matters of skills, personal gifts and education. Here freedom of informed choice is paramount.

The cultural dimension of CSA covers the whole planning of the farm organism. This goes down to the forming of a budget, and is assigned to the specific expertise that only the farmer and people with farming knowledge can cover. Farmers need to be given autonomy, though their budget will later be submitted to the members.

The visionary aspect we are looking at is important in terms of the support the farmers will receive from the community. They need to strike a balance between ability to carry the day-to-day with the right engagement, and the ability to pull back, observe, and envision in accord with nature.

Typical questions of the cultural area of concerns are:

- What is a good crop rotation that fits the needs of the particular farm?
- What animals would help most maintain and enhance fertility?
- What pastures should rotate and which should be kept permanent?
- What tools and machinery should be used?

It is important that practical initiative takes its departure out of the area of the needs of the farm organism as they are understood by the farmer, and only later to consider the legal and economic ramifications. This will predicate the ideal that the land, the capital invested in the operations, and the farmer's labor should not be considered as disposable commodities by the whims of the market.

The social aspect includes legal and social relationships, written and unwritten. An example is the legal relationship between active farmers and legal owners of the land, whether this be a community land trust or individual landlords. Some of the social questions are

- What are the personal needs of the active farmers?
- How can we support the farmers and the farmers' families?
- Should we have equal-cost shares or should we have flexible options considering the socioeconomic reality of the shareholders?
- Should we exchange products with other farms? How would we deal with these?

For these questions, a consensus needs to be reached through fully participatory processes. Involving a multitude of interests and stakeholders is something that requires that some members, or organizing committees, turn their attention to how best to generate common ground and decision-making approaches that have everybody's buy-in.

One of the most enlivening possibilities offered through CSA is that of building new kinds of communities where traditional ones no longer survive. Entering a CSA means in fact entering direct but complex relationships with the earth and other people. Participation takes commitment: members pay money upfront, have to pick up food at the farm or central drop off, have to figure out what to do with the food, are tied to what nature produces seasonally, and must learn new ways to cook and process food. Likewise, members acquire a new relationship with earth, and a new relationship with people: celebrating together social occasions and festivals, the most obvious ones being the solstices and equinoxes

Finally, matters of community building can go even further. Considerations of a CSA's social function concern also the possible access to the land for the benefit of the larger community, not just its shareholders. More and more CSAs allow access to, or act specifically as educational farms for, various populations.

Where CSAs really present new, wide horizons for the future is in their offering a completely new economic model. In fact we could say that they are truly economic whereas the model of agribusiness, profitable as it may be, is the antithesis of true economy. When strawberries, even organic, are produced in California for the Northeast market, the amount of energy that the fruit provides to its consumers is a small fraction of all the energy applied in growing, shipping, conserving, and distributing them. It is society that pays for the shortfall, not to mention the subsidies that go into making this model possible. In contrast, with CSAs not only are all these costs either eliminated or drastically reduced, but consider that the quality and freshness of CSA produce cannot be matched in any other conventional or organic distribution chains.

Fostering a Collaborative Economy

CSAs embody a new kind of economy, which stands in contrast to a market economy: an economy in which each player listens to the needs of the others, instead of placing self-interest at the center as in Adam Smith's idea of the free market. CSAs potentially allow the greatest amount of people and the greatest variety of stakeholders to associate with farming, plus a greatly varied demographic range of ages, occupations, and incomes.

In working within a CSA, farmers and members identify needs and work out of them in an altruistic mood. The shareholders are really committing to the preservation of the farm organism, its needs and those of its stewards. This is a way to take the economy of the free market out of center stage.

In this new kind of associative economy, the focus shifts from fighting for our own needs to listening to the needs of the other stakeholders and seeing how all needs can be met and how new synergies can emerge. It is in effect a major cultural shift.

CSAs' new economy has far-reaching consequences. An example: some crops could be difficult to grow in a given US region; hence the need to partner with farms in another part of the country. CSAs of the Northeast have interest in partnering with grain-producing farms of the Midwest. But in the spirit of CSA economy, they will not just purchase the grain. They will cover all it takes to grow the grains in that part of the Midwest, all the needs the farmer needs to meet while he is growing them. In fact they will share in the risks or benefits of the harvest, whether there is a crop failure or abundant yield. Beyond these collaborations the CSA model has also spawned a great number of variations.

Evolving CSA Models

Below are some examples of how CSA has been adapted to various needs and has taken on new forms. Keep in mind these are snapshots in time that were true until 2007 and may have presently evolved in other directions. For an update look at the information on the websites.

Congregation Supported Agriculture

This set up is ideal in many instances because the congregation already forms a natural community with existing infrastructures (buildings), vehicles of communication (newsletters), yearly celebrations, orientation to service and outreach, and interest in education.

Genesis Farm CSA was spearheaded by Sister Miriam McGillis, member of the Roman Catholic Dominican Sisters, on a 140-acre farm in Blairstown, New Jersey. The land was dedicated to the state's farmland conservation program, precluding future development. In 1987, 51 acres were turned into a CSA (Genesis Farm Community Supported Garden). At present there is also a Learning Center for Earth Studies, allowing a movement of reconnection between farmers, members, and the community at large. This initiative has been imitated, and by the year 2007 there were some 50 "sustainable communities on the land" according to the National Catholic Rural Life Conference.[76]

College- or School-Supported Agriculture

Culture seems to be an ideal avenue for CSA promotion. An advantage of this model is the support the CSA can derive from a sister organization until established and financially independent. Students can learn and develop projects, up to thesis and culminating-experience projects. The farm's work is integrated in the curriculum of various departments such as Biology, Earth Sciences, Environmental Studies, and Geography, and serve programs for the larger community. An example of these is the Dartmouth Organic Farm in the Dartmouth College-owned Fullington Farm in Hanover, New Hampshire, which became operational in 1996.[77]

Tax [Citizen] Supported Farms

Natick Community Farm in Natick, Massachusetts, runs a 22-acre farm, 25 miles west of Boston on town-owned land, and operates under the umbrella of the Natick Youth and Human Resources Committee that works with youth at risk. It occupies public school students in the summer, and serves a variety of demographics: women in drug rehab programs, individuals with special needs or with mental illness, homeschooled students, youth seeking employment, and more. Taxpayers have decided to support the initiative, and this is taken in charge by a variety of civic concerns: the town government, the Natick Public School district, and various nonprofit groups.[78]

---

[76] Henderson and Van En, *Sharing the Harvest*, 203, 246; see also http://csgatgenesisfarm.com/.

[77] Henderson and Van En, *Sharing the Harvest*, 206–7; see also https://outdoors.dartmouth.edu/activities/facilities/organic_farm/.

[78] Henderson and Van En, *Sharing the Harvest*, 210; see also https://www.natickfarm.org/.

CSAs Involving Low-Income or Homeless People

In some CSAs a certain number of households decide to carry an extra membership and make it available to a person in need; often what food is left over goes to the local food bank, soup kitchens, or families in need. Such models can include "work for a share" option for low or no-income people with an hour's labor being set at minimum wage. This necessitates a training program, and therefore offers the benefit of work education. The Santa Cruz Homeless Garden is one such example: one of its main benefits is to provide a meeting place where homeless people meet with other constituencies. It worked out of a 2.5-acre garden on a vacant urban lot. Besides supplying to the shareholders, it sold food to local stores and restaurants, and gave the remainder to homeless shelters and free-meal programs. The garden employed Alan Chadwick's biodynamic French-intensive approach to gardening. Started in 1990, it turned into a CSA in 1991.[79]

Community Food Security

The Hartford Food System (HFS) in Hartford, Connecticut, is considered a model of a systemic approach to the question of food security. It was instrumental in establishing the Downtown Farmers' Market, the first in the state. It also started the Connecticut Farmers' Market Nutrition Program, which provided close to $400,000 in vouchers to purchase fresh produce from those markets for over 50,000 individuals; it did something similar for 6,000 senior citizens. In 1993 it worked to start a CSA in the Holcomb Farm, a 16-acre parcel of fruits and vegetables. HFS partnered with other organizations working with low-income people in a model not too dissimilar from Collective Impact. (see Chapter 4) The Holcomb Farm offered "working shares" of 60 hours/week for an "all-you-can-eat" package. Thanks to HFS's collaborative spirit, some 11 community organizations distributed shares to 1,200 low-income residents.[80]

---

[79] Henderson and Van En, *Sharing the Harvest*; see also http://www.homelessgardenproject.org/.

[80] Henderson and Van En, *Sharing the Harvest*, 235–39; see also https://www.hartfordfood.org/.

Food Banks and CSAs (and Gleaning)

The Food Bank Farm (part of the Western Massachusetts Food Bank) near Hadley provided food to 400 shareholders, while also offering an average of 100,000 pounds of fresh food each year to local food banks and programs that feed people in need. Thanks to its nonprofit tax-exempt status, the farm could ask the Commonwealth of Massachusetts for land below market price. The Food Bank Farm is now financially independent.[81]

Corporation Supported Agriculture

Although it sounds like a good idea, corporate support may be more difficult than the other models because of the fast pace of business and difficulty in harmonizing interests and timetables. A successful example is Fairfield Gardens CSA in Santa Barbara, California, under the auspices of Patagonia Inc. After an initial trial, now Fairfield Gardens was one of many initiatives that the company supported through a 1 percent of its profits.[82]

CSAs and Thinking in Threes

Groh and McFadden give us an enticing definition of what the new economic model, of which CSA is part, could be: "Identifying needs and covering these needs with the least effort (the least input of energy, substance and labor) is true economy."[83] We can see how this simple definition stands in opposition to operating for profit alone.

Why is then CSA an example of an economy that thinks in three? Where do we find the synthesis between two extremes? Capitalism only looks at the freedom of the individual and believes in such a thing as an abstract force of the market that tempers it. The farm becomes a business. Socialistic farm models, now mostly in the past, all but kill the freedom of the individual in the name of equality. The farm will tend to resemble an institution. The CSA is neither a business nor an institution, but a living organism.

In the CSA idea, the farmer is selected to further the interests of the land itself and of the community. Ideally he is chosen because of his keen

---

[81] Henderson and Van En, *Sharing the Harvest,* 212–13; see also https://www.youtube.com/watch?v=_f6GE8Gp0SY.

[82] Groh and McFadden, *Farms of Tomorrow Revisited,* 205.

[83] Groh and McFadden, *Farms of Tomorrow Revisited,* 36.

understanding of the land and the community around it. The farmer is freed to pursue the development of his individuality in accord with the needs of the land. The land trust or nonprofit that ensures the future uses of the land for benefit of environment and community has no resemblance whatsoever with a government agency. The selfish profit motive of capitalism and the equalitarian view of human beings are reconciled at a higher level with the maxim "to each according to his needs." The objective place of individual human needs replaces the notion of the survival of the fittest, or the seemingly generous but abstract notion of human beings' equality in economic terms.

Subscribing to a whole other notion of what a farm is, a whole other way to see the role of the farmer and the role of the market, a whole other way to "purchase vegetables" pays rich dividends to all parties involved. Here are some the potential advantages for farm and farmers:

- The land can build increasing fertility and sustain a very diverse ecosystem.
- Farmers can be sure of a set income since the whole community shoulders the risk. They can have an easier work schedule and be better stewards by observing how their crops grow.
- Farmers don't have to market during the growing season, their busiest time of the year.
- They can alleviate the temptation to overproduce due to economic pressure.

Among advantages for shareholders are the following:

- CSA products have unique levels of freshness and quality. Consumers know where the food comes from and can offer immediate feedback, thereby improving quality.
- Consumers and farmers bypass the middleman and obtain savings. CSAs bypass the intermediary costs of transportation, packaging, processing, storage, and marketing, which add up to 75 percent of the average food price. We are moving toward an economy in which consumers pay the true cost of the produce, and the farmers receive the full consumer dollar. The Food Bank Farm CSA calculated that

the cost of a share ($450) would buy the equivalent of $750 at a local supermarket, and $1,150 at a natural foods store. A similar study conducted by Equiterre, Quebec, found members' savings adding up to somewhere from 10 to 50 percent on costs of organic foods.[84]

- There is little waste; even "unaesthetic" produce can readily be used

And other advantages accrue to the community at large:

- The preservation of open spaces and farmland makes the community a more satisfying place to live.
- Since CSAs need to plan for generous crop yields to alleviate for weather patterns and to be able to cover members' needs, all of the surplus will not be destroyed to satisfy market demands but can be made available to those in need (e.g., food pantries).
- Money remains in the local economy.
- Farms can be places to bring people together around a variety of common concerns. The farm can lend itself to educational and recreational uses for the larger community and particular groups.

Note that all the advantages contribute to the development of a true economy from all perspectives: reducing costs, increasing efficiency, reducing waste, linking most efficiently producers to consumers with the greatest amount of feedback loops. It is true that producing a great variety of crops renders further mechanization difficult. However, this adds motivation and interest to the farmers and is a plus on the consumers' end.

CSAs within the Constraints of the Neoliberal Economy

The kind of collaborative economy for which CSA or other value chains set the ground rules is based on knowing and understanding each other, and operating from the ground of needs to be fulfilled. We have shown that CSA secures the satisfaction of needs with the least expenditure of energy, resources, and materials. Ideally a well-integrated farm with a rotation that includes pastures and farm animals will have little need for extra inputs. And in most scenarios, very little is lost of what is produced.

---

[84] Henderson and Van En, *Sharing the Harvest*, 214, 218.

A shift to a new economy cannot happen until we affirm new sets of values and build the ground for a new culture. As a matter of fact, CSAs can only be established through a firm commitment to new values, through the support of a surrounding culture.

The disastrous consequences of neoliberalism amount to a complete alienation from the environment and from local cultures, and ultimately induces a complete alienation from self, the ultimate anticultural endeavor. The life-negating values shoring up elite globalization will only be countered when life-affirming values have sufficiently taken hold of society as a whole, or in pockets of it and expand from there. In the immediate this means creating settings in which nonprofits and businesses can operate outside of the free market.

CSAs represent an ideal of great potential, but at a very small scale. To maintain its strength within the global market implies taking the bull by the horns and scaling up. As Trauger Groh realized from his farm in New Hampshire, "The community farm has no future without a network in New England of 100 or so similar farms that can support each other through trade and association."[85] Traveling for the last four months in preparation for this book, the fragile health of CSA was a leitmotif that I sadly encountered all too often.

Meeting the challenge that Trauger Groh invites CSAs to overcome means facing two of the paradigms of which we will talk about next:

- Bringing a large number of CSAs to collaborate in spite of their differences: functional CSAs versus more idealistic CSAs, small and large ones, differences of perception as to what constitutes quality food, etc.
- Building organizational models that are neither too rigid nor too loose; some in which the farmers can invest their time knowing that generally speaking they have little to spare; and forms that can preserve a variety of interests without compromising any single one

---

[85] Groh and McFadden, *Farms of Tomorrow Revisited*, 112.

These are two challenges we will face in the next chapters:

- How to bring a variety of stakeholders to work from common ground in spite of their differences (Chapter 3)
- What forms are most natural and organic that can sustain common action, while preserving autonomy and a variety of coexisting interests (Chapter 4)

Resources

Trisector Partnerships

Paul Hawken: *Blessed Unrest: How the Largest Movement in the World Came Into Being and Why No One Saw It Coming* (New York: Viking, 2007), about the emergence of civil society at the global level.

Jon C. Jenkins and Maureen R. Jenkins, *The Social Process Triangles* (Toronto: Imaginal Training, 1997), unfortunately hard to find because out of print.

Henry Mintzberg, *Rebalancing Society: Radical Renewal Beyond Left, Right and Center* (Oakland, CA: Berrett-Koehler, 2015).

Ros Tennyson and Luke Wilde, *The Guiding Hand: Brokering Partnerships for Sustainable Development* (London: Prince of Wales Business Leaders Forum and the United Nations Staff College, 2000).

Steve Waddell, *Societal Learning and Change: How Governments, Business and Civil Society are Creating Solutions to Complex Multi-Stakeholder Problems* (Abingdon, UK: Routledge, 2017)

For how to engage in trisector partnerships see Chapter 3: Multi-stakeholder Logic.

Toward a Tripolar Society

Moving from an either/or to a both/and thinking in social matters. To develop a new kind of thinking, look at the following resources:

David C. Korten, *Creating a Post-Corporate World*, twentieth annual E. F. Schumacher lectures, October 2001, Great Barrington, MA; https://centerforneweconomics.org/publications/creating-a-post-corporate-world/.

Gary Lamb, Associative Economics: Spiritual Activity for the Common Good (Chatham, NY: AWSNA, 2010).

Martin Large, *Common Wealth for a Free, Equal, Mutual and Sustainable Society* (Stroud, UK: Hawthorne, 2010).

Nicanor Perlas, *Shaping Globalization: Civil Society, Cultural Power and Threefolding* (Forest Row, UK: Temple Lodge, 2019)

Otto Scharmer and Katrin Kaufer, *Leading from the Future: From Ego-System to Eco-System Economies* (San Francisco: Berrett-Koehler, 2013).

Blog: Luigimorelli.wordpress.com

Food Systems and a Collaborative Economy

Trauger Groh and Steven McFadden, *Farms of Tomorrow Revisited: Community Supported Farms—Farm Supported Communities* (San Francisco: Biodynamic Farming Association, 2000).

Elizabeth Henderson and Robyn Van En, *Sharing the Harvest: A Citizen's Guide to Community Supported Agriculture*, revised and expanded version (White River Junction, VT: Chelsea Green Publishing Co., 2007).

R Karp: *A New American Revolution? Associative Economics and the Future of the Food Movement*, http://robertkarp.net/wp-content/uploads/2018/03/New-American-Revolution-Final.doc.pdf.

Ken Meter: *Building Community Food Webs* (Washington, Covelo: Island Press, 2021)

Susan Sweitzer, et al., *Value Chain Best Practices: Building Knowledge for Value Chains that Contribute to the Health of Source Communities* (Wealth Creation in Rural Communities Initiative, 2008), https://community-wealth.org/content/value-chain-best-practices-building-knowledge-value-chains-contribute-health-source.

Videos

Here is a list of videos that, although not explicitly addressing a tripolar society, offer many ideas that go in that direction:

A Convenient Truth: Urban Solutions from Curitiba, Brazil, directed by Giovanni Vaz del Bello
"This inspirational documentary shows a city where urban solutions are not just theory, but a reality. The film shows innovations in the areas of transportation, recycling, social benefits (affordable housing), parks, and the great philosophy behind the successful leaders that transformed Curitiba in a model green city."
(https://www.imdb.com/title/tt1018804/plotsummary?ref_=tt_ov_pl)

Who Cares?, directed by Mara Mourao
"*Who Cares?* carries a very empowering message for individuals: anyone can be a changemaker, regardless of leadership or marketable skills. It starts with having a vision for society while seeking accomplishment in one's life through contributions to improving the lives of others."
(http://www.whocaresfilm.com/film-crew/)

Tomorrow, by Cyril Dyon and Melanie Laurent
Cyril Dyon, director, writer, and activist, has joined forces with actress Melanie Laurent to explore present alternative ideas and practices in agriculture, energy production, economics, education, and tools to reinvigorate democracy. They render us conscious of new ways of bringing about change through the work of hundreds of trailblazers. From groups and cities producing their own food, to new sustainable energy generation, alternative currencies emancipating us from speculation and wealth inequality, new emerging social compacts and ground-breaking educational systems, they stimulate new ways of seeing, understanding, and acting for change.

Create Your Own Study Plan

Seeing society as the intersection of the three sectors requires a bold rethinking that moves beyond the dualism of the twentieth century that has framed all social issues in terms of ideology. It requires unlearning and the freeing of the imagination. Here is a proposed study plan to acquire a taste for this unlearning and new learning:

- Review the ideas offered in this chapter.
- Start with a topic that interests you deeply: e.g., education, banking and money, means of production and ownership, or political reform
- Write down notes about your present thinking in this matter.
- Explore these topics from some of the resources listed above.
- Inquire about the most unique and innovative approaches.
- If you can, go on a learning journey and collect stories.
- Relate what you have studied and explored to the larger field and to the intersection with other fields.
- Gather notes from everything you have explored.
- Compare with what you started from. What has changed in you and in your way of seeing and approaching the topic?

An example: land and home ownership

- Write down your current thoughts about the matter:
  - the forces at play
  - the actors
  - the alternative approaches to land ownership and housing in your town, region, country,
- Document each of the following steps:
- Explore the topic: read chapter 10 of Large, *Common Wealth for a Free, Equal, Mutual and Sustainable Society*. Look at the proposed alternatives:
  - Land value tax
  - Community land trusts
- Follow up on the leads:
  - Look at land value tax and what it has done in places near you and/or further away

- • Explore community land trusts near you; virtually or in person
- • Explore/study other forms of shared living: e.g., co-housing and ecovillages
- Review what you have learned from your exploration.
- Compare your notes with your starting point:
  - • What has this exploration offered you?
  - • How has it changed you?
  - • What else comes up that you would like to explore?

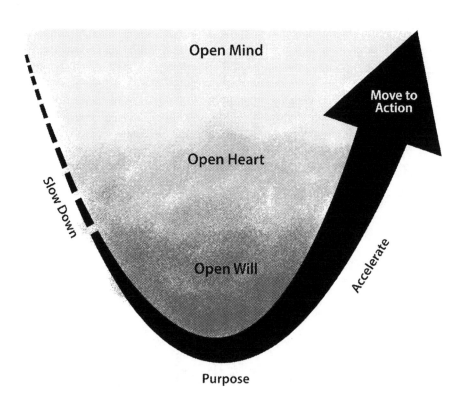

Chapter 3
Multi-Stakeholder Processes

It is through imagination that we cross the apparent raging water that separates us from those who are at odds with us. The wider the gap, the more imagination is needed to discover the human being on the other side.

—Miki Kashtan

Leadership is about creating, day by day, a domain in which we and those around us continually deepen our understanding of reality and are able to participate in shaping the future. This, then, is the deeper territory of leadership—collectively listening to what is wanting to emerge in the world, and then having the courage to do what is required.

—*Margaret Wheatley*

IN THIS CHAPTER:

SETTING THE GROUND FOR EXTRAORDINARY CONVERSATIONS
- Learn what it means to be a conversational activist
- Being both courageous and vulnerable when we want to create new outcomes together
- The best change happens when learning comes with playfulness

INVITE ALL STAKEHOLDERS
- Go out of your way to invite everyone that matters
- Create solutions that have all stakeholders' buy-in
- From fighting against to winning over
- From majority rule to supermajorities

LISTEN TO THE WHOLE PERSON
- Carefully designed facilitation is key
- Meet the whole person: mind, heart, and will
- Listen to the future that wants to come into being
- Promote leaderfulness
- Promote collective change and individual growth

A Defining Moment

I HAVE HAD AT DIFFERENT points in my life the privilege and pleasure of leading practice groups for Nonviolent Communication. I will not forget the experience I had in 2007 through a participant sharing with us his experience and emotions about seemingly losing his battle with cancer. I will call him John. The group had already some years of practice, so it was a safe container of seven experienced people. We listened as the individual went deeper and deeper into the experience, simply reflecting back what we heard in terms of feelings and needs. We plunged into the uncomfortable taboos of death and dying: the loneliness, the fear and idespair, the powerlessness. Nobody offered advice or consolation; we simply stayed with it and remained connected, no matter how difficult. When there was nothing more to say, we simply waited. Then we witnessed the turning point. Having reached rock-bottom the individual seemed to be reborn in stages. His countenance had changed; he emanated confidence in himself and a sense that something could be done, and that he was going to find out what.

Without anybody giving a signal, we just witnessed John emerging from the depths of the darkest emotions into a whole other space of future and possibility. I saw with surprise and awe how he seemed transfixed, altered, and reborn. When he came to a place of inner satisfaction and completion, we all realized what happened in the group. We simply stayed in silence in a collective experience of connection to each other and self. Silence was the most comfortable expression for it. Time lost its familiar dimension for me and for the others. We came out of the experience when somebody simply reminded us that it was nine o'clock, the agreed-upon closing time. We filed out quietly, not daring to break the silence with trivial remarks. I was still holding to the mood on the long way back home. I had just experienced more clearly than ever before something for which I didn't have a name yet. The experience itself was not wholly new; the depth and intensity of it was. Only years later I came across various other experiences and with these the name "presencing" that I can now give to that magic moment and turning point. We will see the importance of presencing in everything we will touch on below.

Tapping into Collective Wisdom

Trisector partnerships, as we have mentioned them in the Pittsburgh example in the previous chapter, offer promising answers to tackling issues of growing complexity. They require out-of-the-ordinary conversations. In this chapter we will look at the science and art of these conversations, of convening a great variety of stakeholders around a common goal.

One way to tackle complex issues is to generate *collective wisdom* through conversations that allow us to break through the perspective of isolated and isolating silos and generate the ability for concerted, collective action. Much of this has been called *emergent conversations, participatory facilitation*, or grouped under the name of *social technology*. The latter is the term that we will refer to most often in this chapter.

We have just seen that societal order no longer rests on two pillars but on three. This means a whole new way of seeing the social world and envisioning possibilities of change. But envisioning is only a first step of bringing about new social realities. In order to generate these new realities, we need to gather from a cross-section of one, two, or three sectors all the stakeholders that together can produce the change that is needed in the matter at hand. For many of these stakeholders, these are conversations that they have never had before; they lay outside of their culture or their immediate comfort zone.

Extraordinary conversations can generate extraordinary results. In practice this means gathering the greatest possible diversity of perspectives and forming new relationships of trust and support, taking time before discerning a concerted common action for change.

Processes of so-called social technologies allow everybody to experience change at the organizational, community, even societal level without having to previously master any new skills. They do not seek to change people directly, but to change the conditions under which they interact. They offer conditions for individuals to experience new ways of relating and collaborating, without being significantly better than they are. Rather, the participants are allowed to tune into different parts of themselves, and with time internalize new, life-affirming values. Likewise, before entering in what can result as an extraordinary conversation, nobody is asked to give up their beliefs or change their minds. They just need to be willing to experiment with new ways of relating and collaborating.

Extraordinary Conversations: The Universal U

The frame of reference we will use below is the result of the work of Otto Scharmer in his Theory U. We can relate to the "U" as a blueprint or, even better, an *archetype* that is quite universal in social processes. We will use this pattern beyond the specific methodology devised by Scharmer that we saw in Chapter 1. This was a discovery that emerged for me progressively in conversations with other people in the social field, quite independently from anything that Scharmer has done or said.

In the weeks and months following my own training through the Global Presencing Classroom in 2007[86] I was often on calls with friends or networks of people involved in various tools for individual, group, or social change.

---

[86] https://www.presencing.org/aboutus/presencing-institute/what-we-do.

When we happened to have a working knowledge of Theory U in common, new understanding would arise of the universal essence of what Theory U calls Open Mind, Open Heart, and Open Will. In other places I have shown how applicable the seven steps of the U are to Twelve Step, Nonviolent Communication, or Focused Conversation (of Technology of Participation) processes. Here the process will be extended to some examples of social technology—Consensus Decision Making, World Café, and Future Search.

Let us try to envision what "collectively going through the U" looks for an organization or community. Let us choose the example of a network deciding to work collectively at addressing large landscape conservation, and let us look at just one step in this process. It could be how to address the preservation of some threatened species, the establishment of easements through private land that would favor migration of a species in critical parts of its habitat, the forming of natural preserves, and so on.

In order to tackle any similar issues we need to have a sample of key stakeholders. One possible way to look at these is offered by M. Weisbord and S. Janoff. This can be thought of the people who AREIN the room, or people who have:

- **A**: authority to act
- **R**: resources, such as contacts and/or money
- **E**: expertise in the issues at hand
- **I**: information about the topic that no others have
- **N**: need to be involved because they will be affected by the decisions.[87]

In any of the above situations, securing the best possible results means inviting a variety of stakeholders from the one, or better two or three sectors. In the last instance these could be scientists, nonprofit agencies that advocate for one aspect or another of landscape protection, representatives of local governments, public agencies that regulate one aspect or another of land use and environmental protection, landowners, representatives of the logging industry, lumber mills, trade associations, chambers of commerce, tourism

---

[87] Marvin Weisbord and Sandra Janoff, *Don't Just Do Something, Stand There; Ten Principles for Leading Meetings That Matter* (San Francisco, CA: Berrett-Koehler, 2007), 17.

initiatives, and so forth. Once this eclectic crowd has been convened, it becomes obvious that none but the most extraordinary conversation could generate positive results. This is precisely the conversation that would allow the group to progressively move through the Open Mind, Open Heart, and Open Will, to the point of collective presencing (see figure 19).

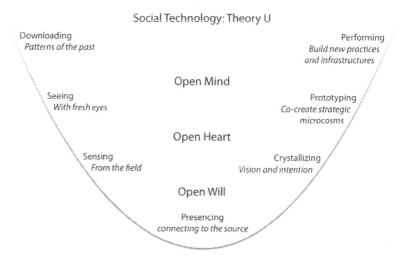

Figure 19: *Theory U*: Going through the Open Mind, Open Heart, Open Will (modified from Scharmer, *Theory U*)

Going Through the U

In a first stage of the process we need to overcome the silos mentality, the natural tendency to see things according to sectoral and organizational perspectives with their accompanying blind spots. An environmental organization tends to thrive in advocacy but not know how to look at the economic perspective of a problem; the reverse is most often true for businesses or trade associations. Government agencies may look at the problem from the purely bureaucratic perspective of existing policies and regulations. Only bringing these groups together can allow us to generate a larger tapestry of information that highlights the interconnections of all the elements of a situation. The assembled stakeholders will go through the Open Mind by collectively enriching and rounding off everybody's perspective. This is a stage of new learning, of truly *seeing*. At this stage the participants are encouraged to refrain from interpreting, countering, responding to each other's perspectives.

Withholding from forming judgments and criticisms is what allows a shift towards the stage of the Open Heart. From the jungle of facts, new relationships, patterns, and themes emerge. Stakeholder groups will realize that this was only possible by breaking the boundaries of the silo perspectives. In a build-up of trustful relationships, in which no one is judging others, individuals and stakeholder groups start to see the part they play in a complex and challenging situation. Collectively encouraging this taking of responsibility is the skill of a well-designed process, carried out by experienced facilitators.

At each step of the process trust and openness are heightened. Seeing challenges in a fuller perspective; realizing the limitations imposed on our perception of a situation when we are only immersed in a stakeholder perspective; experiencing the goodwill of those we traditionally perceive as adversaries or enemies; coming to the conclusion that nothing looks as easy as we thought; maybe reaching the point of thinking that our preferred solutions are not that desirable after all. . . . This is the stage of *sensing*. It will facilitate the next stage of the Open Will leading to Presencing.

When all previous ideas, perceptions, and assumptions are loosened, it is easier to imagine an open field of inquiry. Most, if not all, processes using the U will guide participants to a clear understanding of a common ground from which it is possible to operate, together with the recognition of differences that for the time being cannot be addressed, knowing that the field of operation can be widened in the measure that trust is enhanced by the results that can be reached first.

At the stage of the Open Will, the stakeholders will typically brainstorm loosely ideas for action from which will be selected those that all stakeholders see suitable, most immediately reachable, most efficient in terms of the investment of energy that they require, most strategic, and so on. This process may take many iterations. Success is manifested when a highly satisfying solution has been reached that no given stakeholder could have generated on their own. Even though the scenario at this stage is just an outline, participants have the feeling of being completely aligned with the group, while they are allowed to retain complete personal and organizational independence. This is what presencing allows.

Presencing

Processes that allow the stage of presencing are those in which perspectives coming from past thinking are placed on hold, and we can collectively listen to a future that wants to emerge.

Through presencing the letting go of the past makes room for allowing the new; in Otto Scharmer's words, "letting come." Whether we are fundamentally anchored in the past or whether we allow the future to influence us and our decisions is much more determining for the paradigm of transformation than our political persuasions. The political arena typically operates from the second level, that of change through reform, not that of transformation; very often it approaches complex problems as if they were complicated (see Figure 1 in Introduction). It most often resists presencing in name of favored, predetermined options.

Moving to the Other Side of the U

After the act of collective presencing, thoughts and ideas need to be given form and direction, and the experience of a new way of operating becomes integral part of the organizational culture. These are the stages of crystallizing, prototyping, and performing. At the first stage of *crystallizing*, the group starts giving form to ideas, determining what can be done and how.

Prototyping introduces the step of experimenting with the new ideas, of testing possibilities of change without placing the whole at risk. Prototyping means supporting initiatives at a small scale in places where they have the best possibilities to succeed. These initiatives will receive resources and manpower to succeed from the organizational environment; they will not operate in a vacuum. Once successful, prototyping can be scaled throughout the organization.

Imagine then an organization in which all the previous steps up to prototyping are held on an ongoing basis and change happens in a holistic way. All the steps leading to prototyping now need to be supported so that the culture becomes that of a learning organization or community at the stage of performing. New practices and structures need to be integrated in the internal culture so that the U process is part and parcel of a continuum that supports change on a regular basis.

The process of journeying through the layers of consciousness on one side (Open Mind, Open Heart, and Open Will on the way down), presencing at the center and emerging on the other side (crystallizing, prototyping, and performing) is present in Twelve Step or Nonviolent Communication. In those approaches the moment of presencing is not recognized as such; we could call it the silent, elusive moment of greatest change, a moment that is present only in the consciousness of the beholders, not in a structured step of the process. In Twelve Step presencing appears at the utmost humbling of the personality of the addict trying to overcome old habits (step 9 of making amends). In recognizing one's behavior, how it has affected self and others, and in being willing to offer apologies, the person in recovery touches the place where the utmost vulnerability and seeming powerlessness shifts into a truer power, heretofore unknown.

In Nonviolent Communication, at the moment in which two parties have reached full understanding of a situation of conflict—of how both have been affected in their feelings and needs—new possibilities arise. Usual, fixed perspectives are as if momentarily dissolved; new possibilities seem tangible, including new ways of being. The two parties stand at a crossroads, and something completely new can emerge that was hardly thought possible even minutes before. This completely inner, and often neglected, experience of turnaround, to which no name is usually given, is the experience of presencing.

The Quintessential Process of Decision Making

All social processes relating to the U can be related to the quintessential daily act of decision making. One example can illustrate what its dynamics are in daily life, whether it relates to what I will buy, where I will go, what I will eat, who I will meet, what I will do, and so on.

Suppose I am driving towards an intersection and see the light turning from yellow to red, and I have to decide whether I will stop or go through the intersection. This decision will be taken in a universal sequence, though it can be influenced by a great number of variables, and the process may go back and forth in the sequence.

The first step will consist in discerning the *facts*. The list of those given below is far from exhaustive:

- location of the intersection, volume of traffic; cars behind my own, to the sides; and so on
- speed I am traveling; state of the asphalt (dry or wet)
- drivers' record, impact of a possible fine, known presence of police officers in the area
- sense of urgency about what I am doing

The above, especially the information known to myself alone, generates a background of feelings, which is accentuated as I see the transition of the light from yellow to red. And the feelings I carry in the background are affected by what I register of the facts. An example: if my situation at work were precarious, I may be worried and may want to speed through the light and not arrive late to work once more. But if my driver's license record is also precarious, I may be anxious about getting a ticket, compounding the intensity of the feelings. But the list of feelings doesn't stop there; I may have reasons to be excited, angry, giddy, overwhelmed, overstimulated. Based on the facts, the feelings, which may be already present, are intensified.

Based on the information and what my feelings are telling me about this information, I envision a variety of outcomes, even in such brief lapse of time as it takes to stop at or go through the intersection. In the case given above, the decision could go both ways. I may decide that because I don't see a cop, it is worth going through the yellow light even though I risk doing so when it is actually turning red. Or I may feel paralyzed by emotion and decide to stop.

The above sequence is that of information (external and internal) and corresponding feelings. Based on information first (corresponding to *Open Mind*), feelings second (corresponding to *Open Heart*), exploration of alternatives third (corresponding to *Open Will*), I take one of the possible decisions. All of this happens very fast, and I may soon realize that I did not make a good decision. It takes time and training to be able to take good decisions, ones that are not conditioned by strong feelings and last-minute thoughts. If I am not clear about my feelings and needs, the decision will more likely than not be unsatisfying when seen in hindsight. Making the best decisions means being able to have a better understanding of our feelings and what strategies best meet our needs and other people's needs.

Creating a New Way of Relating

What is said here of one person deciding on a single, small issue is still equivalent to the phenomenon of a large group of people or network of organizations making a decision. Obviously the difficulties increase exponentially.

What social technology does is countercultural to some degree. In passing from the Open Mind to the Open Will, we pass through the critical step of the Open Heart. In our culture and our times, expressing strong emotions, feelings, concerns, gut reactions is not easy, and in many ways the sequence of the steps is often altered in the name of expediency and comfort.

Paradigm of Competition	Paradigm of Inclusion/Participation
Good or bad/right or wrong	Life affirming versus life negating
Needs are most often confused with strategies	Needs are universal and distinct from strategies
Judgment	Evaluation
Majority rule	Large coalitions
Goes most often from mind to action	Seeks to go from Open Mind to Open Heart to Open Will
Debate	Generative Conversation
Victory	Presencing
Works from the past (ideologies)	Works both from the past and from the future that wants to emerge

Table 20: paradigms of competition and inclusion/participation.

Only seldom do we want to dwell at the level of feelings and emotions, because they are uncomfortable, because we do not know how to express them, how to receive them, how to handle them safely. When this is the case, we will often move from a more or less complete view of the facts to a decision that will be influenced by feelings, but only unconsciously. We may very well know somehow that the decision is unsatisfactory and just hope for the best. Since our buy-in is only partial, we know that when the time comes we can pull back and invoke a good reason for the change of mind.

Social technology is thus the art of restoring the natural sequence in decision making, rather than the habitual one. In such a simple secret lies the key to its success. From this simplicity, according to the scale of action involved, interventions of growing complexity can be crafted that still hold these simple principles as their core truth.

Table 20 summarizes what we have discussed so far; it compares the paradigm of competition that is a given in our culture with the new, emerging paradigm of inclusion and participation.

The Breadth of Social Technology

It is not only the clarity reached in social technology that characterizes the 1990s and the turn of the twentieth century in the social field, but also the application of social technology to larger and larger interorganizational scales, rather than just single organizations, and the mixing and blending of participatory dialogue and decision-making techniques.

A compelling example of this is the Global Compact, which brought together worldwide leaders from the private and public sectors, unions, and NGOs, in order to promote socially responsible businesses worldwide (See box on page X). Sustainable Food Lab is another initiative incorporating more than one hundred businesses, government organizations, and NGOs worldwide, working at setting up alternative and sustainable food systems worldwide. Sustainable Food Lab integrates *Theory U* together with approaches from the Society for Organizational Learning. This expanding work of facilitation and integration serves the emergence of trisector partnerships, with public, private, and nonprofit sector collaborations in the food system.

Finally, social technology has expanded in a myriad of ways. The second edition of *The Change Handbook* counts some sixty-one social approaches presently available. And it's far from exhaustive.[6] The first edition of the

Handbook, published eight years earlier, included only eighteen processes. It seems in the last decades approaches to social change have increased exponentially.

What individuals experience in presencing can be discovered collectively in the set of processes that have taken the name of Theory U. To reach the stage of presencing it seems that Open Mind, Open Heart, and Open Will have to precede it. We could call this sequence a phenomenological organic whole, one that can be found in myriads of processes. However, only experience with these processes can allow us to recognize these archetypes at work. One has to resist the temptation of intellectually attributing correspondences without experiencing them firsthand. I will now turn to these places in which I and others have experienced presencing, and in which after the fact can be recognized the presence of the U process. I will look at Consensus Decision Making, World Café, and Future Search. The first two are tools you can immediately try out with a minimum of preparation, or after taking a workshop or webinar.

Another word of caution has to be added here. Most of the processes go down the steps to the bottom of the U, up to the moment of presencing and to the next stage in an organic way. Only an added, deliberate intention to repeat the experiences and integrate them in a larger process of cultural change allows the completion of the process on the right side of the U. And such an experience is not possible for tools of social technology, which are often used as a single part of larger interventions. Therefore we will turn our attention to the first 5 steps of the U process and leave aside steps 6 and 7, or only mention them very briefly.

Consensus Decision Making

My training in Consensus Decision Making came in Albany during the Occupy Wall Street movement. The first half-hour crash course took place under a tree with two young facilitators. They laid out the steps of the practice and advised to take small steps on involvement in the process, such as helping the facilitator by taking notes, stacking the interventions, counting hands in a temperature check, and pointing to people who stood aside or objected in order to hear them. Handling a large crowd in the open implies a large collaboration.

Appreciative Inquiry and the UN Global Compact

In June 2004 more than 500 leaders gathered in New York for the UN Global Compact Leaders Summit. Among these were 250 representing large businesses, 180 medium to small businesses, 31 government representatives, among which were also heads of UN agencies, and more than 40 from civil society and organized labor.

The gathering was facilitated by David Cooperrider, the founder of the Appreciative Inquiry (AI) methodology, which teaches that organizations, in this case networks, are "a solution to be embraced" rather than a "problem to be solved."

AI starts with an exploration of an affirmative topic at the heart of the intervention, then it moves through four stages:

- Discovery: identifying the "best of what is," or "what gives life": the so-called positive core.
- Dream: envisioning, detecting "what might be."
- Design: Co-creating the future. Building on the positive core and the dream allows the co-creation of the ideal design of "how it can be." The ideal is an organizational structure in which the exceptional becomes everyday and ordinary.
- Destiny: learning, empowering, and improvising to sustain the future. This aspect looks at the implementation of "what will be."

At the end of the summit the participants committed to ten core principles embracing respect for labor rights and standards, environmental sustainability, and an anticorruption pledge. In addition they manifested the intention of partnering in projects with others who embrace the principles. Fifteen years later, EcoVadis, one of the world's most trusted provider of business sustainability ratings, has evaluated a large sample of the nearly 12,000 companies that subscribe to the compact, finding that the tools provided by the compact—action platforms for forming partnerships, the UN Business Action Hub, and reporting mechanisms with GRI (Global Reporting Initiative)—are producing tangible results.

Most of the organizations in the sample that have subscribed to UNGC principles performed significantly above the rest on matters relating to sustainability and labor rights along the supply chains. Smaller and medium-size businesses perform and adapt to change better than the larger ones.

Key to the success of particular businesses are:

- Leadership commitment at the level of executives and boards, accompanied by public statements
- Using the resources made available through UNGC
- Measuring and reporting on progress, e.g., through GRI
- The voluntary nature of participation
- The multi-stakeholder and trisector approach to change
- The credibility of the United Nations as a convener
- Tapping into more than 40 country and regional networks.

Using a decentralized model, the global compact addresses primarily economic goals. The partnerships of governments and nonprofit sector organizations are nevertheless very important as was felt by the participants of the Leaders Summit for the following reasons:

- Governments can play an important role by supporting the principles of UNGC, making contributions to the compact, and abolishing trade barriers.
- Civil society is important both as a watchdog in relation to compliance and through partnerships that can provide ground-level knowledge that businesses lack.

Sources
- The Global Compact Leaders Summit United Nations Headquarters 24 June 2004, Final Report, https://appreciativeinquiry.champlain.edu/wp-content/uploads/2016/01/UN-Global-Compact-Appreciative-Inquiry-Summit rep fin.pdf.
- For the particular format followed by the summit see https://appreciativeinquiry.champlain.edu/wp-content/uploads/2016/01/workbook-June-2004.pdf.
- For the Ten Principles of the UN Global Compact, see: https://www.unglobalcompact.org/what-is-gc/mission/principles.
- For an assessment of the UN Global Compact see: "Why the UN Global Compact Is a CSR Commitment That Works": https://www.reutersevents.com/sustainability/why-un-global-compact-csr-commitment-works

Having taken the small steps for some three or four general assemblies, I stepped into the disconcerting/exhilarating experience of facilitating a fluid audience of individuals at all levels of experience with consensus. When a topic would come back for a further stage of consensus, the crowd may have been very different from the original one. This may sound like a losing proposition, as I thought at first. And in fact, it may be hard to get past the repeated breaches of process from one individual or another, the length of some interventions, and the need to go back and forth between the steps. But something else stands out if one observes over a period of time. A process of collective education takes place. The "unruly" individuals who seem to cause the greatest problems are often those who care the most about an issue. When they relax into the experience of being heard, their attitude changes. Many start in fact realizing the nature of the process and the collective benefit it generates; they turn out to be potential assistants to the facilitator. Though not a linear process, progress is visible over a number of general assemblies.

Of the processes we will present here, consensus is one of the simplest since it is, generally speaking, the one that can be accomplished, at least potentially, in the shortest amount of time. Consensus Decision Making has its origin in Quaker practice and has been in use for three and a half centuries. In its highest form Quaker consensus tends to be seen as part of the religious experience at a collective level; it is the avenue for possible spiritual breakthroughs. Thus, it is in a different form that it has been adapted for work in groups and organizations that do not have a spiritual mission. Among those who adapted it first, credit is often given to the feminist and antinuclear movements of the 1970s, who gave it the shape from which it has evolved at present.[88]

Typically a consensus process occurs around an agenda item in one meeting, though often the process has to be prepared beforehand and/ or repeated over time. We will look at the simplest example of a simple, noncontroversial proposal in a single meeting. In a successful scenario, submitting a proposal in Consensus Decision Making implies the following steps:

---

[88] For a book on consensus see Larry Dressler, *Consensus Through Conversation: How to Achieve High-Commitment Decisions* (San Francisco: Berrett-Koehlers, 2006).

- Presentation of the proposal and clarifying questions (these are fact based, nonemotional) to assure a shared understanding of the factual basis of the proposal.
- Raising of concerns and constructive criticism.
- Exploring of alternatives; offering of amendments
- Eventual acceptance of "friendly amendments" to the proposal.
- Testing for consensus and reaching consensus: the possible options are acceptance, standing aside (neutral), and blocking (negative).
- If there are no blocks, implementing the consensus decision to some degree; this may or may not entail further iterations of the process.

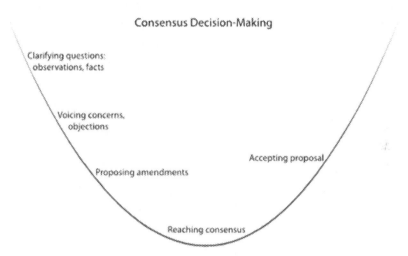

Figure 21: Consensus Decision Making

The pattern of the U is here echoed in the following way:

- Step I: Open Mind: facts are presented and clarity is sought so that everybody can agree on an objective basis.
- Step II: Open Heart: surfacing the emotional content raised by the proposal.
- Step III: Open Will: working to incorporate everybody's concerns for a better final decision; willingly letting go of favorite solutions in favor of what are seen as better ones.
- Step IV: Presencing; the magic of reaching true consensus.
- Step V: accepting proposal.

It is important to underline that in what is called *pure consensus*, a decision can be blocked even by a single person. For this reason it is important to distinguish between pure consensus and consent. Though the steps are very similar in the two variants, the results can be vastly different.

Suffice it to say here that they can be the ends of a spectrum. *Consensus* in the loosest understanding of the term can refer to the possibility of airing objections—and blocking consensus—based on purely personal reasons, or without a reference to clearly articulated and accepted parameters. At the other end of the spectrum, *consent* refers to working within a range of tolerance, without recourse to blocking. As in the case of Sociocracy, which we will see at the end of this chapter, this means being able to object only upon a common set of agreed-upon criteria. Moreover an accepted decision can be linked to sets of criteria and terms of review. The more concerns a decision presents, the more criteria will be added and the shorter the terms of review will be.

Consensus in Action

The form of Consensus Decision Making I have referred to in relation to Occupy Wall Street is not significantly different from the way in which consensus is used in a community or organization. Only the scale of its use and the fluidity of the settings are different.

It is interesting for our purpose to see how the particular form of consensus at Occupy Wall Street emerged. On August 2, 2011, before the occupation of Zuccotti Park in the Wall Street neighborhood that would lead to the Occupy Wall Street encampment, twelve people of the "process committee" met on Bowling Green to project a form of direct democracy to use in the General Assemblies. The daring idea was born to facilitate assemblies of hundreds for collective decision making. Many, even among the twelve, thought this impossible.[89] They envisioned securing the process through spokes-councils in which people send their "representatives" rather than doing it 'live." Nothing of this sort had been done at this scale before.

The General Assembly became the de facto decision-making body for the occupation at the park, renamed Liberty Plaza. Through this form of Collective Decision Making, the paradoxes of equality of input and diffuse

---

[89] David Graeber, "Enacting the Impossible: On Consensus Decision-Making," *The Occupied Wall Street Journal*, October 22, 2011.

leadership are reconciled to a great extent. Nathan Schroeder, who has lived this experience up close, concludes: "Working toward consensus is really hard, frustrating and slow. But the occupiers are taking their time. When they finally get to consensus on some issue, often after days and days of trying, the feeling is quite incredible. A mighty cheer fills the plaza. It's hard to describe the experience of being among hundreds of passionate, rebellious, creative people who are all in agreement about something."[90] He is in effect describing the moment of presencing that forms the culmination of the first part of the U process, and the transition into the second part.

Conversation Cafes

Vicky Robin, Susan Partnow, and Habib Rose, three friends living in Seattle, first evolved the Conversation Café format in the summer of 2001. Each of them simply held conversations around topics of relevance in various coffee shops once a week. The method was soon tested in carrying out conversations for defusing the tensions around 9/11. Soon after Conversation Cafés spread to Toronto, St. Louis, Tucson, many other cities in the US, Canada, and Europe.

The method, though quite simple, is so effective that it can be used successfully to tackle thorny political issues such as in bridging the "red-blue divide" as it is done by Let's Talk America. It has also been used at Bioneers Conference, many Green Festivals, PBS, and even in the British Parliament, not to mention myriad other conferences and meetings.

Conversation Cafés are held in groups of five to eight individuals; the format is structured in four rounds: two introductory rounds to hear each participant at turns around a question. The third, and longest, round is an open exploration; the last, short round serves to gather insights, new questions, and closing remarks. The method can be learned by going to http://www.conversationcafe.org/, where you will also find the manual (http://www.conversationcafe.org/wp-content/docsPDF/docHostCompleteManual.pdf), tips, video training, and more. Having mastered this, you could turn to World Café next.

---

[90] Nathan Schroeder, "How It Came About, What It Means, How It Works and Everything Else You Need to Know about Occupy Wall Street," *The Nation*, September 29, 2011, https://www.thenation.com/article/occupy-wall-street-faq/.

World Café

Experiencing or setting up a World Café conversation is a sheer delight. I have been on either end of it, for work, for conferences, for a host organizations, or for community purposes. The format is the emblem and banner of a new way of engaging as an activist; some call it being a "conversational activist" and set out to "change the world one conversation at a time."

Don't underestimate the power of creating a fun, colorful, and inviting environment as one of the first steps in working on social issues. The joy with which you work, how you welcome stakeholders, and how eagerly you engage and listen to their ideas sets the tone for the way and the goals you want to pursue. World Café is the hallmark of a conversation format that was devised based, among other things, on the observation that in meetings, seminars, or conferences, the most interesting conversation often, and sadly, happened during the breaks. Why not bring the atmosphere of the breaks into the main event itself? Why not learn, connect, and make the best kinds of decisions while having fun? No tool of social technology will in fact fully work if learning does not go hand in hand with deeper connection, humor, and fun.

In 1995, a small group of business and academic leaders were meeting at the home of Juanita Brown and David Isaacs in Mill Valley, California. None of them had any idea they were about to create a form of social technology that would rapidly spread, as its name augured, around the world.[91] Good luck sent a providential rain that prevented the participants from carrying a large group conversation outdoors. They formed small groups and gathered them around tables instead, and recorded their insights on improvised paper tablecloths. Having a good collective knowledge of facilitation, they hit upon the idea of harvesting the ideas generated at one table and circulating them to other tables, with the intent of connecting more widely and deepening the quality of insights generated. They noticed patterns and themes that were progressively enriched by cross-pollination from one round to the next. They felt that the quality of their collective work had been transformed in

---

[91] Juanita Brown, with David Isaacs and the World Café Community, *The World Café: Shaping Our Futures through Conversations That Matter* (San Francisco: Berrett-Koehler, 2005), 16–17.

depth, scope, and quality, and thus emerged what would later be perfected and become World Café.

Afterwards they went back and looked at all the factors that had generated the breakthrough of new insights on critical strategic issues and mobilized a common will. They recognized seven key principles that stand behind the process and that, consciously applied, can favor the emergence of collaborative conversation and leadership. These principles were then tested and refined in a multitude of different conversations.

World Café is most often built around three successive conversation rounds, followed by a large group dialogue, but other variations have also been used. The number, length, specific pattern, sequence, and mechanics of the rounds depend on the focus and intent of the conversation. Rounds of conversation usually take from 20 to 30 minutes in length, sometimes longer. One host usually stays at the table while the others become "travelers," carrying what has been said from one table to the other tables—each of the travelers going to a different new table. During the second or third rounds host and participants start by briefly conveying what has been said in the previous round at the different tables. The host then asks support from everybody at the table in taking notes and summarizing key ideas. He may also encourage everyone to draw and doodle on the tablecloth, adding other perspectives to the more rational deliberations.

The Principles

World Café revolves around seven principles that encourage good conversations:

- *Principle 1: Setting the Context*
  The three elements of context are:
  - purpose: consider the needs that the conversation will fulfill; clarify the desired outcomes;
  - participants: bring in additional perspectives that will enrich the conversation; have in mind who could benefit from this conversation and who will be affected; and
  - parameters: the World Café can be, and often is, a part of a larger facilitation intervention including other techniques.

- *Principle 2: Create Hospitable Spaces*
  - offer access to a beautiful, hospitable, playful setting; craft original and creative invitations, introduce significant and relevant stories; and
  - introduce people to the Café Etiquette: "Contribute your thinking and experience; listen to understand; connect ideas; listen together for patterns, insights and deeper questions; play, doodle and draw." (see figure 22).

- *Principle 3: Exploring Questions That Matter*

World Café organizers spend much time and attention in crafting relevant, provocative, and thought-generating questions.[92] Good questions must feel truly new and relevant, stimulate fresh inquiry, evoke possibility, create a healthy tension, unearth assumptions, and generate new questions.

Figure 22: World Café Etiquette
(Reprinted with kind permission of Avril Orloff and
the World Café, http://www.theworldcafe.com/)

---

[92] Asking truly relevant questions takes a central role in World Café as in many other facilitation tools. Anyone interested in leading a World Café would do well to read Eric E. Vogt, Juanita Brown, and David Isaacs, *The Art of Powerful Questions: Catalyzing Insight, Innovation, and Action* (Mill Valley, CA: Whole Systems Associates, 2003), https://umanitoba.ca/admin/human_resources/change/media/the-art-of-powerful-questions.pdf.

- *Principle 4: Encourage Everyone's Contribution*
Eliciting everybody's contribution lies at the heart of World Café. This acknowledges, however, that not everybody participates in the same way. Input can be offered by slowing down the conversation through use of rounds (speaking in sequence, clockwise or anticlockwise) and talking sticks; by asking for moments of silence and reflection; by offering drawing materials for those who want to use the paper that is most often in the center of the table of a World Café.

- *Principle 5: Cross-pollinate and Connect Diverse Perspectives*
In the setup of a World Café the organizers have a care to invite the greatest variety of stakeholders (Principle 1). The participants move from one table to another, conveying what has been said in the previous round in their own table. This encourages the greatest possible permutation of inputs at each table, and the greatest variety from table to table.

- *Principle 6: Listen Together for Patterns, Insights, and Deeper Questions*
Through deliberate moments of reflection at the table or in the larger groups, participants are encouraged to listen to what World Café calls "the magic in the middle" (what the future wants of us). This is the step from listening, not just to what others are saying, but to the deeper insights and questions that emerge in between the various perspectives.

- *Principle 7: Harvest and Share Collective Discoveries*
The goal of this is to harvest the meaning out of the whole of the conversations and the conversation process itself; to let emerge what is more than the sum of the parts. This is often done in a larger group conversation through a variety of strategies:
  • Asking for a moment of silence and individual reflection.
  • Asking people to offer insights on sticky notes posted on a large board and asking them later to order them to detect patterns and themes.
  • Creating a graphic recording of the event with the help of someone trained for the purpose.

- Producing a report that incorporates artistic contributions such as the drawings generated or other materials contributed, hanging up the tablecloths, etc.

Starting Your Own World Café Conversation

World Cafés are not the easiest of participatory conversations, but they can be mastered with some precautions in mind. Have a clear understanding of the format and the aims to achieve. Key to the intervention is spending time on crafting clear and stimulating questions.

Familiarize Yourself with the Approach

- Hosting Tool Kit: http://www.theworldcafe.com/wp-content/uploads/2015/07/Cafe-To-Go-Revised.pdf.
- Book: Juanita Brown with David Isaacs, *The World Café: Shaping Our Futures through Conversations That Matter* (San Francisco: Barrett-Koehler Publishers, 2005).
- Overview of the World Café Method: http://www.theworldcafe.com/key-concepts-resources/world-cafe-method/.
- Where to get some training (learning programs): http://www.theworldcafe.com/services-programs/signature-learning-programs/.

Props and Tips

- Hosting Toolkit: A Quick Reference Guide for Hosting World Café: http://www.theworldcafe.com/wp-content/uploads/2015/07/Cafe-To-Go-Revised.pdf.
- Café Etiquette Poster: http://www.theworldcafe.com/wp-content/uploads/2015/07/WC-guidelines-small.pdf.
- Table Menu and Etiquette Cards: http://www.theworldcafe.com/tools-store/hosting-tool-kit/image-bank/table-cards/.
- World Café Room Set-up:
- https://api.ning.com/files/S7U7lpmHwWtFV*rCmdoaXSiaV84WA4sqVdFm1-aDZ8JnYLVuJ2uXL3TAayHTyVHyZQvfq0YzxBypeMkcZOcPzDsi7qcw2ukS/WorldCafeRoomSetup.pdf.

- Eric E. Vogt, Juanita Brown, David Isaacs, *The Art of Powerful Questions: Catalyzing Insight, Innovation and Action*: http://www.ncdd.org/exchange/files/docs/powerful_conversations.pdf.
- World Café Stories (with clips): http://www.theworldcafe.com/category/stories-reports/.

Videos and Audios: World Café in Action

- Principles of the World Café (used in a inter-European World Café): http://www.youtube.com/watch?v=_fSnbzUcQ44&feature=related.
- World Café, Video: http://www.youtube.com/watch?v=1cv82Yl0H7M.
- Audio Interview Juanita Brown, David Isaacs on New Dimensions: https://programs.newdimensions.org/products/collective-creating-through-conversations-with-juanita-brown-david-isaacs, 1 hour; $ 1.99.
- See other video and audio World Cafe resources at http://www.theworldcafe.com/videos.htm.

Gary Hammel of the London School of Economics comments on tools like the World Café: "Strategizing depends on creating a rich and complex web of conversations that cuts across previously isolated pockets of knowledge and creates new and unexpected combinations of insight."[93]

We have seen on what lies the success of World Café: the format of rounds and the seven principles that pervade it. Here too the process goes through the U of Otto Scharmer, though in a fluid, less differentiated way than in Consensus Decision Making.

Reviewing the Process

What appears as almost discrete steps in Consensus Decision Making is rather an overlapping sequence of steps in World Café; we merge from the Open Mind to the Open Heart, and from the Open Heart to the Open Will, and from there to presencing and beyond.

---

[93] Juanita Brown, *World Café*, 190.

In the first step of the Open Mind, the organizers have care to gather all possible kinds of stakeholders that have a say in the matter. At the time of the World Café people are asked to simply hear what others say, to spend much time listening, gathering information, and sharing it with others. For this purpose the crafting of relevant questions is crucial, and the facilitators will do well to devote time and attention to them and test their questions beforehand.

The Open Heart is mixed in with the Open Mind; it grows as the other recedes. It is encouraged by the sequence of questions. In the step of moving from one table to the other, we are asked and openly encouraged to embrace all the perspectives we have heard by conveying them to others, thus moving away from our perspective to embracing with empathy those of others. We will then hear other perspectives at the new tables. For those who play with it, art encourages something other than factual listening; it moves us into our feelings.

The Open Will emerges as we go deeper into the Open Heart; here too one emerges from the other, and from what the participants are asked to contribute. Something new emerges from being asked to reflect back in silence, from contributing insights and new questions, from looking at patterns and themes. It starts with the gathering of insights at the last table round and is rendered more concrete in the open large-group conversation or process. It leads to what World Café has called "the magic in the middle," which we have called presencing so far.

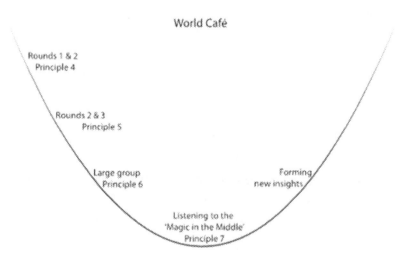

Figure 23: World Café

In looking at this moment of presencing, Finn Voldtofte comments: "It is essential to understand that the magic in the middle is more than an idea. It is a reality that can be experienced, and which I may have a poorer or a better ability to recognize, participate in and possibly to take leadership of engaging in my organization. As such it is very appropriate to ask: *Which practices can help me and my people to engage the magic in the middle?*"[94]

World Café most often ends with a gathering of insights and possibly their clustering into actionable items.

World Café for a Nation

World Café is more often than not a tool of change used in conjunction with many others. It is difficult therefore to assess its impact, or illustrate it through large-scale case studies. An exception has been in recent years its widespread use in institutions and government agencies in Singapore.

It has been said that Singapore wants to become a learning nation, entrepreneurial, creative, and innovative. And World Café has been adopted as one of the tools for this national learning in many ways. The new approach to generative dialogue was first introduced by Daniel Kim, cofounder of the MIT Sloan School's Educational Learning Center, and his partner, Diane Cory. Following are some of the examples of its use.[95]

What best place to avail oneself of World Café than in systems thinking? This is what the Temasek Polytechnic uses to introduce youth to an exploration of complex issues, close to their immediate concerns, such as teenage pregnancy and youth smoking. After exploring the issues from an academic perspective, a World Café is held in which are invited some major stakeholders, such as the National Youth Council, the Center for Fathering, and the Ministry of Health. At the Café tables, not only do the youths have a wider understanding of the issues; they also overcome the fear of engaging older adults.

At another end of the spectrum, no less than the police have decided to emphasize hearing and listening in new ways and the World Café is a tool of choice. One example: the conversation around the ways in which officers are impacted by a new computerized tracking system used in police cars,

---

[94] See the six-part series by Finn Voldtofte from 2005 at http://www.theworldcafe. com/tag/magic-in-the-middle/.

[95] Juanita Brown, *World Café*, 198–201.

encouraging a better integration between junior and senior officers. And the police department also uses World Café conversations at their annual corporate planning exercise.

The World Café has been seen as a tool of choice for embracing the culture of the traditional *Kopitiams*, local coffee shops that sell traditional specialties. Through the National Community Leadership Institute, the People's Association of Singapore hosts People to People conversations through an adaptation of World Café it calls Knowledge Kopitiam. At its tables sit government representatives and grassroots leaders.

The Knowledge Kopitiams have been used by other government agencies and institutions. The Ministry of Defense has used them to explore the question of how to expand their purpose from deterrence to nation building; the Housing Development Board to hear the concerns, hopes, and aspirations of new officers; the InfoComm Development Authority and the Ministry of Manpower to cross-pollinate learning across departments and to explore how to promote a culture of creativity and innovation in Singapore.

From the above we can see how concretely the World Café is promoting a culture of emergent dialogue in the island state. The widespread use of World Cafés helps bridge levels of authority and build a path from past to future. Yaacob Ibrahim, secretary for the Ministry of Communication and Information Technology offers: "Today we want to spark a revolution, not to overthrow the government, but to reinvent ourselves. . . . These people-to-people or P2P discussions are essential to our development as a cohesive and well-informed people."

World Café has been a conversation tool that has fitted well local culture, allowing effective communication between the various ethnic groups, providing a relaxed setting where differences can be bridged, while inspiring movement forward. Moreover change can be encouraged while partnering with the authorities. Samantha Tan, who gathered this information, concludes that World Café activism "is not an activism *against* the authority structure, but *for* the world we want. It's a humanistic activism, because in the Café you are responding to a common question, but you are called from wherever you sit in relation to the question. It's fundamentally a very respectful process—a form of *pro-activism* rather than *re-activism*."[96]

---

[96] Juanita Brown, *World Café*, 201.

Future Search

The facilitation approach known as Future Search was formulated by Marvin Weisbord and Sandra Janoff in 1985. It has some similarities with Eric Trist and Fred Emery's Search Conference methodology.[97] It helps stakeholders address three wide categories of use:

- Create a shared future vision for organization or community.
- Discover shared intentions and take responsibility for their own plans.
- Implement an already present vision.

Among the conditions for its success are the following:

- The whole system must be present in the room: this encourages the formation of as many new relationships as possible! The greater the diversity of encounters, the greatest the potential for innovation.
- Global context/local action: Placing local issues under a global perspective is a way to defuse tension and bring cohesion.
- Focus on common ground and future focus, not on problems and conflicts. Common ground is the prerequisite for action planning.
- Work with small, self-managed groups. This reduces passivity, conflict, and dependency on experts, and is facilitated by a shared leadership format with rotating roles.
- Public responsibility for follow up: Intentions are declared publicly, and people are encouraged to sign up for action groups.

Future Search has been applied in a great variety of settings; in business (from community bookstores to the New England fishing industry) to communities, (Children infected with AIDS in Tanzania, Seattle Human Services Coalition, holistic city development plans,...) in congregations, in education, (particularly for developing vision) in government (Vermont, Copenhagen, Center of Government in Flanders, Belgium,...) for environmental problems, (water management, eco-tourism, waste

---

[97] Marvin R. Weisbord and Sandra Janoff, *Future Search: An Action Guide to Finding Common Ground in Organizations and Communities*, Second Edition (San Francisco, CA: Berrett-Koehler, 2000).

management,…) in healthcare (alcohol and drugs abuse, home birth, early childhood, job injuries, reproductive health, …).

Selecting and Organizing the Stakeholder Groups

As we have seen previously, stakeholders are people with key information, people with authority, knowledge, and resources to act, plus those who are affected by the organization/community's actions. The organizers themselves may add criteria they find important.

Separating the groups by demographics risks accentuating stereotypes and differences. However, demographics can be used to ensure inclusion across the board (across the stakeholder groups). So ideally a Future Search would include as wide a demographic representation as possible, but it would not work around this distinction.

A major criterion to be set in view of the event concerns the envisioned timelines in relation to the age of the organization; these are most often divided in decades (1960s, 1970s, 1980s, 1990s, etc.). The group needs to envision the future as far as the planners can tolerate, so that the participants can let go of limitations and dream big. Ten years is reasonable; twenty is better.

Structure of a Future Search

One conference most typically involves from sixty to seventy people. The structure involves a movement from past trends, to present potential, to desirable/ideal future, alternating work in mixed groups, stakeholder groups, or self-selected groups. It is based on five tasks of two to four hours each, spread over three days. Below is the sequence of the days and tasks.

FIRST DAY
Afternoon
- Review of the past (mixed groups)
- Exploration of the present: external trends (stakeholder groups)

SECOND DAY
Morning
- Trends continued
- Focus on present: taking responsibility (stakeholder groups)

Afternoon
- Creation of ideal future scenarios (mixed groups)
- Identification of common ground

THIRD DAY
Morning
- Confirmation of common ground
- Action plans (stakeholder groups and self-selected groups)

Let us review the above in detail

Day 1, afternoon (4 1/2 hours): Past to Present

FIRST TASK (mixed groups): Past
Large swaths of butcher paper are set on the walls with the following themes: "personal," "global," and "x" (community, organization, issue), and dates set every five or ten years apart. People discuss trends and patterns, write milestones on their notes, and then transfer them onto the butcher paper. The task is done in mixed groups.

SECOND TASK (stakeholder groups): Present
This is the stage of the building of a "mind-map."[98] The methodology of mind-mapping was developed in the mid-1980s. It is designed to allow ownership of the "collective mess." It renders visible a broad pattern of concerns around the common topic.

In the mind-map the conference task is written at the center. On the sheet are mapped all the trends that converge on the theme. Each new trend is added with a line of a different color. The trend is accompanied with concrete examples. The purpose of the mind-map is for all to face the confusion and live with the anxiety that is generated from it.

The mind-mapping task takes on average 45 minutes. Strong feelings most likely come to the surface. After the map is complete, people place some seven dots on it, color-matched by stakeholder groups. The dots show which group cares about what. This is a visual tool for the dialogue the next day. People will slowly start seeing patterns out of the "mess." The

---

[98] For a general introduction see: https://en.wikipedia.org/wiki/Mind_map

confusion helps people realize that no person or group has the absolute truth or solution and that these will have to be sought together.

People are left overnight with an interrupted task and with what often is an amount of overwhelming information outlining a great complexity, on the basis that chaos and confusion can have a positive role, and that allowing them can create the conditions for new opportunities. Staying in the "confusion room" with a certain amount of anxiety negates the temptation of retreating and rationalizing.

Day 2, morning (stakeholder groups): Present

SECOND TASK
The stakeholder groups first identify trends that are important to them, then tell the large group what they are presently doing and what they want to do. Practically this is done by returning to the mind-map. Each group highlights the branches that have significant clusters of dots. There is a large group discussion, without interpretation, in front of the mind-map before returning to work in small groups. At this stage stakeholders make their own version of the mind-map and focus on what issues they find more important. Now the groups can return to sensing and owning, together with taking responsibility through the "prouds" and "sorries" (celebrations and mournings). When groups share, there is generally a sense of surprise at who cares about what. Hope starts to emerge from the previous state of confusion. By expressing publicly what they perceive as their own behavior and owning it, the participants get beyond blaming and denial.

Day 2, Afternoon (mixed groups): Future

THIRD TASK
The individuals return to mixed groups to prepare ideal future scenarios. They note common future themes, potential projects, and areas of unresolved differences. Lists are first made by the small groups and then merged and posted on the wall.

It is important to act out the future one wants as if it has already happened. This provides a contrast and reason for seeking to close and bridge the gap with the present. The group is asked to place themselves some fifteen to twenty years into the future and provide images of what has been achieved and what obstacles have been overcome. People are also asked to provide creative presentations of their scenarios (e.g., through skits), listen to other presentations, and write themselves notes about patterns that they see emerge from what they hear. Participants may now be feeling on top of the world, a situation they could not have reached had they not been in the abyss previously.

FOURTH TASK

The participants need time to revisit their places of agreement (from the day before) before willingness to commit is formed. Each group is asked to prepare three flip charts: one relating to the common future that mostly lists general values and aspirations, a second about potential projects, and a third listing the unresolved differences (all issues that have not been addressed and that will not be worked on). Lists are cut into strips so that the participants can place related items together later.

Day 3, Morning (stakeholder or self-selected groups): Future

FOURTH TASK

The whole group reviews the lists to detect common ground. Areas of conflict are not worked on. People gather at the wall and individuals group similar themes by moving the strips around until they feel satisfied that all related items are joined together. At this point anxiety often rises again. This is no longer a time based (past–present) anxiety but mode based (from thinking into action) anxiety. Now is the time to decide to act on what is possible rather than looking at the past.

FIFTH TASK

Finally the group moves into action planning. This can be done by stakeholder or by self-selected groups. This is the task that can be extended for another few hours, particularly if people live far from each other. The action planning is about dividing up work, setting up goals, figuring who to involve, making public one's commitments, and setting timetables.

Future Search Conferences generally propose two rounds of planning. In organizations people generally meet in stakeholder groups or already-formed taskforces to begin planning. In communities or issue groups, the Future Search may go either through the stakeholder groups or immediately build voluntary coalitions.

In the first round of planning people start determining their actions, what they will do and with who. Then they report to the larger group. After the first round a chance is offered to reorganize in any way the groups wish. Individuals are asked to "place a stake in the ground," to publicly state on which issue they want to work, so that others may join if interested.

The Whole in Review

The structure of a Future Search Conference is built over a number of criteria of contrasts:

- Alternation of awake time and soak time (overnight), with two of the tasks being divided by a night
- Alternation of looking outward and looking inward (as in the first day and in the "prouds and sorries")
- Alternation of formats of individual work, small groups (stakeholder or mixed groups), and large group
- Tasks moving between information, interpretation, and presentation
- Creation of links between personal, organizational, and global levels

The sets of contrasts above enable the group to pass through the stages of Open Mind, Open Heart, and Open Will to presencing, and into the other side of the U. Here too, as in World Café, we witness a continuous shift between the stages rather than discontinuous steps.

In the first task people explore trends and patterns. They create a mind-map that renders concrete the level of complexity. They expand the Open Mind to encompass a view of reality that no individual or stakeholder group can generate alone. With the second task people start seeing patterns and start realizing what part they play in them. They carry these feelings of confusion and overwhelm overnight, sowing the seeds for the Open Heart phase.

The Open Heart ultimately signifies taking responsibility for one's actions, and that is brought to a climax during the completion of the second task in the second day in what has been called the "prouds and sorries."

The third task transitions from the Open Heart to the Open Will. On one hand the Open Heart is acknowledged through what divides people (areas of unresolved differences) and the resolve that they can only act on what is common ground. In the building of creative scenarios, participants enter the stage of the Open Will. This is generally accompanied with feelings of elation.

The fourth task requires a harmonization of purposes with a letting go of preferred scenarios of one stakeholder group or another; the group determines what it is possible to act on. This generally entails a sense of surprise in relation to the solutions people carried in their minds when they entered the Future Search Conference. It is the prelude to concerted action that passes through the moment and experience of presencing, the forming of a higher resolve in a group in which stakeholder groups and individuals retain their full individuality but feel united in a common purpose. The fifth task enshrines all of the above stages and moves to the right side of the U in terms of "placing stakes in the ground" and taking resolves.

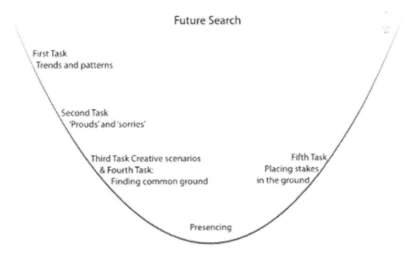

Figure 24: Future Search

Case Study: Byward Market (Ottawa)[99]

The ByWard Market had been in existence for almost 180 years when a Future Search Conference was called for in 1998. This was followed by other conferences in 1999, 2003, and 2005. Gentrification and urban development threatened the future of this established market. Increased taxes and rents led to fewer grocers and farmers selling their produce. There had been efforts to salvage the market since the late 1980s, but they had created mixed results and led to growing divisions in the community.

Another added reality needed to be addressed. Ottawa is bilingual, and a split was reflected in the majority of farmer-vendors being francophone and the business owners mostly anglophone. Thirty percent of the market customers are French-speaking. Documents needed to be translated and simultaneous translation offered during the conference. Finally, some groups worked in English, others in French, and some bilingually.

The first Future Search was held with the help of Marvin Weisbord and Sandra Janoff, the founders of the methodology. The planning of the conference took the steering committee some thirteen months. The conference took place between January 18 and 20, 1998. It led to an understanding of the existing common ground, the drawing of a master plan, and the formation of ten working groups. The care and concern to accommodate both communities has been kept ever since in the market meetings. Bilingual collaboration has been met with success.

At various points after the successive conferences three cross-sector, multi-stakeholder committees were formed: the Safety and Security Committee, the Advertising and Promotion Committee, and the Transportation and Parking Committee, which continue to work successfully. Another association represents all of the vendors. A "buy-local" initiative was formed and called "Savor Ottawa/Savourez Ottawa," which reaches to a number of regions and provinces. What had been a top-down administration is now an inclusive, multi-stakeholder participatory structure.

---

[99] See *ByWard Market Future Search - A Case Study: The Results; Outcomes of the Conference Ten Years Later*, December 2008, and *Future Search Canada Market*, National Education Association, Washington D. C.

The Safety and Security Committee has achieved improved lighting to extend the hours of operation of the market and render it safer. OC Transpo has agreed to offer a late-night bus service. Parking garages have been made safer and cleaner.

The Market Advertising and Promotion Committee regularly offers special events and activities, such as ByTown Days, the Stew Cook-off, Market Mardi-Gras, and Tastes of ByWard. Most of all, people who work for the market have now learned that the only solutions that will last are those that work for all.

What has been said about four processes here can be extended much further to all participatory, emergent processes. What Theory U offers is an understanding of an organic process that underlies many well-devised and tested methodologies of change that unite the apparent contradictions of greater participation, efficiency, and consensus.

Multi-stakeholder Logic: Summing Up

It is time to review what we have seen so far. Consensus Decision Making, World Café, and Future Search are but a few examples of a very large field of social interventions that we have called "social technology." Elsewhere I have looked at the modalities of focused conversation (from Technology of Participation) or Citizen Deliberative Councils.[100] Citizen Deliberative Councils are a good example of the farthest reach of stakeholder practices. They expand the interventions of dialogue and deliberation to the whole political field, to the crafting of legislation, indicating clearly that these tools can help us replace traditional partisan politics.

It is good to remind ourselves that we have explored but the tip of the iceberg. A look at the index of *The Change Handbook: Group Methods for Shaping the Future* shows us what large topics we have had to leave out, including Appreciative Inquiry, Open Space Technology, Collaborative Loops, Integrated Clarity, Whole-Scale Change, Ancient Wisdom Council, Conference Model, Conversation Café, Dynamic Facilitation, Genuine

---

[100] Luigi Morelli, *Visions for a Compassionate America*: Chapter 3: The Evolving Horizon of Equality (Bloomington, IN: iUniverse, 2015). See also https://luigimorelli.wordpress.com/2013/10/27/citizen-deliberative-councils-revolution-for-a-new-democracy-2/.

Contact Program, Leadership Dojo, Real-Time Strategic Change, Study Circles, and Scenario Thinking.

In this paradigm too, as in the multi-sector we have previously seen, change happens at two levels. We can apply social technology simply as a methodology. If we are at the recipient end, it may just be a pleasant experience. If we are among those who invite groups in these spaces of encounter, we cannot help but being touched and changed. Step by step we will walk into and become more proficient in the new paradigm.

Social Processes and Social Forms

Social processes, the main object of this chapter, and social structures, the object of the next, continuously interphase. In her very perceptive and insightful book *Engaging Emergence: Cultivating Leadership for Complex Times*, Peggy Holman explores how to host high-level conversations and cultivate the culture that facilitates emergence. From her extensive experience she reaches to the question of new social forms that encourage emergence. She concludes: "Hierarchies are giving way to networks. Single points of control for story ideas, follow-up information, accuracy, and other aspects yield to networks better able to handle complexity that is impossible to address any other way."[101] These kinds of networks will be explored in the next chapter.

Coming from the opposite end, Brian Robertson, who has devised the whole new social structures of Holacracy, recounts that in the elaboration of this revolutionary new form of governance, clarity had to be reached in social processes. He writes: "After a couple years of predominantly cultural experimentation, it became clear that we needed to focus at a process level as well—we were growing pretty quickly, and the lack of clarity in structure, process, and decision-making was becoming painful."[102]

We will look at Holacracy in the next chapter. Here we will take some time on one of its predecessors, Sociocracy, also known as Dynamic Governance. In the next pages, through Sociocracy we will start to address

---

[101] Peggy Holman, *Engaging Emergence: Cultivating Leadership for Complex Times*, Chapter 15, "How Do We Renew Coherence Wisely?" (San Francisco: Berrett-Koehler, 2010).

[102] https://blog.holacracy.org/history-of-holacracy-c7a8489f8eca.

the question that this chapter implicitly explores but leaves unanswered: What of top down and/or bottom up? Does participatory facilitation inherently predicate bottom up? We will also build the link between social processes and social forms.

When we think of full participation, transparency, and inclusion, we tend to imagine more equalitarian organizations than is the norm in society at large. And the question of top down and bottom up naturally comes to the surface. It is not the task of multi-stakeholder processes, however, to pronounce themselves on matters of social structures.

This contrast has also come up indirectly during the chapter in relation to the idea and practice of consensus decision-making, which is generally associated with equalitarian organizations. And in the short exploration above, we mentioned briefly the difference between consensus and consent. Here we return to it.

Sociocracy achieves a synthesis of top down and bottom up, which is more than either term. Holacracy operates wholly from beyond this frame of reference. It bypasses it and ignores it. Looking at Sociocracy will link this chapter to the next one, and it will announce the theme of emergence. We will return to Holacracy in the next chapter.

At the Intersection of Social Processes and Social Forms: Sociocracy

I have first worked with Sociocracy in a cohousing situation at Ecovillage Ithaca, which went from pure consensus to the Sociocratic model. Since I love facilitating, I jumped into the experience of consensus decision-making with enthusiasm. In a short time I realized what obstacles lie in the capacity of everyone being able to block decisions, no matter how refined the blocking criteria. A committee may have spent hours and hours crafting a proposal, yet when it is presented to the whole group, it is blocked. When this happens over and over again, the system has a dampening effect on initiative-taking. Why risk so much effort and trouble only to risk throwing it all away at the roll of a dice?

When Sociocracy was accepted, we experienced a sort of rebirth. We did not need to always be present for all decisions. Committees, renamed circles, had autonomy, and their work could be effective and appreciated.

They would ask for input from those interested and let us know a decision was due. But most of the time I would trust them and let them do their work. And decisions could be held lightly, with the proviso that they did not need to be perfect since we would revisit them and adapt them to our needs. A lot of energy was freed to tackle questions that had been left aside for a time.

Finally, Sociocracy has proved to be a very adaptable tool. Ecovillage Ithaca is now one of many cohousing communities in the United States that have adopted the Sociocratic model in a situation in which people are all volunteers, and the organization is very flat, contrary to the business model from which Sociocracy originated.

Gerard Endenburg was an inventor, engineer, and entrepreneur before turning his attention to organizational management. He was educated in physical sciences and was the son of Anna and Gerardus Endenburg, very keen political activists. Thus the thinking around Sociocracy evolved from Gerard together with his family. From their activism the Endenburgs had reached the conclusion that neither capitalistic models nor socialistic ones would move the Netherlands forward in the aftermath of World War II. Both paradigms were caught in the either/or mindset of the past, and they wanted to move on to a both/and synthesis that would not pit management against labor in new organizational forms.

Endenburg was at the forefront of the cultural intellectual ferment of his time. He had studied open systems and chaos theory, and the systems thinking that emerged from the work of Kenneth Boulding, Ilya Prigogine, and John Forbes Nash. From the work of Norbert Weiner he was also familiar with cybernetics, which concerned itself with communication and control in electronic systems, and the corollary of positive and negative feedback loops.

Endenburg's exposure to Quaker decision-making had been very important in his formative years. He had been a pupil in the school that Kees Boeke had started and which was modeled along Quaker self-governance models. Boeke's school took decisions through a self-governing body of almost 400 students and teachers. These principles predicated that it was important to incorporate everybody's input, reach solutions that had everybody's buy-in, and make sure everybody followed up on these.

Gerard had long thought about how to reorganize his enterprise, and for that purpose he gave himself a week-long retreat to let something emerge that would be genuinely new and different. When it looked like his retreat was not yielding the fruits he was hoping for, he decided to pack and return home. It was at this moment that all insights started trickling down and that Endenburg developed the key elements for the scaffolding of his new governance model. Much else obviously flowed from experience.

The Endenburg enterprises, which went from producing lamps and electrical parts to electrical installations on oil rigs, ships, nuclear reactors, and large buildings, has been in operation for over 50 years. Since then Sociocracy has been successfully adopted in over a hundred organizations in the Netherlands, such as a municipal police department, a Buddhist monastery, a nursing home, various schools and a chain of hairdressing shops. In all three sectors, it is an eminently adaptable and agile approach to system change. Case studies have shown that it leads to high levels of job satisfaction, lower levels of sick leave, higher employee commitment, increased productivity and innovation, and organizational efficiency as shown by a reduction in meetings frequency.[103]

Decision-Making Processes

Sociocracy ensures through its processes the build-up toward explicit leaderfulness. It does so in rendering communication and transmission flowing upward in the organizational layers as important as the one moving downward. And it adds an explicit element of empowerment in its processes, such as the one of election/selection that we will see below, or in its governance through "double-linking," among others.

The organizational model of Sociocracy still resembles an evergreen tree, tapered at the top, widening at the bottom. The differences lie in how communication travels both up and down that tree and in the autonomy granted at each operational unit, called a "circle." The circles are integrated within the whole through double-linking.

Sociocracy emphasizes three core values, beyond those that each organization can add for itself. The most easily understandable is

---

[103] See https://home.kpmg/xx/en/home/insights/2014/12/engaged-people-deliver-value.html

transparency. The second one is *equivalency* (or full participation of all), which is conjugated with *efficiency*. It is precisely in conjugating full participation with efficiency that Sociocracy reconciles the tension between the concerns of management and those of labor. At the level of a new synthesis, apparent opposites can fully be reconciled. We will look first at the function of the circles, then at the processes that encourage participation and transparency as well as leaderfulness, and finally at the specific governance structure.

Circles

Endenburg's unique thinking allowed the decision-making power that is present at the top or in the board of directors to trickle down to the basic operational unit of the circle, equal to a department or a committee. It is in these circles that the elected roles and the workers make decisions affecting policy, which modify the organization's constitution by consent. John Buck, who has helped introduce Sociocracy from the Netherlands to the United States, specifies that in Endenburg's choice of words from the Dutch, "circle" stands for more than it does in English: "The Dutch *kring* indicates circle but also 'arena.' It is more encompassing than just circle and it also means 'roundtable' or place for discussion between peers."[104] The sovereignty of the circle is enshrined in its ability to spell out its vision, mission, and aims (VMA).

- *Vision*
  Through vision the circle relates to the organization and the world. It defines how the circle wishes to affect the world beyond the organization; how the world can be changed in the best possible scenario through the work of the circle.
- *Mission*
  With mission the focus shifts inwardly. It looks at what the circle needs to achieve in relation to the vision. This vision is completed in the spelling out of the aims.
- *Aims*
  Whereas vision and mission predicate an ideal, aims look at the deliverables, whether products or services. This is best done by

[104] John Buck and Sharon Villines, *We the People: Consenting to a Deeper Democracy* (Washington, DC: Sociocracy Info, 2007), 44.

taking the perspective of the recipients; it can best be established by receiving input from the clients, both actual and potential. Aims are also yardsticks through which the circle can measure success and gage how policy decisions satisfy and reinforce the circle's vision and mission.

Vision, mission, and aims become operational tools, especially the articulation of aims. They are very important because the circles are responsible for their learning, training, and research, and they plan an additional role, as we will see, in relation to reaching consent.

Central to the working of the circles is what Endenburg adopted from cybernetics: the understanding of positive and negative feedback loops. He designed a process of learning and evaluation that he called the "circular process" of Leading (preview) – Doing (action) – Measuring (review), which is key to improving services and/or products.

Some Processes

Sociocracy uses consent not for operational decisions but for anything that impacts policy. Table 25 shows the process in its details. It basically follows the pattern we saw on figure 21, referring to what we know as rounds of concerns and objections.

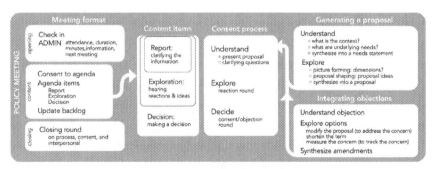

Table 25: Sociocratic Consent Decision Process
(Jerry Koch Gonzalez, Ted Rau, Sociocracy for All)

Consent moves from what we have described as pure consensus under consensus decision-making to consent through the inclusion of the following criteria:

- "Paramount and argued objections" in relation to the group's VMAs
- Inclusion of terms and criteria of review

Paramount and argued concerns spring from the perception that a proposal, if enacted, would negatively affect the needs or concerns of the circle, as they are expressed in the VMA, or have negative consequences outside of the circle. Consent manifestly removes from the consensus process the power to block a proposal. "The principle about consent is not about the power to veto, but the power to argue."[105]

The above picture is completed with the second set of criteria. If a decision has been relatively easy to make and if the dissonances have been resolved, the proposal will become policy. If full agreement has not been as easy to reach, the proposed policy once adopted can be reviewed at a later time according to the criteria that raise the most concern. The greater and deeper the concerns, the shorter will be the review period. In the meantime the proposed change is considered "good enough for now, safe enough to try." The above is an important change from pure consensus and the power to block. It removes the obstacles of too much focus on the bottom up.

To give a further idea of how Sociocracy encourages leaderfulness, we will describe below the role of selection process. It is customary in many traditional settings to encourage those who want to be leaders to step forward, or let higher-ups determine who has developed skills in that direction; in bureaucratic settings it may just be a matter of seniority. The Sociocratic process bans the idea of volunteering for a job because it wants the selection process to be one of discovery, learning, and mutual appreciation.

As it can be seen from Table 26, the selection process is made in three rounds for a couple of reasons. It is important to hear about people's choices *as well as* hearing what reasons people bring up for the choice. Based on these reasons, people are invited to change their minds. I may have chosen one person, but based on the reasons I have heard from the whole circle, I may switch to another choice, realizing I did not have a complete picture during the second and third rounds (Submit Ballots and Share Reasons Round).

---

[105] John Buck and Sharon Villines, *We the People: Consenting to a Deeper Democracy*, 70.

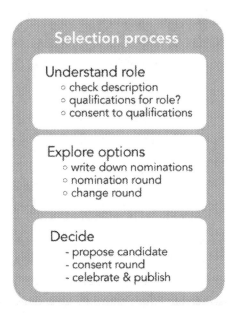

Table 26: sociocratic role selection process
(Jerry Koch Gonzalez, Ted Rau, Sociocracy for All)

The important criterion for choice is not the number of votes but the amount of skills and attitudes that the candidate brings to the role. This is what the participants are invited to articulate in the process. Every person in the circle discovers what others see in him/her. A natural-born leader may hear what she is already accustomed to hearing, or come out sobered. A shy, unassuming person, on the contrary, can suddenly discover his latent leadership skills and accept the group's invitation to step forward.

Double Linking and Governance

We are coming here to the key process that makes Sociocracy an effective combination of hierarchy and "bottomocracy," the "double linking."

In the Sociocratic model the connection between two circles at two contiguous levels is assured through two representatives whose function is complementary: the operational leader and the representative. The higher circle selects the operational leader of the circle immediately below it. The circle itself selects the representative based on its ability to encompass the logic of the circle and of carrying its concerns. The operational leader conveys the needs and concerns that come from above; the representative what emerges from below, so to speak. And this is repeated at the juncture of all hierarchical levels. Additionally, for this to work, the two roles are present in both circles. The representative, chosen by the circle, is present in the higher circle when the selection of the operational leader takes place, and he has to consent to the choice. Having this double-linking mechanism ensures that feedback has to be taken into account not only within circles but also between circles of different levels. Hierarchy is present but balanced by "bottomocracy."

Another important innovation occurs at the top circle, a modified board of directors. The top circle includes members not only of the profession and industry but also of those stakeholder groups that are closest to the organization's spheres of interest, so that the enterprise remains an open system. The CEO works with both elected representatives and external experts as partners. The whole gives the enterprise the multi-stakeholder dimension that we have seen to be so essential in encompassing all aspects of complex, open systems.

Through double-linking and through a fully integrated open system, top circle Sociocracy assures that energy in the system travels both up and down and leadership emerges at all levels. Solutions can emerge at any point in the system, not just at the top. Two examples from Endenburg's enterprises will illustrate this reality.

In 1976 Endenburg Electrotechniek went through a crisis. The firm depended on the orders for heavy wiring for the ships in the Dutch shipyards, when there was a downturn due to Japanese competition. Since half of their employees worked in the shipyards, the firm was faced with the prospect of having to fire much of its workforce. The top circle was called to figure out alternatives and solutions. One of the members of the Fabrication Circle, not affected by the layoffs, came up with the solution: retrain the workforce, mostly for purposes of marketing. The person who came with the idea was selected as special representative to the top circle. Overcoming the skepticism of some managers, the machinist's ideas were put to the test and resulted in success.[106]

---

[106] John Buck and Sharon Villines, *We the People: Consenting to a Deeper Democracy*, 45-46.

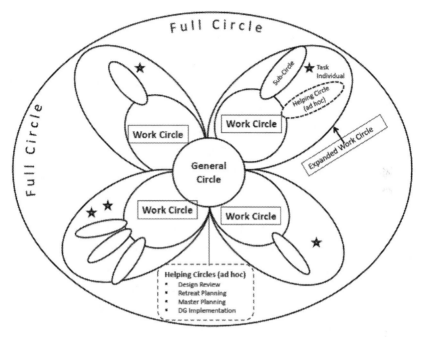

Figure 27: sociocratic organizational structure
(Jerry Koch-Gonzalez, Ted Rau)

The above is a first indication of different relationships between labor and management. The second one came from the Dutch government, in a country that gave a lot of importance to workers' ability to form trade unions. Provisions for trade unions have been lifted from Sociocratic organizations, recognizing that the workers are actually better protected in those firms.[107]

Finally, Sociocratic firms have the means to address the thorny problem of the market and hostile takeovers. The goal and ideal of a Sociocratic organization is to become independent from the stranglehold of the stockholders' power. This is what Endenburg Electrotechniek first successfully achieved by determining that the company could not be bought or sold other than with the consent of all its employees. The configuration of the top circle is already a great tool for preserving the integrity of the organization.

---

[107] John Buck and Sharon Villines, *We the People: Consenting to a Deeper Democracy*, 47.

Success Stories

Rainbow Community School Asheville North Carolina[108]

Rainbow Community School is a kindergarten through 8th grade private alternative school in Asheville, North Carolina. At the point in which it was studied, the school that prided itself in offering holistic education for thirty-five years was going through very difficult times. Among the difficulties stood out a lack of clarity in the functions of the board and in the qualifications of its executive director. Accompanying these were diffuse, dysfunctional behaviors. In 2007 the school called on John Buck, consultant and CEO of the sociocracy consulting group, to offer an introduction to Sociocracy to some of the school's management. It was decided to pilot the governance change together with the faculty. Renee Owen, the executive director, was surprised at how quickly change was generated, even in such difficult endeavors as rebranding and renaming the school. She observed that the new system allowed quick generation of ideas and ease in testing them out. She appreciated how the efficiency of hierarchy at the operational level could be balanced out with full input on policy changes that affect everybody. "Hierarchies are very efficient," explains Owen. "If there is an emergency, the person on top issues orders. Dynamic governance doesn't throw out the baby with the bath water. When you need hierarchy, it's still there."

The CEO role itself changed in the process. Renee noticed that when she assumed the job, she tended to overextend herself with the time spent in meetings or attending to small but urgent matters in person. When these concerns were shared with her staff, through consent various individuals stepped forward to relieve her of the excessive load. She could devote more time to focus on longer term issues, delegate to others, and make her experience overall much more pleasant. Four years in the experiment, the school has doubled the size of its campus and is thriving financially, with full enrollment and full waiting lists.

---

[108] Sarah Lozanova, "What Can a School Teach Us about Organizational Agility?" https://www.triplepundit.com/story/2014/what-can-school-teach-us-about-organizational-agility/41261.

Sociocracy in Eldercare[109]

Dee De Luca came from the world of business into eldercare twenty years ago. She invested her energy in two senior care facilities at the same time that she decided to look into Sociocracy and its practical uses. The two facilities are Living Well Care Home in Bristol (http://livingwellresidence.org/) and the Ethan Allen Residence in Burlington (http://ethanallenresidence.org/).

As can be expected, Sociocracy has led to a greater employee involvement in a sector in which quick turnover is the norm. What keeps both employees and residents more fully involved is their participation in long-term planning as well as daily operations. Employees are more proactive in bringing up concerns and have more buy-in in the solutions they are part in shaping.

And transformation touches everyone at all levels. De Luca herself finds her job more manageable and rewarding: "I spent several decades of my adult life owning, creating, buying and selling small businesses.... I was tired of having it all sit on my shoulders. I did it alone and I was done being a worker bee.... [With dynamic governance,] my job is to steer the creativity, which is exhilarating, instead of being a policewoman and disciplinarian most of the time."

Where the change tells most is on the recipients' end. An elder council addresses the residents' input once a month. Much has come through it and through a holistic approach to health. The elderly are offered meals from local farms during the growing season; some food is preserved for the cooler part of the year. And this higher-quality nutrition is achieved in comparable financial terms to what semi-industrial catering can offer. Adding to this that the elderly receive naturopathic care and have access to yoga and Tai Chi classes, it may not be so surprising that these senior care facilities have lower medication expenses than similar ones.

From Social Processes to Social Forms

We have addressed two layers of paradigm change so far. The first one was the matter of sectors. If we realize that society is more than the interplay of political and economic forces, our polarized world emerges from an impasse.

---

[109] Sarah Lozanova, "How This Residential Care Home Bumped Employee Engagement Into Overdrive," http://www.triplepundit.com/story/2014/how-residential-care-home-bumped-employee-engagement-overdrive/42566.

With the recognition of the role of Civil Society as a shaper of the cultural arena, we can start thinking beyond the either/or of the past and its recurring variations of capitalism against socialism, and move into the recognition of three equally important poles of society. When this is done, we move from two to three and from dualistic thinking into new insights into what change is possible. We realize more and more the need for the three sectors to sit at the table and constructively dialogue and work as equals. When we start recognizing the specific powers and competencies of the three sectors, new solutions emerge that have rarely been tried previously.

The second large paradigm addresses the variety of stakeholders involved in any given issue. Here it is a matter of relating and collaborating. We are following here the proposition best exemplified by the organic and holistic processes of the U. When human beings meet in mind, heart, and will, new perspectives emerge, allowing new synergies and the wisdom of something that is more than the sum of the parts. Those who have traditionally stood as rivals can start to see that all needs can effectively be met when everybody is heard. New evolutionary possibilities emerge when consent appears through the experience of presencing.

In this chapter we have explored the reality of presencing—what occurs when a group can start to operate at a higher level than it has been used to, when it has fully differentiated and integrated. We have heard new expressions in relation to Sociocracy, such as overcoming top down and bottom up, and promoting leaderfulness. We will now look at what happens when familiar systems of our present reality dissolve and either of two phenomena take place. The first is a pure dissolution leading to chaos; the second is the rise of a new, stable system operating at a higher level of complexity, which cannot be predicted from what we know from the past. This phenomenon has been known as *emergence*. We will explore what it takes to foster it.

Resources

This is far from exhausting resource guide, but it could get you going for a long while.

Some Foundational Books

- Margaret J. Wheatley, *Leadership and the New Science: Discovering Order in a Chaotic World* (San Francisco: Berrett-Koehler, 1999).
- Joseph Jaworski, Betty Sue Flowers, editor, *Synchronicity, the Inner Path of Leadership* (San Francisco: Berrett-Koehler, 1996).
- Peggy Holman, *Engaging Emergence: Turning Upheaval into Opportunity* (San Francisco: Berrett-Koehler, 2010).
- Theory U
  - Otto Scharmer, *Theory U: Leading from the Emerging Future; The Social Technology of Presencing* (Cambridge, MA: Society for Organizational Learning, 2007).
  - Executive summaries: https://www.ottoscharmer.com/publications/executive-summaries.
- Tom Atlee, Empowering Public Wisdom: A Practical Vision of Citizen-Led Politics (Berkeley, CA: Evolver Editions, 2012).

General Resources in the Field

Communication and facilitation skills
- Peggy Holman, Tom Devane, and Steven Cady, *The Change Handbook: The Definitive Resource on Today's Best Methods for Enlarging Whole Systems* (San Francisco: Berrett-Koehler, 2007), for an overview of many approaches to social technology.
- The National Coalition for Dialogue & Deliberation, a network of innovators who bring people together across divides to tackle today's toughest challenges. NCDD serves as a gathering place, a resource clearinghouse, a news source, and a facilitative leader for this extraordinary community: http://ncdd.org/.
- Revolution of Hope blog: https://luigimorelli.wordpress.com/.

Among the most well-known facilitation approaches

- Larry Dressler, *Consensus Through Conversation: How to Achieve High-Commitment Decisions* (San Francisco: Berrett-Koehlers, 2006).
- World Café Book and link

- Marvin Weisbord and Sandra Janoff, *Future Search: An Action Guide to Finding Common Ground in Organizations and Communities* (San Francisco: Berrett-Koehlers, 2010).
- Harrison Owen, *Open Space Technology: A User's Guide* (San Francisco: Berrett-Koehlers, 2008).
- David L. Cooperrider, *The Appreciative Inquiry Handbook: For Leaders of Change* (San Francisco: Berrett-Koehlers, 2008).
- Dynamic Facilitation and Wisdom Circles (and blog link)
- Art of Hosting and Harvesting Conversations that Matter: http://www.artofhosting.org/.
- Programs relating to Theory U: www.presencing.org.

Formats you can try right away

- Conversation Café: http://www.conversationcafe.org/.
- Focused Conversation: Brian Stanfield, *The Art of Focused Conversation: 100 Ways to Access Group Wisdom in the Workplace* (Gabriola, BC: New Society, 2000).
- Trainings through Institute of Cultural Affairs (ICA): https://www.ica-usa.org/top-training.html.
- For other simple formats see also information in *The Change Handbook* listed above.

Foundational training

Nonviolent Communication is one of most effective resources for thinking in terms of needs rather than strategies, developing self-connection, authentic expression of needs and empathy.

- Marshall B. Rosenberg, *Nonviolent Communication: A Language of Compassion* (Encinitas, CA: Puddle Dancer, 1999).
- The Center for Nonviolent Communication, https://www.cnvc.org/.

Civic Engagement

- Tom Atlee, *Empowering Public Wisdom: A Practical Vision of Citizen-Led Politics* (Berkeley, CA: Evolver Editions, 2012).

- Wisdom Councils: https://www.wisedemocracy.org/3-wisdom-council-process.html.
- Citizen Deliberative Councils: https://www.co-intelligence.org/P-CDCs.html.

A step further towards social forms: Dynamic Governance (aka Sociocracy)

- Sociocracy for All (SoFA): https://www.sociocracyforall.org/.
- The Sociocracy Consulting Group: http://sociocracyconsulting.com/co-ops/.
- Ted J. Rau and Jerry Koch-Gonzalez, *Many Voices One Song: Shared Power with Sociocracy* (Amherst, MA: Sociocracy for All, 2018).
- John Buck and Sharon Villines, *We the People: Consenting to a Deeper Democracy* (Washington, DC: Sociocracy Info, 2007).

**ORIGINAL
ORDER**

DISRUPTION

DIFFERENTIATION

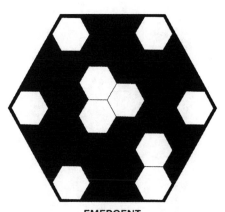

**EMERGENT
ORDER**

Chapter 4
Multiscale Logic: Emergence and Self-Organizing

Traveler, your footprints
are the only road, nothing else.
Traveler, there is no road;
you make your own path as you walk.
As you walk, you make your own road,
and when you look back
you see the path
you will never travel again.

—*Antonio Machado*

I think that those of us who wish to see a truly, radically different world must demand of ourselves the possibility that we are called to lead not from right to left, or from minority to majority, but from spirit towards liberation.

—*Adrienne Maree Brown*

IN THIS CHAPTER:

EMERGENCE AND COMPLEXITY
- Transformation and Emergence
- What fosters emergence?
- Self-organizing: inclusiveness and entrepreneurial spirit

SPONTANEOUS EMERGENCE
- Keep it simple
- Large scale emergence; from chaos to opportunity
- Limits to spontaneous emergence

FOSTERING EMERGENCE
- Beyond top down and bottom up
- Roles not individuals
- Acting simultaneously at a multitude of scales
- Mastering paradoxes and seeming opposites
- Leaderfulness and stewardship
- Socially generative networks

IN THIS CHAPTER WE WILL look at new social forms/structures that accompany the phenomenon of emergence. In the introduction we discussed complex systems in contrast to complicated and simple ones. We showed that simple and complicated systems can be approached within the boundaries of an either/or approach. In fact the analogy for a complicated system is that of a machine that can be taken apart and reassembled according to a user's manual, a typical deterministic approach in which the whole corresponds to the sum of the parts. The parts allow us to understand the whole without the need for anything else. Incremental change and reform can effectively address these levels of complexity.

The above approaches are of limited impact, however, because most social systems and most situations faced at present are complex and require a holistic approach that acknowledges that the whole is more than the sum of the parts, and that most isolated interventions in the system will cause nonlinear and therefore unpredictable reactions. And when we come to higher complexity we have shown how, not reform, but transformation is the response needed.

We did not look more closely yet at what this complexity is, what we will call "emergence." In a nutshell, emergence indicates the dissolution of old orders of reality and the birth of new ones that cannot be predicated from the old, even though they keep elements of it in metamorphosed fashion.

Emergence and Complexity

In the previous chapter we have determined the central phenomenon of presencing. Restated here, we could describe it as the ability to accompany people through a process in which they will experience change together in such a way as to generate insights and a movement forward that is more than the sum of the wisdom of each individual. In presencing, various individuals and stakeholders feel aligned with the group, without sacrificing their individuality and independence. We can think of emergence as something of equivalent nature but affecting higher orders of reality—no longer just the people convened for a decision-making process, but a whole social system. Presencing is the phenomenon of a group of people passing through an experience that leads to a wholly new stage of collective cohesion; emergence is a new state of cohesion for a whole system.

The concept of emergence was first expressed in biology as the capacity of natural systems to go through a state of dissolution, as can happen in the wake of a disruption, to then reappear (emerge) at a new evolutionary stage of higher complexity. The term has been gradually extended from natural to social systems. In simplest possible terms, emergence is new order arising out of chaos.

Every system, whether natural or manmade, contains polar forces that hold each other in balance. One we could call a drive for order and coherence that preserves what exists: cells held together in an organ, people held together by institutions and associations. On the other hand stands a drive for differentiation, for separating and forming something new: a species differentiating under some unique ecological conditions, a group of pioneers starting a social experiment. All of this can happen under natural conditions but can be highly amplified under exceptional ones. Disruptions can occur of varying nature and intensity, from a yearly drought to a prolonged one, from a 1-year budget deficit to a 10-year-long one. And occasionally the disturbances can take the form of immediate disasters: an earthquake, a tsunami, or a popular rebellion. The above forces are in a continuous interplay with each other. Coming back to emergence, we can detect the following sequence:

- *A prevailing state of order that has been in place for a length of time*
- *Disturbances accelerating and disrupting the status quo*
- *Differentiation and innovation arising among the parts of the system*
- *Formation of a new system emerging at a higher level of complexity than the original one (see figure at head of chapter)*

We have said that emergence is a new order arising out of chaos. More precisely we could borrow Peggy Holman's definition of a "higher-order complexity arising out of chaos in which novel, coherent structures coalesce through interactions among the diverse entities of a system."[110] In emergence the system incorporates greater diversity, larger webs of relationships, and greater interdependence.

When social systems are disrupted under great pressures, the system becomes chaotic. When traditional hierarchies can no longer address the constraints, something new can appear that is another key element of emergence: the system's capacity to *self-organize* and create higher states of equilibrium. The other possibility is a spiraling down into social chaos.

Just as producing moments of presencing in social processes cannot be predicted but can be fostered, likewise emergence cannot be predicted; yet it can be invited through new and unusual responses.

Whereas disruption usually stimulates knee-jerk reactions of isolating ourselves, looking at differences with suspicion, and inciting violence, we can decide to work with it, to take a reverse stance. In fact until we decide to engage with emergence, we may be facing more and more violent and chaotic upheavals. If we decide to work with it, we can decide to welcome differences by creating safe spaces of dialogue, see challenges as evolutionary opportunities to birth the new, listen to what the future wants of us, and set clear intentions for change; in effect, much of what we have heard in the previous chapter. In this chapter we will look not at what fosters this change but what specific forms can arise spontaneously through the processes of

---

[110] Peggy Holman, *Engaging Emergence: Turning Upheaval into Opportunity* (San Francisco: Berrett-Koehler, 2010), 18.

emergence, and how we can stimulate this self-organizing response toward higher degrees of complexity.

The two examples we will explore next correspond to change that has happened spontaneously, or with relative ease—Buurtzorg in Dutch health care, and Argentina's Horizontalism. In both instances it was deep crisis that encouraged innovation. After these we will look at how this change can be sustained intentionally within an organization—through Holacracy—or for higher levels of collaboration, such as the coordination of a great number of individuals/organizations in the example of "socially generative networks."

Spontaneous Emergence: Buurtzorg; Keep It Simple

The Dutch health care system may not sound all too different from what we know in other countries. The nurses work under cumbersome levels of regulations and complex management structures, which impact their freedom, judgment, and the attention they can offer to their patients. In practice this means regimented interventions prescribing how much time they can spend with a patient, according to the problem or illness they are approaching. Accompanied with layers of paperwork, this implied losing perspective of the whole patient in the context of his or her physical and social environment and world of meaning.

In the early days that led to the forming of Buurtzorg—which simply means "neighborhood care"—two people met: a young pioneer nurse, Jos de Blok, and Ard Leferink, who had long worked within the system at improving all levels of management according to the dominant view, which is basically the model of health as a business.[111] Leferink had come to realize how little he had managed to improve the system after years of trying management ideas, and how unsatisfied were its ultimate recipients. Then came his meeting with Jos, who showed him that he was going into a dead-end and who came up with a very strong alternative. He basically envisioned to simplify to the extreme in order to innovate. He was going to intentionally disrupt the system.

The two were driven by new ideas, chiefly the desire to create small-scale initiative, getting rid of management and attracting dedicated nurses.

---

[111] https://wiki.businessagility.institute/w/CaseStudies:The_Buurtzorg_Story

They were inspired by a Dutch author who preached the idea of keeping companies at a small size and splitting them up when they reached a certain scale. Another resource was *The Starfish and the Spider: The Unstoppable Power of Leaderless Organizations*, by Ori Brafman and Rod Beckstrom.

De Blok got the idea off the ground in 2006, together with three other nurses, emphasizing the approach of taking care of people in their homes. The same idea of empowerment of the team beyond levels of management and red tape was offered to the clients by strengthening their independence through their natural networks of support—family, friends, even neighbors are enrolled in the task.

Nurse-Led and Client-Centered

"I believe in client-centered care, with nursing that is independent and collaborative," says de Blok.[112] Putting the client at the center goes hand in hand with trusting most of all the perspective of the community nurses and their understanding of how best to support their charges.

The nurse-led and client-centered model of holistic care rests on some basic principles:

- Individuals want control over their own lives for as long as possible.
- They strive to maintain or improve their own quality of life.
- They seek social interaction.
- They seek "warm" relationships with others.[113]

Empowering the clients means reducing the nurses' intervention time, a net benefit for all in the health system. This is measured by the fact that Buurtzorg has managed to halve the time the patients stay in care and to avoid a third of emergency hospital admissions.[114]

The growth of the seemingly simple idea has been nothing short of astounding. In 2016 Buurtzorg generated €330 million from its natural growth (no mergers or buyouts), employed 12,000 employees, and served

---

[112] https://www.buurtzorg.com

[113] https://www.buurtzorg.com

[114] Frederic Laloux, *Reinventing Organizations* (Brussels: Nelson Parker, 2016), 66.

80,000 clients 10 years after its founding.[115] The organizational structure, pretty flat, includes no departments of any kind and little policy beyond the stated mission; nor does it need strategic meetings. In fact the nurses are supported by an administrative body of just 50 and an additional 22 coaches. This leads to a very simple organizational structure (Figure 28). The 6 percent support personnel compares to 25 percent in the rest of the Dutch system.

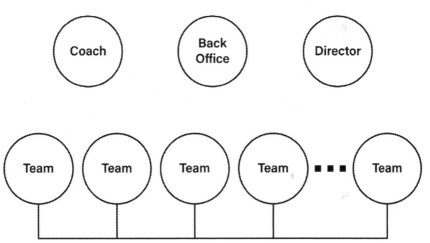

Figure 28: Buurtzorg organizational structure
(Source: Strategic Health Network, https://www.strategichealthnetwork.
com/2016/05/change-from-bottom-community-nursing-in.html)

At the center of Buurtzorg vision lies a circle unit of care of ten to twelve nurses. They tackle all aspects of care, internal management, administration, contacts with professionals, finances, and so on. Together they serve about some fifty clients within a small area, and nurses tend to see the same clients in order to better know them. All roles otherwise normally performed by a leader—planning, finances, administration, relationships with other organizations—are distributed among the members of the circle. The model encourages entrepreneurial spirit and leaderfulness (see section Leadership/Stewardship below, for a definition of this term), and in turn innovations coming from anyone within the circle.

---

[115] The Buurtzorg Story video by Ard Leferink at https://wiki.businessagility. institute/w/CaseStudies:The_Buurtzorg_Story (April 2018)

The coaches are called upon to assist the teams on demand to brainstorm and support, not to direct or prescribe. Most of them are older, experienced nurses with great listening and interpersonal skills. The support offered by the head office to the whole lies in taking care of payroll and invoicing, following up on new regulations, trying to learn from discussions and trends, and stimulating collective learning.

Support Tools

Most importantly, Buurtzorg offers the nurses a key element for self-organizing: trainings called Solution-Driven Methods of Interaction, upon which the teams can build listening, communication, facilitation, and decision-making skills. These are critical steps for the teams' success, and they can further be reinforced when a team gets stuck with recourse to a coach or to outside help. The coaches' role is to let the team strengthen their capacities through understanding the process tools they have available, build on their own strengths and resources, and figure out solutions on their own.

Another tool offered by headquarters is the Buurtzorg Web, a software platform very much enjoyed by the nurses both as a resource and a way to connect.[116] These are some of the areas addressed: performance, assessments, a comprehensive classification system, how to empower patients, and all aspects of holistic care and interventions. All is made accessible in understandable terms, built in a transparent way, and rendered accessible to all teams and coaches. Access to Buurtzorg Web has even been extended to some other thirty organizations in the Netherlands that have adopted the Buurtzorg model with similar, positive results.

The flattening of the organization is only made possible through higher efficiency of care and higher direct involvement of the nurses in quality of service. The model encourages leaderfulness within the teams. Everyone has different tasks and levels of competency, but everyone is encouraged to express entrepreneurial spirit.

The role of the CEO himself, Jos DeBlok, is greatly changed from the typical. As a visionary he is highly placed to embody the values that he has helped to shape in the organization. The ideas that he offers have value on

---

[116] https://www.buurtzorg.com/innovation/buurtzorg-web/.

the basis of the insight they reveal, not on a higher authority. The nurses may or may not applaud all proposals he offers.

The agility of the system, its leaderfulness, and its low overhead are accountable for two complementary aspects. According to the KPMG Case Study Buurtzorg allows a savings of the order of 40 percent to the Dutch health care system, achieved through empowering the patients, increasing the extent and quality of their natural supports, and reducing the hours of direct care by 50 percent.[117] Not least of all the nurses' job satisfaction, lower absenteeism, and lower turnover contributes greatly to all of the above. Buurtzorg has been named the Netherlands' best employer four times in the last five years.

Planning, Innovation, Competition

Contrary to more hierarchical organizations, since it does not count on ad hoc departments for the purpose, it is not surprising that Buurtzorg has a whole different approach to long-term planning. Add to this that being in the service industry means not having significant purchases, inventory, or investments. Thus the teams find they have no need for any elaborate budgets, other than the month-to-month cash flow. The larger Buurtzorg will determine how many new teams can start operating and where. And even here, Buurtzorg is not your typical aggressive corporation, as we will see later. No mergers are on the horizon, only the natural growth from within.

Innovation has marked the growth of Buurtzorg in many ways and in various directions. None of it was the result of careful and deliberate planning from headquarters. New ideas stand the litmus test of life: if effective, they will be replicated; if not, they will simply die out.

Buurtzorg+ was launched in a very natural fashion from a physiotherapist who joined the company after returning from the United Kingdom. The idea emerged from the already existing collaboration between nurses, physiotherapists, and occupational therapists. Her innovation came from seeking a more conscious collaboration. She elaborated the idea and

---

[117] https://home.kpmg/xx/en/home/insights/2014/12/engaged-people-deliver-value.html.

discussed it with Buurtzorg, who agreed to launch a pilot in two of its teams that sought PT and OTs to work closely within their area.

The move makes sense in rounding off holistic client care, since the most immediate goal was to address client safety at home. The collaboration of the Buurtzorg+ teams most often takes place in the client's home; at other times it takes the form of multidisciplinary meetings.

The pilot's results were encouraging, showing that the patients could increase self-management skills and achieve higher safety and independence in their homes. Once more this was a win-win for the nurses, who could reduce interventions and leave more of the care in the hands of the patients themselves, who acquired greater mobility. Since then the remaining Buurtzorg teams naturally see the advantage of becoming Buurtzorg+ teams and are in the process of becoming so, without the need of formalized planning or incentives.

Among other innovations that have been successfully replicated is Buurtzorg Jong (Young), which addresses children—newborn to 23 years old—in conjunction with families and guardians. Buurtzorg Jong took a whole-systems view of the young, addressing all matters of health in relation to awareness, educationm and social well-being, integrating variables such as unemployment, financial burdens, psychiatric and behavioral challenges, drugs and addictions, child abuse, and teenage pregnancies. In the holistic perspective Buurtzorg Jong wants families' empowerment to be the first line of defense.

The second level of systemic change sought is that concerning the health system's hurdles, such as:

- the tendency to over-diagnose, overtreat, and overmedicate
- the overspecialization of care and the maze of organizations involved
- the lack of coordination between specialists
- the weight of bureaucratic requirements and layers of management
- the lack of a point person to coordinate information and resources

By cutting through the layers of complexity, Buurtzorg Jong wants to simplify the system and provide faster and more flexible service. The first line of intervention is called "first things first." By this are meant all those changes that are easiest to implement and most effective in relieving stress, and which can give the families a taste for success, creativity, and empowerment. After these initial successes, Buurtzorg Jong will develop a plan of support with the family's input, addressing such things as how to best use the natural network of support, return to a more stable life, offer support for parenting, and organize collaboration with the professionals. The focus remains on enabling as much independence as possible on the family's end.

With things evolving this fast and covering so much territory, and an employee force continuously growing, it would not be surprising to see Buurtzorg trying to capitalize and expand. However, as we have seen from Buurtzorg Web, the company does not have a proprietary behavior. On the contrary: Jos de Blok spends much time giving advice for free to others who want to replicate the model; he acts like a coach to the "competition." And further, the model is being exported abroad through Buurtzorg International. As of the last estimates, 24 countries including Sweden, Japan, the United States, China, Japan, and Taiwan are joining and experimenting.[118] These will be independent initiatives that receive Buurtzorg's free advice and expertise, not subsidiaries or franchises. The real competition remains the old, corporatized model of health care.

The Buurtzorg Model and Self-Organizing

In reviewing what has come up so far, we can discern a trend that continues our preliminary exploration of sociocracy. Buurtzorg is all about promoting holistic view of care, of professional and organizational development. Both sociocracy and Buurtzorg diminish or eliminate the distances between management, direct line workers, and patients; Buurtzorg blurs the very notions of it. They encourage leaderfulness and innovation from across the system, especially the margins. In fact it's hard to find anything else than the margin in the spaces created by Buurtzorg. It would be inconceivable to direct innovation from headquarters.

Buurtzorg, through its founder Jos De Blok, is interested in diffusing and exporting the idea, not the brand. It is working at supporting similar initiatives in the Netherlands and exporting the model abroad, creating avenues and minimal forms of support for others to replicate the system.

---

[118] "Find Buurtzorg near you," https://www.buurtzorg.com.

By making their model so easily available, de Blok and Buurtzorg can hope to accelerate the obsolescence of the health care corporate model that has lost touch with reality and can no longer satisfy immediate needs in any significant way.

Finally, if the model looks deceptively simple, it's because it is so. Ard Leferink sees that others who want to adapt Buurtzorg's innovation may be tempted to merge them with elements of the prevailing paradigm, or attempt gradual transitions. To this, his answer is to keep it simple. This is what makes it work.

To temper the above views, we should just remind the reader that, yes, the model is "simple," but it requires a new way of operating. The training that the nurses receive in all matters of communication, facilitation, and decision making is essential in creating a new reality of collaboration among equals and an entrepreneurial spirit. The coaches add support and strengthen capacities in the teams.

Buurtzorg and the service industry may appear as an exception to the rule, special spaces in which self-management can have a latitude of freedom. That this is not so can be understood by looking at just one example, at the other end of the spectrum: FAVI in the European manufacturing business. FAVI is a brass foundry company in the north of France, employing about five hundred people in the production of parts for the auto industry, mostly gearbox forks.

FAVI is an enterprise that goes back to the 1950s, but has received a new impulse with its present self-managed model with the arrival of Jean François Zobrist at its helm in 1983. He was responsible for converting the whole business into thirteen self-managed "mini-factories," most of which serve a specific client.

Resisting the push for cheaper labor that has expanded the markets in China, FAVI has remained the only gearbox manufacturer left in Europe. Not only does FAVI compete successfully with their Asian counterparts; their lines of product cover 50 percent of the market, and they are renowned for both quality and timeliness over the last twenty-five years. And their workforce is highly rewarded for their pains. To see more about this, and about other similar examples, see Frederic Laloux's *Reinventing Organizations*.[119]

Emergence and self-organizing have occurred at higher levels of social reality. For this we will turn to just one example that has involved a nation.

Emergence at the Level of a Nation: Horizontalism

We will now turn our gaze from a particular organization to a more diffuse movement, which has occurred at the scale of a nation: Horizontalism in Argentina. Something similar has taken place in Chiapas, Mexico, through Zapatismo, where indigenous communities have been organizing autonomously from the state since 1996. The indigenous communities have organized themselves at a grassroots level in a process honoring their cultural identity, independently from the state or political platforms.

In rural Brazil the landless movement (Movimento dos Trabalhadores Rurais Sem Terra—MST) has been reclaiming the land and reconstructing their communities. Similarly, the United States experienced the phenomenon of Occupy Wall Street, which took the nation by surprise. Similar answers have emerged with the popular assemblies in Spain and Greece in response to the dictates of neoliberal policies.

Argentina's Turnaround

Marina Sitrin, who has written at length about Horizontalism, calls this a "prefigurative revolutionary movement" that announces in the present what forms will be more and more possible in the future.[120] To better understand it, we will review Argentina's history very briefly.

Argentina has been one of the most industrialized countries in South America; it is also one with the richest and most diversified agricultures, to the point of being called the "granary of the world." It has known the welfare

---

[119] Laloux, *Reinventing Organizations*, for FAVI see 65–67, 137–42. Among other organizations see: Sun Hydraulics (manufacturing), Heiligenfeld (mental health hospitals), Morning Star (tomato harvesting, transport, and processing), ESBZ (grades 7 to 13 schools in Berlin), Patagonia (outdoor apparel), AES (electrical products), BSO/Origin (IT services), and Sounds True (multimedia publishing company).

[120] Marina Sitrin, ed., *Horizontalism: Voices of Popular Power in Argentina*, 4.

state in the 1940s and 1950s before the advent of Juan Perón (1946–55), an authoritarian populist. When the system started to crack, the reaction came in the form of violent revolutionary movements: from the ERP, which received first a Trotskyist, then a Maoist inspiration; and from the Montoneros, left-wing Catholic and Peronist. The Montoneros conducted campaigns of kidnappings of political figures and business executives. The ERP was successful in occupying towns in the impoverished Tucumán province, and in robbing banks. Both movements rallied little political support. On the contrary they served as rationale and excuse for the Dirty War of 1976 to 1983, which saw the disappearance of some estimated 30,000 people, mostly from the political opposition of the Left, unionists, and students. The disappearances were accompanied with torture and murders of great cruelty.

One of the first movements of reaction originated during this dark page of Argentinian history: the Mothers of the Plaza de Mayo. Some of the mothers of the *desaparecidos* ("the disappeared") took to rallying weekly on the Plaza de Mayo in the capital, wearing white scarves as a symbol of peace and displaying pictures of their missing loved ones. The regime could not silence them, even though three of the fourteen founders of the movement disappeared. Most of the demonstrations came to an end in 2006.

In its hubris, the Argentinian military even decided to confront the English in taking control of the Falkland/Malvinas islands. In all its attempts, the army left the country saddled with debts and vulnerable to the requests of the International Monetary Fund for neoliberal and contractive fiscal policies. Chief among these, in Argentina as almost everywhere in the world, are labor deregulation and privatization of national companies (e.g., water, energy, telecommunications). In the 1980s when the government was still unable to repay the debt, inflation grew to up to 200 percent per month, peaking at 3,000 percent annually in 1989. Corollaries of the above were a flight of the dollar from the country, the deterioration of the industrial infrastructure, and high levels of unemployment.

The transformations in agriculture speak volumes for the neoliberal agenda of the IMF. Soy was the cornerstone of the new policies. The crop displaced a thriving dairy sector all around the capital and a diversified agriculture in the rest of the country. Argentina, with Brazil and the United

States, now produces more than 80 percent of soy worldwide, and 90 percent of the national soy production is exported.

As an indication of the devastating effects of soy, consider that its share went from 27,000 metric tons in 1970 to 34 million in 2004. Soy displaced more basic staples like wheat, corn, rice, and sunflower, offering 50 percent of the country's grain harvest in 2003. Internal beef consumption, for which Argentina is famous, declined as well; an estimated 16 percent between the years 2002 and 2003 alone.[14]

Benefiting from infrastructure in large part subsidized by the Argentine government, the soy conglomerates now cultivate the land for the short term, offering only seasonal employment and exposing the bare land to erosion. Add to that that the soybean crops most often grown are GMO strains and Roundup Ready, exposing the land to large amount of toxic substances. Not surprisingly, a nation of abundant agricultural resources started to know hunger. Agronomist Alberto Lapolla estimated that between 1990 and 2003 some 450,000 Argentines died of hunger.[121]

With the rise of unemployment, another movement started giving shape to new responses and forming the background to Horizontalism: the MTDs or Movimientos de Trabajadores Desempleados (Movement of the Unemployed Workers). They organized first in the north and south of the country to resist government policies and pressure for government subsidies, by taking to the street and blocking major roads. They assumed forms of diffuse leaderships and took their negotiations directly and collectively at their blockades, rather than sending a representative. They obtained the first unemployment subsidies in South America.

In the precarious economic situation Argentina spiraled in, the events of December 19 and 20, 2001, formed a watershed. In the 1990s Argentina entered a phase of recession, leading to a flight of foreign investments from the country. The economic situation was mirrored with vast social disengagement: all sense of community seemed to be disappearing in the country, be it in neighborhood groups, libraries, union locales, social services, or even neighborhood cafés.

---

[121] Rush, Cynthia R. "Cartels' Soy Revolution Kills Argentine Farming," *Executive Intelligence Review*, November 19, 2004.

With a complete loss of confidence in government policies, the trigger came when people started withdrawing money from the banks, and the only response the government could offer was freezing their accounts. The days of December 19 and 20, 2001, marked the critical turning point. Spontaneously, large crowds took to the streets, banging pots and marching to the center of the capital. The middle class, relentlessly attacked and demoted over the decades, extended solidarity toward the unemployed or those who survived recovering recyclables from the capital. New chants were heard in the streets of Buenos Aires: "Nuestros sueños no caben en sus urnas" (Our dreams do not fit in your ballot boxes), "La verdadera democracia está en la calle" (The true democracy is in the streets), and "Ocupar, Resistir, Producir" (Occupy, Resist, Produce), among others. President De la Rua declared a state of siege, but little could be done at that point to stop the popular uprising. In fact, after his resignation, four other governments followed in quick succession.

What happened after December 19 and 20 formed a true departure from Argentina's often tragic recent past. Economic and social upheaval can easily spiral down toward anarchy, as it had in Argentina's recent past. The protestors in the capital and elsewhere risked a showdown with the police and authorities. Fortunately, the anger that was present in the beginning gave way to new discoveries and collective, creative breakthroughs, to an unfolding of new possibilities, which Marina Sitrin characterizes as a *rupture*, a term not too different from *emergence*, as we will see shortly.

The New Forms

The events of December 2001 gave way to new social initiatives. In a completely spontaneous way, the so-called General Assemblies were established, often very informally, in which people in a neighborhood assembled to explore questions of common interest and took decisions in completely transparent ways. It is estimated there were up to 200 neighborhood assemblies in urban Buenos Aires, most of them gathering from 200 to 300 people. The most successful were those that tackled concrete projects and/or occupied buildings.

The *tomas* were repossessed factories and buildings. Among these were an auto mechanical factory (La Forja), a tile and ceramic industry (Zanon, now FaSinPat), a printing press, medical clinics, a hotel (Bauen in Buenos

Aires), and a daily newspaper. In conjunction, or separately from these, were popular kitchens, bakeries, cafés, media and art or education collectives, and theater and music workshops. The movement had started already in the late 1990s but picked up steam after 2001.

Another change worth mentioning is that of the MTDs after 2001. Many of these joined in a loose network called Anibal Veron, and later into the Frente Dario Santillan. They too espoused the ideas of Horizontalism and took steps toward strengthening their own self-sufficiency, lessening the importance of roadblocks in their strategy.

Horizontalism

A host of new words have constellated the Argentinian experience. We will recognize part of what has already emerged, with new shades and nuances. Most of the people and movements included under the umbrella of Horizontalism oppose capitalism in its neoliberal expression and most also oppose political parties. Many also oppose the state itself.

Horizontalism is the word to express that the movement wants to change the way people relate to each other, moving away from the vertical structures that are found in all of society, including traditional leftist opposition parties. A close ally to horizontal is the word *autonomy*, which does not bear resemblance to the term as it is used in Marxist circles. In the negative it indicates independence from the government; in the positive it lays the stress on the capacity to self-organize through direct participation and wider democratic practices.

Emilio of a Tierra del Sur neighborhood assembly summarizes it thus: "The traditional leftist configuration is like a tree, where the central committee is the trunk. . . . On the other hand, the relations we are experiencing between different movements resemble web-like formations. It's like a network, a real network, where no single group leads. It's a web of independent and interrelated communities, which don't work around a single consolidated project; rather relationships form around concrete projects." The central idea of autonomy is intimately linked with the capacity to self-organize, which leads to fluid enactment of new ideas and initiatives, rather than the consolidation of new permanent structures. Emilio concludes: "We're not creating the opposite, but are creating something else. We aren't building the opposite to the capitalist system, that's been tried and it doesn't work."[122]

It is important to underline this sense of new creation, which distances Horizontalism from a typical opposition movement. The participatory goes hand in hand with the entrepreneurial spirit: great emphasis is laid on the realization of concrete projects. Starting a community kitchen or an organic garden is more important than laying out a coherent ideological platform. In fact, you will not find a Horizontalist ideologue speaking for the movement. When new ideas emerge, they are part of a collective endeavor coming from the aggregation of experience and practice.

The new and the sense of discovery emerge from all the interviews by Marina Sitrin. As one of many, here is Ezequiel, an activist in a neighborhood assembly: "What began angrily, with people coming out on the street in a rage, quickly turned joyful. People smiled and mutually recognized that something had changed. . . . It was a very intense feeling that I will never forget."[123]

It is not surprising to hear whole new terms of reference, and most of all a sense of departure from the past, captured in the word *rupture*, which indicates the feeling of being placed in a choice between two worlds, two diverging realities. The economic crises Argentina has suffered are seen as part of something larger, as an opportunity to reflect, see the whole of neoliberalism in context, and be able to articulate a fuller answer from within. These are movements that want to prefigure the possible futures.

At the center of it all lies the insight that new relationships are possible that reject the rigid structures of the past. In Marina Sitrin's words, "People spoke of rupture as a break, but also, and simultaneously, as a freeing or an opening thus capturing the new energy created by changed circumstances."[124]

The breakdown of the structures of the past is not seen as an end in itself, but rather as a beginning of new possibilities. It frees energy for loosening

---

[122] Sitrin, *Horizontalism*, 175.

[123] Sitrin, *Horizontalism*, 26.

[124] Marina Sitrin, 2007, "Ruptures in Imagination: Horizontalism, Autogestion and Affective Politics in Argentina," *Policy and Practice, a Development Education Review*, no. 5, Autumn 2007. https://www.developmenteducationreview.com/issue/issue-5/ruptures-imagination-horizontalism-autogestion-and-affective-politics-argentina.

people's imaginations, changing the forms and quality of social relationships and freeing them from old social structures. Because it is an opening to the new, the path to take cannot be preset or mapped without smothering the energy and dampening the imagination.

The revolutions South America has known were means designed for an end; here means and ends walk hand in hand. The means that are being worked with are possible emerging ends. Others will be discarded as failed experiments. All in all, we may say that what has been called a rupture stands very close to the term we have chosen, *emergence*.

Horizontalism, autonomy, and rupture come with a corollary of host phenomena, such as increased creativity, leaderfulness, and prizing of diversity of voices. Creativity has been compared to "constructing with a happy passion" by Toty of MTD La Matanza. "Happiness isn't something you can postpone until tomorrow—we must live with total fervor today," echoes a fellow unemployed member.[125] Creating the new obliges these pioneers to face fear, the most effective instrument the government has for debilitating the movement. It is such a challenge that many will experiment with the new and withdraw before returning with new energy. Horizontalism is transformative; it is not an experience for the faint of heart.

The new Argentinian experiment is one that embraces paradoxes and integrates polarities. Having given up "power over" for "power with," it commits to value the individual as much as it does the collective. And being entrepreneurial in spirit means encouraging all to be leaders when the time comes to express one's strengths for the good of all.

If all voices are to be valued, then listening and giving people the feeling of being heard becomes paramount. This means being able to listen beyond people's stated persuasions. Argentina has known polarization in terms of political stances and religious choices, among others. Feminists are now willing to face women strongly anchored in Catholic or traditional beliefs. Issues like abortion can spur creative dialogue in the spirit of rejecting dogmatic stances and listening in a nonpartisan way. True dialogue is sought, and when it comes to decision, true consensus arises rather than weak compromise. The spaces for new ways of meeting are central to the definition of the movement.

---

[125] Sitrin, *Horizontalism*, 246.

Seeds for a New Culture

Much of what Argentina has witnessed in the days after the 2001 economic debacle is now subsumed, subdued. Many factories and workplaces continue to work, operated collectively, and other groups continue to hold the spaces created with the new spirit. You may not find the Chilavert press or the La Forja auto factory (from the movie *The Take*). This is not to say that all has been in vain. The seeds of a new culture have been sown to be reborn at the best opportunity.

Horizontalism aims in fact at a whole redefinition of values, which are not seen as something definite and immutable. The question asked by Emilio, of the Tierra del Sur neighborhood assembly, is as crucial as ever: "How do we change ourselves and our communities? This is as important as getting rid of the IMF. . . . More important, even." A woman from MTD La Matanza echoes: "We believe that in some way we're going to change the education system from what we experienced. . . . All the things we're taught are carried inside ourselves and they are difficult to remove later. We think that it's more difficult to struggle with the enemy inside of ourselves."[126]

As we have seen in other parts of this present exploration, all of the above is eminently cultural, rather than political in nature, though it will affect political change over time. Horizontalism is in fact an almost circular process that goes from the individual to the collective, then to the changed individual and back to the changed collective. These have been called *subjectividad* (subjectivity) and *protagonismo* (individual becoming protagonist). In short, the individual and the collective are seen as interconnected: you can only change one if, and while, you change the other. And this means that we can become agents of change without waiting for external events to motivate our actions. We need to create the change we want to see in our day-to-day relations, in effect attempting to prefigure future society.

Horizontalists aim at expanding beyond Argentinian borders. They have ongoing relationships with the Landless Movement of Brazil (MST) and are constantly exchanging ideas with the Zapatista Movement of Chiapas, Mexico. Their networking has started to expand at a continental level. In 2005, a "First Gathering of Recuperated Workplaces" was convened

---

[126] Sitrin, *Horizontalism*, 151.

in Caracas, Venezuela, with representatives of 263 workplaces from eight countries.[127]

Horizontalism in the Present and Its Limitations

A 2013 article in *The Guardian* indicates that some three hundred recovered factories are still in existence in Argentina, half of them in the Buenos Aires area.[128] In fact new sectors have been added, such as restaurants, trash collection, construction, health, and transport.[129]

Most of the above operate as typical co-ops: horizontal management, cooperative employee ownership, same or very similar salaries. In most instances executive roles are filled for short terms and rotated every few years. The movement as a whole, however, has suffered from divergent views, leading to the forming of various federations.

It seems that the emergence of the new has not led at least in the organizational field to any breakthrough in terms of social forms but rather a return to the cooperative form, familiar to much of European and Latin American cultures and beyond. The ideas that were cultivated in cultural terms did not generate emergent options in the economy.

Co-ops mostly oppose the bottom-down model to the top-down and struggle with its limitations. For all its good intentions and future potential, the co-op movement risks remaining at the other end of the continuum of top down, and fighting it with little success. We have seen in the previous chapter sociocracy as a successful attempt to honor and integrate both approaches, rather than antagonize them. We will now turn to more deliberate and intentional forms, both at the organizational level and at larger scales, that move completely beyond the dilemmas of the past.

We will look at two indicative phenomena: Holacracy and so-called socially generative networks. The first is a way to restructure an organization

---

[127] https://www.handsoffvenezuela.org/venezuela-expropiations-encuentro.htm.

[128] Oliver Balch, "New Hope for Argentina in the Recovered Factory Movement, *The Guardian*, March 12, 2013, https://www.theguardian.com/sustainable-business/argentina-recovered-factory-movement.

[129] Matt Kennard and Ana Caistor-Arendar, "Occupy Buenos Aires: The Workers' Movement that Transformed a City, and Inspired the World," *The Guardian*, March 10, 2016, https://www.theguardian.com/cities/2016/mar/10/occupy-buenos-aires-argentina-workers-cooperative-movement.

LUIGI MORELLI

in a way that mimics natural systems in which parts and whole work in autonomy and integration. The second will look at how large commons issues can be tackled by a variety of organizations from one to three sectors. In the same fashion, the work of the parts operating autonomously can be integrated in the larger vision of the social good. Autonomy and collaboration mutually reinforce each other.

Allowing Emergence: Holacracy

We have seen with Buurtzorg how management roles are distributed among individuals in a circle, eliminating the need for a specific CEO title, for management, and organizational departments (HR, sales, administration, etc.). This has been achieved at a low level of complexity. We can now move to more complex organizational models, where the roles will be distributed among a larger number of units than the single team. Like Sociocracy, Holacracy aims at recognizing and integrating the reality of an open system, at seeing the organization in constant relation with a changing environment.

Definitions

Literally speaking *Holacracy* breaks into the idea of "holon" and "cracy," the term for governance that we know in democracy, or sociocracy. A *holon* is a term that has come in vogue in describing an autonomous entity (a whole in itself) that is part of a larger whole. In nature, a cell is a holon that is part of an organ. The organ is a holon that is itself part of the body, which we can term a *holarchy*, which in turn interacts as an open system with larger orders of reality.

The above example of holons will serve as an analogy that we will find expressed in how Holacracy overcomes traditional structures that apply to closed systems. In Holacracy an ensemble of holon/roles overlaps with the holon/circles, which are nested within the larger holarchy of the organization, itself an open system. Holarchy aims at rendering the organization a reality that is more than its individual components, therefore independent from them. It simultaneously honors *autonomy* and enables *self-organization* at every level. The organizational holarchy looks a like a series of nested circles, rather than the typical tree.

178

As we will see from the details, Holacracy is an ensemble of processes and governance ideas that completely bypass and replace top-down hierarchy and need for management. In a thought-provoking statement, Brian Robertson, the major architect of the system, calls it "governance of and by the organizational holarchy; *through* the people, but *not of or for* the people"[130] (emphasis added). The official website defines Holacracy as a "new way of structuring and running your organization that replaces the conventional management hierarchy. Instead of operating top-down, power is distributed throughout the organization, giving individuals and teams more freedom to self-manage, while staying aligned to the organization's purpose."[131]

The Still Evolving History

Brian Robertson recognizes that what is now called Holacracy is indebted to a great variety of thinkers and social experiments. In his research he credits the initial sources of Jim Collins, Peter Senge, Barry Oshry, Patrick Lencioni, and Linda Berens. Among later sources are David Allen's Getting Things Done method (GTD) and the writings and teachings of Kent Beck, Ken Schwaber, Jeff Sutherland, Mike Cohn, and Mary Poppendieck, among others.

From a practical perspective, Robertson found that he had to hold these ideas, as well as his own preferences, lightly in order to let best design practices emerge from a continuous movement of experimenting, testing, recording feedback, and adapting, so that in retrospect he could say, "I did not *create* [the Holacracy ideas]; the process was more like discovering some basic laws of physics, through a lot of experimentation."

Robertson inquired in many directions toward established theories and practices. One of the critical pieces of the whole came from the "Manifesto of Agile Software Development," which was published shortly before Robertson started his own Ternary Software company.[132] It was natural to turn his attention to the agile software development approach, which

---

[130] Brian Robertson, "History of Holacracy; The Discovery of an Evolutionary Algorithm," July 28, 2014, https://blog.holacracy.org/history-of-holacracy-c7a848 9f8eca.

[131] https://www.holacracy.org/what-is-holacracy.

[132] https://agilemanifesto.org/.

predicated recourse to self-organizing teams that devise their own ways of working. This type of software development relinquishes extensive predictive analysis and planning in favor of repeated iterations with rapid feedback and adaptation to changes, which will let the software evolve in collaboration with the community of users. It was only natural to want to extend this approach, not just to the development of software, but also to the whole organizational culture. This approach gave the impetus for many more years of experimentation and adaptation.

As ideas started to coalesce, Robertson and his team found the need to come to clarity with group facilitation and decision-making processes, the natural complement to all governance ideas, in order to integrate a multitude of perspectives. At this point he turned to the *Facilitator's Guide to Participatory Decision-Making* by Sam Kaner, and in time for the crucial encounter with Sociocracy.

In Sociocracy the evolving Holacracy found to some extent the key concepts of consent rather than consensus, but most of all the idea of double-linking—in short, a natural way of conveying feedback across layers of complexity and in all directions. Sociocracy offered the fuel for new practices and for quite some time. Still Robertson saw its limitations in its dependence on hierarchic structures. He wanted to further emancipate the roles from the individuals and of those from the organization, increase autonomy and distribute authority at every level, acquire greater orientation toward organizational purpose, and increase decision-making speed and evolutionary capacity. He wanted to avoid concentration of power in individuals or its dilution into the group, by placing organizational purpose full center.

As a champion of adaptability, Holacracy has reached at least its fourth version for the present, and Robertson further imagines that "its future evolution will be driven more and more by its larger user community."[133]

[133] Brian Robertson, "History of Holacracy; The Discovery of an Evolutionary Algorithm," July 28, 2014, https://blog.holacracy.org/history-of-holacracy-c7a8489f8eca.

How It Works

Holacracy wants to place the organizational purpose above personalities, even that of its founder(s). The purpose is the highest manifestation of organizational potential, which needs to be found in relation to objective needs of the world. This can only be discerned through listening and adapting, and Holacracy places this goal above all others and at every step of the way. People in the organization will come and go; the organization's purpose will endure.

Among its most important components Holacracy counts:

- autonomy of the organizational circles and a definition of the roles and accompanying responsibilities that people absolve within the circles;
- unique processes for detecting what roles are necessary, and how they should evolve;
- specific meeting processes;
- dynamic steering; and
- an evolving, living constitution, which captures all of the above.

Circles and Roles

Starting from the simplest level, the greatest innovation of Holacracy is not the function of the individual, but of the role an individual fulfills within a circle (equivalent of a team). "Holacracy aspires to result in a natural hierarchy focused on work [roles] instead of individuals."[134]

An individual can fulfill more than one role in more than one circle. The roles are nested in circles and these are nested in the larger circle, which Holacracy calls the "anchor circle" (or "super circle") containing the whole organization. The roles and circles are like the cells and organs (holons) of the organizational holarchy. The circles themselves are subdivided in sub-circles (Figure 29).

---

[134] Pepijn van de Kamp, "Holacracy—A Radical Approach to Organizational Design," in *Elements of the Software Development Process: Influences on Project Sources and Failure*, edited by Hans Dekkers, Will Leeuwis, and Ivan Plantevin, 9 (University of Amsterdam, 2014). https://www.researchgate.net/publication/264977984_Holacracy_-_A_Radical_Approach_to_Organizational_Design/link/53fa346a0cf27c365ceed4fe/download.

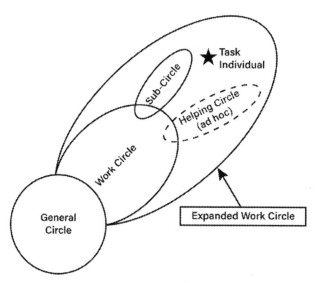

Figure 29: Basic circle structure

The circles are self-organizing teams. They have to naturally emerge and evolve over time; so do the roles. The individuals themselves no longer have job titles; they simply assume roles that can change over time. This separation of individuals from roles is what Robertson calls "separating role and soul." Step by step the process of evolution is recorded in a constitution that defines the domains of action, responsibilities, and limitations of roles.

An emphasis on self-organization and empowerment of the roles encourages those with managerial experience to let go and other employees to step forward. What is often seen as mutually exclusive becomes a matter of fact; initiative/autonomy and collaboration are mutually reinforced. Leadership is assumed everywhere in the system, since there is no real top.

Roles contribute to the aims of the circles and the organizational purpose. Each role has several qualities:

- A purpose that explains what the role wants to achieve. An example of role in a small company could be marketing or accounting.
- One or more domains over which it exerts power: the domain is the area of autonomy over which other roles will not interfere. In the case of marketing, some domains could be online orders, social media accounts, or website contents and upgrades.

- Accountabilities over which the role has complete control; these are specific activities that the role is intended to perform. Accountabilities for online orders could include promoting services and/or products on the website, or maintaining and expanding presence on social media.

The domain is the general area of action of the role. The accountabilities will break down targeted areas of this specific role: the how, when, where, and what. The individual will have specific authority over the whole of the role. In the day to day, a role will enter in creative tensions with another role, for example in overlapping areas of action. Individual leadership addresses the tensions, and Holacracy has developed efficient processes for addressing them.

Everyone in the organization is a leader in his role(s) and a follower in all other roles, thus distributing responsibility over the whole organization. And roles will emerge from need over time and dissolve when and if their purpose is fulfilled or no longer functional. The founders have their own roles defined by respective domains and accountabilities and cannot overstep their boundaries. The constitution serves as the safeguard.

Facilitation

Holacracy purports to have a focus on one tension at a time; it aims at most successfully addressing tensions with the minimum investment of energy for the sake of the role. Individuals are encouraged to discern and address tensions in their roles to better address organizational purpose. These tensions can appear in either of operations/strategy (the processing of the work) or tensions on governance (impacting organizational structure). See figure 30.

Operational meetings, most often called "tactical meetings," involve minimal and fast-paced facilitation in what is called the "integrative decision-making process." Here too we can recognize the stages of Open Mind (clarifying questions), Open Heart (reaction round, objection round), and Open Will (integration round). Governance meetings, as in Sociocracy, address policy decisions and also the evolving description of roles. Addressing governance means slowing down in order to gain clarity, but this is done in order to speed up operations. Good governance stimulates good intrinsic motivation in the fulfilment of roles.

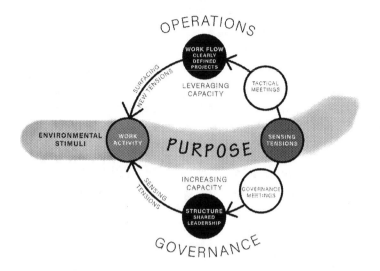

Figure 30: Operations and Governance in Holacracy

Double-Linking and Dynamic Steering

Holacracy has evolved and refined features we have already uncovered in Sociocracy and in the example of Buurtzorg. From Sociocracy it has adapted double-linking.

The so-called lead link and rep link act like two channels across a membrane cell. The lead link is chosen within the super-circle to represent its needs within the sub-circle. The rep link conveys the needs of the sub-circle within the super-circle. They are simultaneously present in both circles, providing complementary views and feedback: the lead link has authority to remove a person from a role, though not to fire; the rep link relates the tensions he sees to the super-circle in order to free energy for the roles. The two reps are chosen through what is called an "Integrative Election Process."

Not unlike Sociocracy, important decisions are based on consent and are tested through rapid feedback, in what is called "dynamic steering." There is no need for thorough prescriptive planning but rather adjustment to external variables through rapid feedback. This is particularly important for matters concerning organizational structure, which can continuously be improved based on experience.

Recourse to strategic planning would limit ability and readiness to sense the tensions and adapt to evolving trends. The goal is to reach workable decisions and let reality inform the next step, rather than follow a road map and risk resisting reality in the name of long-term goals.

There is a medium-term strategy that is framed around sets of polarities, both defined in positive terms. The group as a whole decides which direction seems more desirable in the present circumstances. Through the Integrative Decision-Making Process each person, with input from the whole, can see how they can adapt their role to the strategy.[135]

Holacracy is a relatively young organizational form that has received positive reviews in academic circles and has been applied in small and medium-sized enterprises. Of late it has shown positive results in larger ones, such as Precision Nutrition and Zappos, to which we turn next.

Success Stories

Precision Nutrition

Toronto's Precision Nutrition defines itself as "the home of the world's top nutrition coaches: coaching clients and certifying professionals since 2005."[136] And it adds, "Over the last 15 years, through our Men's and Women's coaching programs, our in-house coaches have helped over 100,000 men and women get into the best shape of their lives.[137]

In 2012 cofounders Phil Caravaggio and John Berardi decided to implement a transition to the Holacracy model in the organization. The change yielded results even in its first year. In an interview with Brian Robertson, Caravaggio explains that a motivation for innovation was his distaste for commodity work, the work-for-paycheck exchange.[138] Added to this was the very successful growth of the company from its inception, which generated a tension between holding on to its core values, growing in numbers and volume of business, and adapting to a rapidly changing

---

[135] Robertson, *Holacracy*, 132, 138.
[136] precisionnutrition.com.
[137] https://www.precisionnutrition.com/our-story.
[138] https://www.holacracy.org/precision-nutrition/.

environment. The founders did not subscribe to the idea of limiting growth as a way to hold on to what made the organization special, but knew the risk that comes from rapid expansion.

Caravaggio observes that Holacracy has extended entrepreneurial spirit and leadership, though not in a managerial sense, since there isn't really a top to the business. In fact a big change has occurred at what was the top.

Before the change, due to the company's amazing growth, Caravaggio found himself doing all the important and urgent tasks in the company—he was the leader and decider, and felt he could manage less and less. It was a demanding task to step back and let other talent and leadership emerge and to trust it, to the point of realizing that the company could go on without needing as much from him. And he knows that he cannot overstep his boundaries and have the last word, because the Holocratic constitution just doesn't allow him. However, he still has a unique role in it, as he specifies: "[Holacracy] gives you, as the custodian of that [organizational] specialness, enough to keep it. You're not going to delegate that part of the organization. As the founder, that's my primary role and task."[139]

Noticing that the company has continued to grow in people and revenue between 25 and 50 percent per year, Caravaggio is sure that this has only been possible by moving whole-heartedly into the new paradigm, not just doing a halfway transition.

Zappos

Zappos, an online firm offering apparel, was founded by Nick Shurman in 1999. It shone the light on Holacracy, as the first large-scale company—counting a workforce of 1,500—to convert to Holacracy in 2013. The transition has favored what Zappos sees as a culture of "collective individualism" and of "mini-entrepreneurs."

The lessons learned from Zappos emphasize cultural coherence at all levels, starting with a stringent recruitment process, continuing in the structure, operations, and strategy, plus individual motivation. No doubt this was the reason for 18 percent of the company employees to leave after the transition. This is in fact an expected conclusion since Holacracy requires a shift to autonomy, commitment, risk-taking, and self-organizing, and the

---

[139] https://www.holacracy.org/precision-nutrition/.

transition may not be easy after fourteen years of the prevalent culture. Robertson himself explains that you cannot do a halfway transition to Holacracy; however, you can pilot change within parts of the organization.

Zappos's stated core values seem quite aligned with Holacracy: delivery of superior service, embracing and creating change, adaptability and flexibility, learning potential, risk taking, and highly committed and motivated employees. Finally, though difficult, the conflict between old and new generations needs to be embraced, without sacrificing the needs and values of the senior employees.

Comparing Sociocracy and Holacracy

Sociocracy predicates the autonomy and interdependence of the circles. Holacracy goes one step further: it separates the role from the individual and predicates the autonomy of the role from other roles, obviously autonomy only in so far as there is integration and no role is hurt by another role. This means that the CEO is only a role that can operate within the parameters defined by the Holacratic constitution of the organization.

Since the role becomes central, over and against the circle and the individual, there is no need for continuous consent; it is sufficient to keep rewriting the role descriptions when new tensions between roles arise, strictly between the parties involved. This is done by giving satisfaction to the individual in the roles.

There is equally no need for core values or for promoting a special culture. The culture simply emerges because everybody is operating in the best of conditions, conditions in which tensions are continuously addressed and extreme clarity reigns in the function, domains, and accountabilities of each role.

Socially Generative Networks

We are moving now to the most important piece of our explorations in this chapter. It becomes more understandable in light of what has emerged so far, including the two previous chapters.

Networks bring the art of engaging with emergence to its ultimate level at present. Enterprises like Buurtzorg or FAVI have illustrated what is possible and successful at the organizational level when autonomy is allied with inclusion, transparency, and efficiency. Holacracy brings this science and art to a new level by incorporating the apparent simplicity of self-organizing into higher organizational complexity, into the new reality of a nested holarchy of autonomous levels of operation. Argentina's Horizontalism gives us a feeling of how networking can naturally emerge between all kinds of initiatives in a territory the size of a country. Sustaining that natural, spontaneous emergence by giving it forms that depart from the past has proved challenging. It seems that spontaneous self-organizing can work only to a certain extent. Beyond that it needs the help of a living understanding of how to promote and sustain conscious emergence.

We will now have a look at how larger, complex goals can be addressed through what seems a complete paradox, that of organizing the movement toward self-organizing. How can we sustain networks in such a way as they continue to self-organize, not just dissolve, when one practical goal is reached? And why not let them do their own thing?

In the face of the mounting challenges that defy being addressed by few actors in isolation, we need a systems approach. We need to be able to apprehend the whole system in order to identify the leverage points upon which concerted action will lead to the greatest results with lowest, or lower efforts. This work of first identifying and then taking concerted actions means encouraging greatest inclusion of all stakeholders within one, two, or three sectors, and developing leaderfulness at all levels.

A Network to Preserve an Ecosystem: Celebrating 25 Years of the Yellowstone to Yukon (Y2Y) Vision

Recent scientific data show on one hand that the Yellowstone grizzly population is moving northward, while the northern counterparts are moving southward from the Yukon. At present, in west central Montana these bear populations are within one hundred miles from each other, something that has not occurred in the last one hundred years. Much of this is the result of the work of the Y2Y network. While it gathers primarily scientists and conservationists, it also counts representatives of government agencies, Native Americans, landowners and ranchers, and the support of the local governments and populations. The strength of this network lies in meeting all stakeholders' challenges and needs by forging strong partnerships.[140] Though a rather informal network in relation to the ones we will explore later, its successes in ushering in a new vision of landscape preservation are remarkable.

Some Milestones before Y2Y

1980–1990s: Advances in technological devices such as radio collars allow wildlife biologists to track wildlife movements. A wolf is tracked over 800 miles; lynx and bull trout's recorded movements span over 1,000 miles. The research of Dr. Bill Newmark indicates that not even parks the size of Banff or Yellowstone can counter patterns of extinction. He identifies human developments (settlements, roads, fences, etc.) as the major factors hindering migrations and other life processes.

1983: Parks Canada installs wildlife underpasses along a section of Trans-Canada Highway in Banff National Park to ease the patterns of movement of elk and other wild animals. This is a win for motorists as well.

1991: The idea of "continental conservation" takes root, spearheaded by biologists and conservation leaders. Founders of the Society for Conservation Biology initiate the Wildlands Project, with the intent of interconnecting protected areas across North America.

Birth of Y2Y

One of the early adopters of the above views was Harvey Locke, future founder of Y2Y. In the summer of 1993, after a 14-day hike followed by a horseback riding trip, he clearly saw at that point that for many species the land uniting Yellowstone to the Yukon was a natural gigantic ecosystem.

He remembers that, while sitting at a campfire, "I wrote the words 'Yellowstone to Yukon' for the first time with the conviction that this was the right scale at which to think and act."[141] He also wrote an essay that became a rallying cry. He then managed to convene a first meeting in December of

---

[140] The following information comes mostly from y2y.net. See also https://www.youtube.com/watch?v=eqHinMdejEc (Karsten Heuer, Y2Y conservation senior advisor, on 20 years of Y2Y progress) and https://www.youtube.com/watch?v=1mDnkTxOy8E (Harvey Locke presents "From Yellowstone to Yukon" at the Buffalo Bill Center of the West, located in Cody, Wyoming).

[141] https://y2y.net/about/vision-mission/history/.

the same year, attended by 30 scientists and conservationists from the US and Canada, who accepted the Y2Y idea.

Achievements

Various milestones steadily followed in the years to come. Some among the many:

November 1994: Wolves are reintroduced in Yellowstone.

1994: More than 40 academics and conservationists form the Y2Y Council with the mandate to create an interconnected system of parks and reserves from Yellowstone to Yukon. A Coordinating Committee is empowered to implement the Council's decisions.

December 1997: Public Launch of the Y2Y Vision. The Connections conference in Waterton Lakes National Park, Alberta, gathers about 300 between land trust and government representatives, scientists, Native Americans, and news media operators. The Y2Y vision goes mainstream.

1997: More wildlife crossings—38 under- and six overpasses—are built to ensure connectivity between animal habitats. Wildlife responds readily with enhanced connectivity between habitats, and animal-vehicle collisions drop by 80 percent.

1998: 16 million acres in British Columbia are set aside as the Muskwa–Kechika Management Area, which includes parks, protected areas, and special management zones where some development is allowed.

2008: 136,000 acres of land in the southern Selkirk Mountains of British Columbia are placed under conservation. This offers a refuge for wildlife, including one of the last herds of southern mountain caribou.

February 2010: The movement for large-landscape conservation is embraced by the U.S. government through the forming of various cooperatives. Among these is the Great Northern Landscape Conservation Cooperative, whose area covers the southern two thirds of the Y2Y region.

2010 to 2012: As a result of concerted conservation efforts and pressure, ConocoPhillips and BP voluntarily relinquish oil and gas leases in the U.S. portion of the Flathead. Shell Canada abandons plans to frack for gas in the Sacred Headwaters region of top salmon–producing rivers in British Columbia. This is followed by legislation in the United States banning oil and gas development in the Flathead in 2011, and in 2012 British Columbia bans oil and gas drilling in the Y2Y area.

In summing up Y2Y can claim among its successes:

- increased surface of protected areas as illustrated above;
- promoted the vision the Y2Y vision to more than 90 million people through the media and inspiring numerous art, video, and book projects that publicize and promote the Yellowstone to Yukon region and its preservation; and
- protected the survival of bears, caribou, pronghorn, and other previously endangered species, and reconciled the needs of wildlife with those of landowners and ranchers.

The Case of RE-AMP

We will continue our exploration with a typical "wicked problem," that of energy, sustainability, and climate change. It is in this kind of situations that a network approach pays the most. We will therefore look at the work of a relatively simple network operating mostly from the nonprofit sector. We will explore the wildfire phenomenon that has swept the upper Midwest: the work of RE-AMP in eight states of the Midwest, initially Illinois, Iowa, Minnesota, North Dakota, South Dakota, and Wisconsin, and later also Michigan and Ohio.

I had heard and read much about RE-AMP when I visited Melissa Gavin, the Chief Network Officer in downtown Madison, Wisconsin. I was looking for the name RE-AMP as I approached the building but could only see Clean Wisconsin, a nonprofit that champions clean water, air, and energy, which is where I met her. I met others of the network team in Madison and in Wisconsin Dells. The team does not have a main headquarter and is in fact dispersed throughout Wisconsin (and Minnesota)—but that doesn't lessen its impact. So what makes its strength?

From its inception in 2003 to the time it was first studied (2010), RE-AMP grew to include 113 nonprofits and 12 foundations whose focus embraced climate change and energy policy. The original name of the network stood for Renewable Energy and Mapping Project; arguably it has exceeded the mission at present. In fact even after its first seven years, the results obtained by the network were impressive.

Part of the success is due to the unusual and thorough care with which the Garfield Foundation laid the groundwork for the formation of the network. RE-AMP started with 12 nonprofits and 7 foundations, selected very carefully, and sustained by a $2.5 million investment in 2003. It spent the first year simply mapping the system to acquire a fuller perspective of the work at hand. From the mapping four key leverage points were identified by all the stakeholders for the ambitious goal of reaching an 80 percent reduction of carbon emissions from the electricity generation sector by 2030.

When this was done the original participants selected four leaders who worked for nonprofits and asked them to help form working groups of 6 to 10 other organizations that would devise action plans for each of the four target areas. This meant an expansion from the 12 initial nonprofits to almost 40.

To anybody who would have declared the goal unrealistic in a region of the United States dominated by the coal industry and its lobby, RE-AMP has responded with hard facts. Below are some of the outcomes generated by RE-AMP before we return to how the network achieved them. RE-AMP has

- successfully prevented the building of 28 coal-generated electrical plants over four years;
- launched campaigns that were effective in reducing coal electrical generation by 5.8 percent from 2005 to 2010;
- pressured for and obtained more stringent renewable energy standards (RES) in Illinois, Ohio, Michigan, Minnesota, and Wisconsin, and obtained the same results with energy efficiency portfolio standards (EEPS) in Illinois, Iowa, Ohio, Michigan, Minnesota, and Wisconsin;
- through the Midwest Governors Association pushed for and obtained the toughest cap and trade programs in the nation; and
- contributed to defeating federal antienvironmental legislation.[142]

---

[142] Heather McLeod Grant, *Transformer*, 13.

Another successful networking initiative led to the International Campaign to End Landmines, signed by 146 countries in 1997, stopping the production of 2.5 million new landmines per year and leading to the destruction of 30 million of them. The initiative was launched by a network of 1,400 NGOs from 90 countries.[143]

Understanding networks can be challenging for those of us who are not part immersed in their work. We will therefore look at the larger picture, returning from time to time to the example of RE-AMP or ACENET—a network operating in the food system—before looking at networks involving more than one sector, or networks interacting with each other within a region. We will occasionally point to the larger reality of global networks, those that Steve Waddell calls "Global Action Networks" to highlight the ultimate potential of networks to address the needs of the global commons.

Network Terminology

Networks can be defined as "human operating systems for generating change activities."[144] Peter Plastrik calls them "generative social impact networks" because they are adapted to explore change in multiple directions, experiment and replicate their successes, and share the lessons learned with each other. Such networks operate through membership requirements and a mix of voluntary action and peer pressure. Joining a network also implies the willingness to engage in some common sets of behaviors and refraining from acting in ways that would harm other network members.

Important terms for understanding networks are "nodes," corresponding to people or more often to organizations, and "links" or effective operational relationships between nodes. A node with many links will in time be called a "hub."

Members of the network operate by offering access to and exchanging information and knowledge, and rendering available their skills, resources, and connections for joint efforts with other members. Networks are able to adjust their structure and ways of operating relatively quickly and to set in motion pilot experiments that can be replicated and scaled up when successful. The following are some of the most important core assumptions:

---

[143] June Holley, *An Introduction to Network Weaving*, 10.

[144] Peter Plastrik, Madeleine Taylor, and John Cleveland, *Connecting to Change the World: Harnessing the Power of Networks for Social Impact*, 25.

- Stakeholders define together what is best.
- Negotiations should be complemented with dialogue among stakeholders.
- All stakeholders bring expertise.
- Experience should drive action.
- Participation in decision making is key for generating member compliance.[145]

From what has been said above, it should be clear that networks differ from social movements, although they may support them or derive from these. An important difference between these is that networks place requirements upon membership, and therefore are more narrowly defined and more action oriented than most movements.

What networks allow is the transformation we have referred to in contrast to reform or incremental change. June Holley defines this as a series of shifts:

- In how we relate to each other; working as peers to co-create
- Toward appreciation of our differences, and knowing how to use them to foster breakthroughs
- From controlling to enabling, supporting, and reflecting back on our work[146]

From what has been said so far, we can surmise the reason for the networks' efficiency. Networks focus on *processes* more than on structures and outcomes. Socially generative networks create new grounds of relationships between individuals and organizations and produce new core assumptions, behaviors, and results. Through the key element of self-organization, they create the premises for emergence of new order, movement forward and new capacities within the system.

Central to what networks are and do is their ultimate reliance on emergence as the way for change. Emergence cannot be predicted, or used as a technique. However, it can be sought and encouraged, through understanding of the conditions that foster it. For this reason, strategies

---

[145] Steve Waddell, *Global Action Networks: Creating Our Future Together*, 94.
[146] Holley, *An Introduction to Network Weaving*, 7.

for dealing with complex systems need to be robust, flexible, continuously adaptive, radically innovative, and diverse.

Building Trust/Targeting Leverage Points

Key to fostering emergence is the ability to approach the targeted area through the systems thinking that results from mapping a system in its multitude of steps, interactions, and feedback loops, and interpreting these through network member participation. Critical to this is the building of a tangible trust between participating members. This takes time and is essential to the further development of the network.

Trust revolves around a number of issues and can therefore be defined in relation to these as trust of *intent*—knowing that we are aligned on a same goal; trust in *competence*—that we all have knowledge and skills to address an issue; and trust in *understanding*—that we have created a shared frame of reference and of common work.[147] The corollary of this trust is being willing to forego previous patterns of competition, of seeking to obtain advantages at the expense of other organizations in the network.

After a thorough process of mapping of the players and processes impacting energy generation and consumption in the states of the Midwest,[148] RE-AMP was able to formulate an overall ambitious goal based on targets/leverage points where it would place most of its energy. These were the following four: "stop the building of all new pulverized coal-fired power plants; retire most of the region's existing coal plants; replace coal-generated electricity with renewable power; and reduce overall electric consumption through increased efficiency."[149]

Previous to the forming of RE-AMP, single organizations targeted one, two at most, of these goals. Although the four goals are not necessarily surprising, what the mapping process allowed was the insight that no concerted action would have the desired effect if the goals were not pursued in parallel. We can notice that such a collectively pursued process of understanding already had a strong connection-building element. When this was done, the original participants selected four leaders who worked for nonprofits and asked them to help the forming of working groups of six

---

[147] Waddell, *Global Action Networks*, 23.

[148] Grant, *Transformer*, 8.

[149] Grant, *Transformer*, 7.

to ten other organizations who would devise action plans for the targeted area. This meant an expansion from the twelve initial nonprofits to almost forty.[150]

Together with the newly unleashed energy emerged challenges. After all, this was an unprecedented approach to system change, and the inertia of old ways naturally resurfaced. One very important foundation did not immediately see the possibilities of such a transformative approach and withdrew. Before the RE-AMP experiment, by and large foundations were used to operating on their own; in fact, forgoing its exclusive hold on the network was a unique and courageous step on the part of Garfield Foundation. Similar reactions emerged from nonprofits who failed to detect the advantages of this collective approach or feared they would lose their dominant positions in the field.[151] What pulled the effort forward was the determination and enthusiasm of those who had bought into the idea.

I met people within RE-AMP and some of its member organizations in 2019, only to realize that the way of working has completely evolved from what I have given above. The initial goal of reducing emissions by 80 percent in 2050 has now been updated and more in line with scientific analysis to eliminating emissions 100 percent. Key to the emerging new structures was a network-wide retraining, placing equity at the center of all considerations. The focus on equity has shifted the locus of participation to action teams and state tables.

Action teams have replaced some of the functions of the initial working groups with shorter-term goals. State tables have moved to adapt to the conditions of each state in order to form coalitions of RE-AMP members and nonmembers.[152] They form partnerships with frontline communities, which they can support with information and database systems, thus extending the network's reach. In addition, RE-AMP provides small grants to support minimal staffing and sustain the work of a small number of organizations' representatives in each state.

---

[150] Grant, *Transformer*, 8.

[151] Grant, *Transformer*, 11.

[152] See https://www.reamp.org/about/state-based-collaboration/.

Creating a Common Vision

Once the first hurdles are overcome, the benefits of joining efforts in a network become apparent. Sharing of and prompt access to key information means that each organization need not replicate efforts and possible failures. Each voice at the table is strengthened; all vessels rise together.

Through the unfolding of a common culture, mutual support becomes a quickening element. It is possible to adapt to emerging possibilities more quickly and to reach greater scale in less time. A well-oiled network adapts to local conditions, and members can form subgroups around special or regional issues, knowing that they have the backing of the larger network.

After six years in existence, RE-AMP provided a number of benefits to member organizations. Because the platform brings together funders and nonprofits, the improved relationships led to greater strategic coordination and alignment. The original mapping and common resolve meant each participant had better understanding of the issues and greater access to common best practices, leading to more effective local action. The coordinated action led to greater advocacy, power, and influence over legislation. All nonprofits acting in concert can exert more clout and better reach the ears of legislators.

Pooling resources meant being able to create new communication infrastructure, such as the first Commons platform, created in 2005. This interactive online technology—at the time quite novel—had to undergo a series of iterations to become a better tool for transparent sharing of information and coordination of efforts. RE-AMP was also able to foster the birth of a Media Center, which soon after launched *Midwest Energy News* in 2010 through Fresh Energy, an organization that promotes clean energy, sustainability, and climate change solutions.[153] *Midwest Energy News* aggregates all relevant media coverage of energy issues, and works to change the energy/climate change narrative. The media outlet was given independence from the network, which did not review or approve its content.

Midwest Energy News garnered credibility and respect from local media and even further through national publications, such as *Huffington Post*, *Grist*, and *Salon*. The publication reaches the specific audience for people in the sector, be they nonprofits, agencies, the legislature, or utilities. It

---

[153] See https://energynews.us/region/midwest/ and https://fresh-energy.org/.

is also a very effective tool for countering publicity campaigns from the industry with facts. All in all, *Midwest Energy News* is helping to fashion a new narrative. No single nonprofit could have mounted such an effective initiative on its own. The presence of founders in the network helped to turn this idea into reality.[154]

Other obvious pluses for all members are greater access to funding and better targeting of the funds made available. Funders have access to better information and are thus able to target more effective action for change. The opportunities for local joint action are powerful levers for increased leaderfulness and capacity building for single nonprofit organizations and the network as a whole.

Types and Stages of a Network

Networks can serve a variety of purposes. They can emphasize some goals more than others. Central to the following conversation is the understanding of some key concepts. At the first step are hubs, nodes that acquire prominence due to the number of their links to other organizations. Clusters in a network are formed by nodes (member organizations) connected by numerous relationships (links).

At the heart of the network is its core, those member organizations most immediately connected with the established goals and purposes, the places where the most intense activity of the network takes place. In the case of RE-AMP these will be organizations that target specifically or to a large extent energy and climate change. At the periphery are those organizations that have a looser relationship with, or a lesser investment in, the network and its goals. These may be organizations with multiple targets that overlap in just one or two of the goals of the network. They may be concerned with social justice and only marginally with energy and climate change. Core and periphery are equally important. At the core is found closer similarity of intent; from the periphery comes vital input of a different nature, from which the network can receive impetus for new ideas and for greater vitality. Similarity cements trust; diversity introduces vital new perspectives and insights.

---

[154] Media Impact Funders, "Case Study: RE-AMP and Midwest Energy News," https://www.slideshare.net/mediaimpactfunders/tce-casestudy-reampfnlonline.

Connect, Align, Produce

Research on socially generative networks has detected two fairly consistent patterns. The development of a network's capability, what its members are able to do together, progresses from connectivity to alignment to production. At the same time the development of a network's connective structure, which channels flows of information and resources among members, progresses toward greater intricacy and decentralization.

In the connecting phase, a network builder's principal task is to weave members together. In the alignment phase, members capitalize on their connections to discover, explore, and define goals, strategies, and opportunities that they share. As they do this, their connections deepen, and their desire grows for taking collective action. In more detail these are the characteristics of the three phases:

- Connectivity network: the initial phase of building a network takes time. Since it is a new way of working at social change, organizations and individuals within a network must let go of old habits. Forming strong personal connections and a common image of the issue took one year for RE-AMP and was critical to foundations learning to work with each other and with nonprofits. Rick Reed, who helped to weave RE-AMP, recalls that the early network building "was entirely personal. I formed one-on-one relationships with the individuals who were going to be in the network core. For the first years I never thought about the organizations behind these people." At the intersection of connectivity and alignment we find the exploration of the system, which is often an essential prerequisite for creating alignment.[155]

- Alignment network: links people to create and share a set of ideas, goals, and strategies. Members coordinate with each other as a group. Many of the growing number of so-called collective impact community collaboratives (see the example of Vermont Farm to Plate in Chapter 1) started as alignments of local organizations designed to improve a local system.

---

[155] Plastrik, Taylor, and Cleveland, *Connecting to Change the World*, 88.

Aligning means entering together in an experience of presencing, the creation of a new consensus upon which readiness to act with common intent emerges. When RE-AMP completed its mapping project, the members could see the need and possibility to act together toward ambitious goals. The energy that was formed through deepening connection allowed the alignment around the key four goals and toward the overall purpose of the network, reducing atmospheric carbon generated by the electric sector by 80 percent by 2030.

- Production network: fosters collective action by members to produce innovative practices, public-policy proposals, and other outputs for social impact. Once the production stage is reached, a whole new set of challenges naturally arises in how to maintain the optimal health and keep evolving the structure and working of the network.

We can detect in network development something similar to the stages of the U: from Open Mind in Connectivity to Open Heart in Alignment to Open Will in Production. As just mentioned, the shift from connection to alignment and production is accompanied with higher degrees of complexity, to which we will return later.

Knowing the Network and Its Goals

June Holley sees the evolution of the network as "an iterative process of *knowing the network* and *knitting* [weaving] *the network.*"[156] Knowing the network means regularly gathering information about the state of the network and evaluating its progress. Weaving the network entails following a specific but quite organic growth process, of which more will be said shortly.

Central to knowing the network is "mapping," though other more conventional tools can complement this approach, such as review of internal documents, surveys, and interviews. We are here exploring the mapping of the network itself, not the mapping of the system the network is targeting that was referred to earlier on. If there is no deliberate attempt to gain self-knowledge and subsequent focused efforts, networks evolve under two forces. Geographical proximity leads to small-scale results; ideological proximity, implying a small degree of diversity, leads to little innovation.

---

[156] Holley, *An Introduction to Network Weaving*, 141.

Mapping, done through a variety of software, allows the surveying of a vast reality and bringing network members to add their perspectives. Mapping serves the group to detect areas of activity and their specific nature—expertise, leadership, innovation, relationships that emerge, strengths and weaknesses, gaps, and much more.

Visual diagnostic mapping, generated through software programs, is very useful for handling complexity and making it accessible for faster understanding, and for bringing different ways of thinking closer to each other. Sarah Shannahan of RE-AMP realizes that it takes even network members one to two years to fully understand the reality of the network itself; visualization through mapping software shortens this process considerably.

Maps help people think in terms of systems. However, in order to come to use these tools effectively it is important to use *participatory processes* to bring the data generated to speak through the interaction of all stakeholders.

Weaving the Network

When the network has set out its intention and has been built up with care, a tipping point is reached where the community starts operating in a qualitatively different way. When the network core has been knitted, new network building activities can be introduced, such as the planning of annual meetings or offering of network workshops.

Questions to ask at this stage are: Does the network core include enough people/organizations? Does it embrace enough diversity, resources, and energy? How could it be improved? What important perspectives are missing?

The most important task at the beginning, and one of the highest forms of leadership, is that of a network weaver. The weaver not only connects people but also helps others do the same. The network weaver looks at everything that creates connection. The wider the spectrum of interpersonal ties, the better; these range from anything relating to professional challenges and successes to the individual's dreams and aspirations, without leaving aside hobbies and family interests.

Finally, network weaving is more than an activity. It can become a consciousness, a second nature of network members, and be part of every meeting, in person or online. Connection needs to be an integral part of the art of designing meetings. Each of these can be a mix of time devoted to content members care about and time to allow the forming of new connections and strengthening of existing ones.

Network Phases

We have already announced the general lines of evolution of a network in the connection-alignment-production cycle, and in the phases of knowing the network and weaving the network. On the other hand, and parallel to it, there is a movement toward greater complexity and decentralization. Let us look at these closer (See figure 31).

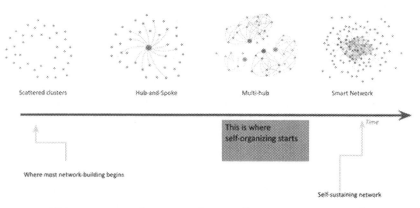

Figure 31: Development of a socially generative network
(Courtesy June Holley)

We can recognize some four basic stages in the building of a vibrant network. At each step the network acquires greater strength and adaptability, while increasing in complexity:

- Scattered Emergence
- Single Hub-and-Spoke
- Multi-Hub Small-World Network
- Core/Periphery[157]

We will follow this evolution in relation to the ACEnet, the Appalachian Center for Economic Networks in eastern and southeastern Ohio. The network's goal is to "grow the regional economy by supporting entrepreneurs and strengthening economic sectors."[158]

---

[157] Holley, *An Introduction to Network Weaving*, appendix 1.
[158] See https://acenetworks.org/about/mission-history/.

1) Scattered Emergence

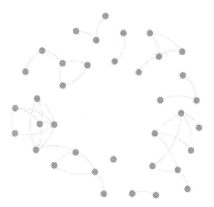

Figure 32: Scattered emergence

At this stage, which precedes intentional networking, there are weak clusters of activity, isolated from each other, of one to five people or organizations, connecting out of necessity—the system is poorly connected and weak. This is the place where a network weaver can detect a possibility and start fostering new interactions between the loose clusters.

Before ACEnet emerged in southeast Ohio, there were some food microentrepreneurs, farmers markets, and worker-owned restaurants. ACEnet started convening them through a state-of-the-art kitchen incubator for preparing and packaging a large variety of food items.

2) Single Hub-and-Spoke

Figure 33: Hub and spoke

The network weaver is the de-facto hub of the emerging network; she helps organizations and individuals connect, spreads information, sets up web-based platforms, and brings in resources and innovation. As said above, the weaver reaches to the disconnected clusters; she finds out about their expertise, needs, and challenges and helps them connect with others, so that they can then start doing the same on their own. The weaver knows that dependence upon herself should be only temporary. The goal is for her work to be picked up and replicated by others. Eventually her role can be taken by an organization—as is the role of the backbone organization in Collective Impact, as we will see shortly—and then spread out across the network.

In ACEnet's licensed incubator kitchen, there was access to ovens, stoves, a processing line, and storage space. ACEnet used the space to bring together restaurateurs with small farmers who wanted to transform their produce for added value. The farmers learned what they could produce from restaurateurs, and eventually sold it to them; the restaurateurs used the storage space for large orders from their suppliers.

The example of Vermont Farm to Plate brought up in Chapter 1 also belongs here. It closely corresponds to a Collective Impact scenario in which a "backbone organization" has been created to ensure and foster growing collaboration. The backbone organization does not do work for its members; rather, it aligns them around a common vision and coordinates their efforts through commonly devised goals, reinforcing activities, and measurement of outputs. Collective Impact coordination attempts to eliminate duplications, sterile competition, and gaps.

Another example of Collective Impact worth mentioning is what led to reforming New York State's juvenile justice system. Before 2010 the majority of incarcerated youths filled the prisons for misdemeanors and recidivism amounted to 90 percent, at a very high cost to New York taxpayers. Attempts at reform were initiated around 2010, but in the jungle of public and private agencies, organizations, and courts, no significant headway occurred. Recognizing the high complexity of the issue, Collective Impact was approached as an integrative methodology. Agency leaders from Albany and New York City decided to attempt a Collective Impact approach. Mapping the system, receiving the necessary input of all stakeholders, and building a common vision that balanced out community safety with youth

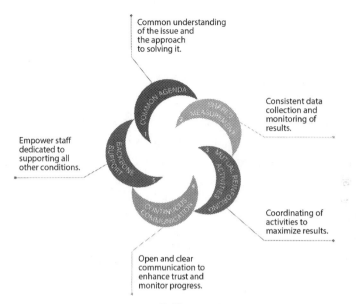

Figure 34: Collective Impact

education and rehabilitation took six months. The vision led to the "Close to Home" legislation signed into law in 2012. In the same year incarceration dropped by 24 percent, and between 2012 and 2013, 45 percent less youth were incarcerated, without increasing crime rates.[159]

3) Multihub Small-World Network

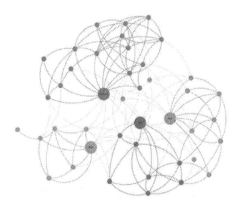

Figure 35: Multihub

[159] Emily Tow Jackson, "Reforming New York State's Juvenile Justice System," https://www.fsg.org/blog/return-investment-new-york-state-juvenile-justice-reform.

At this stage, various businesses and nonprofits start building their own network environment, expanding to new nodes and creating new links.

At each step of a network, the leadership style changes. To facilitate continuous emergence, the network weaver needs to step back from his initial role and become more of a network facilitator, especially in order to span across boundaries and divides, be it for simple and short-term collaborations or for more complex and long-term ones.

In the decentralized structure of a network, a single strong hub presents a limitation. Getting past this stage allows the formation of a multihub network. Having more than one hub eliminates the dependency upon and fragility of a single crucial link.

At this stage ACEnet taught others to weave the nodes within their neighborhood and expand the network to other areas of interest or geographic areas, even outside of Appalachia. The network started paying attention to the weaker ties between clusters. Similar groups within a cluster naturally shared a common focus and way of working. At the intersection of the clusters was found the potential for breakthrough and innovation. The network facilitator focused on connecting hubs to each other so that a greater flow of information and connection could give the network greater resiliency.

At this stage within ACEnet new hubs developed beyond the kitchen incubator, such as:

- a Farmer's Market Café set up by four local organizations, where people could network;
- a co-op-owned Mexican restaurant that played the role of hub among restaurateurs; and
- Big Chimney Bakery's proprietor, which helped entrepreneurs develop recipes and build their strategy.

Working toward its periphery, ACEnet developed "innovation learning clusters" (the equivalent of Communities of Practice), bringing together leading-edge organizations nationwide to share their innovations with each other. For the next stage, it is crucial to strengthen weak ties.

4) Core/Periphery

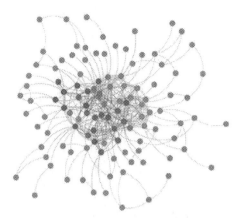

Figure 36: Core and periphery

Moving to the next phase is only possible after some years of working as a multihub network. Having acquired great resiliency, the network can now form links with other networks in its environment. At the periphery of such a network, June Holley finds three kinds of groups forming mostly weak links with the core:

- "The organizations new to the community and working to get to the core
- Bridges to diverse communities elsewhere
- Unique resources that operate outside of the community, and may span many communities"[160]

A sort of symbiotic relationship arises between core and periphery. From the edges flow to the center new information and ideas. The core can see where the greatest potential lies and act on it. The periphery allows the core to sense its larger environment. Too great of a density at the center without a living relationship to the margins carries the risk of both work overload and lack of flexibility.

The network facilitators' tasks consist now in maintaining activity at the core and building bridges with other networks, through their respective

---

[160] Holley, *An Introduction to Network Weaving*, 147.

peripheries. In the example of a network promoting local food systems, we will find at its periphery organizations whose focus includes food systems as a secondary concern. Such could be community development, health, environment, climate change organizations, and others. The contact with these additional concerns will allow the network to deliver new products and services. Together with others it will be in better position to strengthen advocacy in the region and promote policy.

When it reached the fourth stage, ACEnet and other organizations formed the Appalachian Ohio Regional Investment Coalition (AORIC) to empower and offer new supportive infrastructure for entrepreneurs who collaborate for a healthier regional economy.

Network Design Issues and Competencies

Everything that we have described so far does not give us a fuller understanding of the inner dimensions of networking, the critical elements of design. Among design issues are network purpose; membership; value propositions; coordination, facilitation, and communication; resources/funding; and infrastructure. We will turn to these before we look at governance and leadership and the competencies necessary for running a network.

Purpose

A network can be defined by a narrow and specific purpose or by a wider one. Either way, its statement of purpose should address three basic concerns:

- Who is the network for?
- What problem is it working on?
- What type of collaborative activities will the network undertake?

The alignment around the purpose and a coordination of resources and initiatives allow measurement of the evolving collective performance.

Membership

To entice member engagement and focus toward their goals, networks typically

- offer members a menu of varied activities in which to engage, possibly implying different levels of time and commitment;
- strive to engage the unengaged;
- bring new members on board in ways that accelerate their engagement, using ideas such as a buddy system, probationary period, and a requirement for a minimum level of participation;
- use engaging processes that involve members' collaboration and opportunities to know each other;
- monitor and enforce participation expectations; and
- raise participation standards.

Four basic characteristics are central to the building of an effective network: size, eligibility, type of membership, and requirements. Criteria most used for membership revolve around recognized expertise in the field, wealth of relevant connections, and capacity to collaborate and build the network. In networks that have organizations as members, these typically choose a representative to participate in the network.

Based on whether there would be different kinds of memberships, the requirements and benefits placed upon member organizations vary. The Central Appalachian Regional Network offers various levels of membership. There are founding, regular, and affiliate members. Both founding and regular members are organizations involved in a policy work group and in the sustainability of the network. Each member organization contributes one vote to decision making. Founding members have the additional benefit of veto power in admitting new members and in setting of network policies. Affiliate members also participate in a policy work group and are requested to support the network, but are not required to attend quarterly network meetings and monthly conference calls. Most of the affiliate member benefits lie in the added web of relationships, access to information, and opportunity to share ideas and research and create further connections.[161]

---

[161] Plastrik, Taylor, and Cleveland, *Connecting to Change the World*, Appendix A, 209–11.

Value Propositions (Benefits of Membership)

Value propositions—the mutual benefits accruing to network membership—increase in relation to a careful determination of purpose and choice of members.

Too wide of a purpose does not offer specific benefits or reasons to join and remain for its members. On the other hand, there needs to be a recognition that members look for varied value propositions. The selection of members is based upon the recognition of what value they each bring to the table, be it their expertise, connections, resources, or capacities. Thus, a skilled network builder will offer a palette of choices in adding value to the network, to increase the appeal to the newcomer, and the chances that members will meet others with whom they can collaborate.

The value proposition offered by RE-AMP at its inception was the mapping of the energy system, the availability of a Commons platform that allowed sharing of information in full transparency and coordination of initiatives, and the presence and concerted coordination of foundations.

Coordination, Facilitation, and Communication

All of the above issues address the way in which members will connect with each other. Coordination addresses the three issues that to some degree build upon each other: logistics, operations, and strategic management.

- Logistics cover everything that has to do with members' connectivity and sharing of information.
- Operations goes a step further in enabling logistics. It looks at the running of a website and the network's internal information platform, facilitating meetings of all kinds, extracting relevant information from and documenting network decisions, creating an archive of easily accessible documents, managing the network's finances, and applying for grants and funding.
- Strategic management looks at the development of the network itself. It supports those network members who assume network roles and responsibilities, and steers the network to its next stages of development. It loosely plans the directions toward which the network will evolve and explores the kinds of relationships with

partners and funders that the network needs most. Finally, it also supports network members.

Resources/Funding

Networks at the initial stages may have to rely on fees levied on their members and on sweat equity. Funding a network is still a novel initiative for a foundation. By definition a freshly started network has no track record, and in the initial stages it has to turn its resources to the building of its infrastructure and capacities rather than producing outcomes and impact. A new kind of funding outlook is needed, as the Garfield Foundation understood when it set out to design RE-AMP.

As soon as they can, networks will start to diversify their funding as much as possible, looking at different kinds of sources. They may turn to corporations to sponsor some of their ongoing operations, such as annual meetings or websites. Inviting some foundations to be part of the network and collaborating with them on projects seems to be an ideal symbiosis—as in the case of RE-AMP—for mutual learning and for aligning the funding more closely to the needs and uniqueness of generative social networks. Finally, networks have to be aware of the possibility of competition, since some of their members may be individually tapping funding from the same foundations.

Network Infrastructure

In terms of infrastructure, the following areas need to be addressed: gathering and spreading of information, staffing, education, and governance.

Gathering and spreading of information is vital at all stages of a network evolution. This means collecting and processing information of initiatives throughout the network. There needs to be a consistent recording, archiving, and reviewing of information supporting effective decision making.

Additional staffing should be considered, not only in relation to its present needs, but also with an eye toward the network's unavoidable evolution. Some of the tasks can be carried out by part of the network, by external consultants, or in partnerships with other organizations.

Central to a new way of working is the need for ongoing education in two directions: the learning that is necessary to improve initiatives on the ground, and the learning that allows adaptation to the new paradigm of emergence.

Matters of governance go hand in hand with handling of conflict and change, the scope of social technology. This is an area in which networks often lack sophistication. Setting in place systems thinking, and convening great variety of stakeholders, means being able to have moments of presencing through generative dialogue and envisioning conducted at all levels and in all mediums: in face-to-face meetings, teleconferences, online discussions, and local activities.

Network Culture: Participation and Planning

Key to the healthy development of a network over time is whether members learn to undertake actions with others, how much value is generated from connection, and how much decision making becomes a collective proposition.

Network weaving blends elements of top down and bottom up in completely new ways. "Without some element of governance from the top, bottom-up control will freeze when options are many. Without some element of leadership, the many at the bottom will be paralyzed with choices," argues Plastrik.[162] At the same time leadership would be completely counterproductive in a network if it were not exerted for the empowerment of the members. No need to have the network create outcomes for its members!

Planning a network means fostering and opening the doors to newly emerging possibilities. Long-term planning is the antithesis of this. A network will only plan for the relatively short time and primarily in two directions: projects in which the network sees future potential, and the evolution of the network as a whole. We could call this a "provisional planning" of the kind we have seen in Buurtzorg or in the organizations that have adapted Holacracy.

Networks work creatively at the edge of chaos, from which new order emerges. The network must be sensitive to the element of surprise from which creative outcomes can be generated. For this reason, it is crucial that facilitation and decision making do not shirk creative conflicts and seemingly disruptive conversations, from which uncharted territory can be

---

[162] Plastrik, Taylor, and Cleveland, *Connecting to Change the World*, 74.

explored. In the worst-case scenario new directions could be taken up by a splinter network that could keep collaborating with the mother network.

Putting It All Together: Network Governance and Management

Who decides and how is a crucial question in a network. Enabling self-governance and emergence dictates a flexible governance. Peter Plastrik and Steve Waddell advocate keeping governance informal for as long as possible, and letting it evolve organically. Here more than anywhere else, it is a matter of shifting from command and control to sense and respond. Three basic elements of governance are the who, the what, and the how:

- Who is enabled to decide? Most networks will design different kinds of memberships. Often, in larger networks, members will elect representatives to form a steering group that governs the network.
- What is decided? Here a balance needs be established between centralizing and decentralizing.
- How are decisions taken? Here we find great varieties of options, also depending on the stage of development of the network. Different forms may serve a function for a time. Among these are
  - Decisions by the funders: especially at the beginning, network engineers or a big funder set the tone for the directions the networks will take.
  - Decision by democracy: though easier to implement, this style will tend to perpetuate polarization that networks are built to defuse.
  - Decision by consensus: this can be by the members or by their representatives. But reaching consensus may cause unnecessary delays and unduly burdensome decision making.
  - Decision by emergence: this has the advantage of organically letting members decide where they want to place their energy and participate in decision making that directly affect them, rather than on all matters. It can ideally maximize efficiency and participation, while building trust in the dynamics of self-organizing.

Ultimately, socially generative networks tend to evolve toward decisions by emergence.

Leadership / Stewardship

We have already highlighted the role of the network weaver/coordinator and the evolution into network facilitator. More can be said in terms of leadership and the network culture that it strives to build.

Socially generative networks work purely voluntarily. A central authority works as well as no authority. Rather, a network is at its best when leadership is encouraged and distributed in all parts of the system. Highly participatory processes and a shared understanding of and buy-in into the vision are prerequisites. Moreover, the highly fluid and paradoxical nature of networks calls for an evolving style of leadership at each of the stages of their development.

Steve Waddell argues that with such a paradigm shift from traditional organizational structures, even the word *leader* is inappropriate, and he prefers the word *steward*. A network steward leads from behind; he does not look at outcomes but fosters the conditions for a network to fulfill its greatest potential. He needs to be alive to the moment and be able to anticipate future needs.

Such are the skills that are required of an ideal steward that they may seem an unrealistic or unattainable goal, but that is also why such stewardship should better be pursued with a team spirit. Among key qualities a network steward needs to have are some of the following:

- Mindful: A steward can form quality connections, looks at assumptions with detachment, is eager to explore and to learn from experience.
- Collaborative and entrepreneurial: A steward knows how to engage with others, convert opportunities into concrete initiatives, and come up with innovative solutions and carry them through.
- Leaderful: This goes a small step further than the above in as much as a steward is self-assured and confident in herself and therefore able to be compassionate with and trusting of others. A steward must find ways to reconnect people to the network's vision.

- "Systems intelligent": A steward is continuously aware of how she is part of an interconnected system and of the influence that its culture has on her and the other way around. Being able to tolerate paradox and uncertainty is a given condition of network evolution.
- Modest: A steward, just like a facilitator at a smaller scale, works best when he is least seen; he offers praise and distributes appreciation, but may not get much recognition himself. My experience with RE-AMP in the Midwest is that the network doesn't claim much visibility with the larger public, nor does it want to overshadow its member organizations. It is there to empower and highlight members' success.

Steve Waddell concludes, "To develop such qualities requires a lifelong commitment to grow as a human being in ways not well understood in contemporary culture."[163] Table 37 compares organizational leadership and network stewardship.

The Paradigm Shift Beyond Top Down or Bottom Up

Socially generative networks have emerged from a systems thinking that welcomes complexity, and they mirror complexity themselves. They want to become self-organizing living systems.

Networks operate at the boundary between order and chaos; hence the necessity of continuously seeking new states of balance at each step of evolution. The tendency toward chaos is maximized when members exert their independence, pursuing their own goals; order appears as a state of emergence when connection leads to alignment and common pursuits.

Chaos is an inescapable necessity from which, as in living systems, networks find renewed vitality. When a network goes from one hub to multiple hubs, chaos leads to a new place of order; the same when a network enters into partnerships with its periphery. This is the condition of living with paradox and uncertainty, which is part of the continuous creativity needed to converge autonomous, self-seeking members toward collective goals—"the paradox of combining intentionality (that comes with the development of

---

[163] Waddell, *Global Action Networks*, 152.

a common agenda) and emergence (that unfolds through collective seeing, learning and doing)."[164] This edge-of-chaos tension requires a balancing act: too much planning can reduce the network's openness to emergence, while too little planning can reduce the network's capacity for cohesive, collective action. The activity of planning itself acquires a different relevance; plans are made for the short term, and the quality of the planning is more important than the results themselves.

Networks span boundaries. Their operational mindset, argues Waddell, goes beyond the leadership logic of each sector: the *administering* of laws and rules for government; *managing* with the sight of goals in business; *co-developing* with much community input familiar to civil society.[165] Networks must emerge with something that is not only one of the above, but rather a mix of the above, even when their work is set within just one sector. *Ability to connect* is central to what a network can do, between individuals, organizations, and sectors.

We could say that, contrary to organizations with a set, prevailing structure, networks' nature is that of an evolving process rather than of a structure. The cycle of connecting, alignment, and production reflects the archetypal pattern of the U, seen in Chapter 3. At the stage of connecting, members are co-sensing. In alignment a breakthrough of presencing is rendered possible, which leads to a determined common goal and common agenda. Producing leads the network into co-creating on the other side of the U. We could say that networks are social entities that move collectively and continuously through a U process.

Going through the new means creating a new collective culture, one of whose aspects has been called "complex reciprocity" or "generalized reciprocity," which leads to networks being the foundation of a gift economy. Members are continuously sharing with others their time, resources, knowledge, and connections, without expecting a return. "When this member-to-member exchange happens, the network's structural advantages magnify the value of the gifts, efficiently spreading the benefit to other members who, in turn, enhance it and spread it even further. As a result, members don't just bond with the members with whom they have engaged;

---

[164] Plastrik, Taylor, and Cleveland, *Connecting to Change the World*, 136.
[165] Waddell, *Global Action Networks*, 150.

they develop a feeling for, a loyalty toward, and a willingness to support the network as a whole."[166]

Incremental Change and Reform	Emergence leading to Transformation
Imagines and works well within predictable scenarios	Encompasses disruption leading to emergence
Either efficiency (entrepreneurial spirit) or inclusion (democratic spirit) paramount, but rarely both	Seeks both efficiency and inclusion
Long-term planning	Self-organizing, short-term planning
Organizational forms are mostly top down, sometimes bottom up (pure consensus)	New forms that are neither top down or bottom up
Forms are given and evolve slowly	Forms are meant to continuously evolve
Organization as a mechanical model	Organization as a living organism
Leadership, including servant leadership	Stewardship

Table 37: From reform to emergence and transformation

Table 37 summarizes the findings of this chapter.

---

[166] Plastrik, Taylor, and Cleveland, *Connecting to Change the World*, 38.

Resources

Books and Articles

June Holley, *Introduction to Network Weaving*, (Athens, OH: Network Weaver Publishing, 2013). https://networkweaver.com/network-weaving-handbook/.

June Holley, Network Weaver blog, https://networkweaver.com/category/blog/.

Peggy Holman, *Engaging Emergence: Turning Upheaval into Opportunity* (San Francisco: Berrett-Koehler, 2010).

Frederic Laloux, *Reinventing Organizations, an illustrated Invitation to Join the Conversation on Next-Stage Organizations* (Brussels: Nelson Parker, 2016).

Heather McLeod Grant, *Transformer: How to Build a Network to Change a System: A Case Study of the RE-AMP Energy Network*, Monitor Institute, https://www.reamp.org/wp-content/uploads/2014/01/Monitor-Institute-RE-AMP-Case-Study.pdf.

Peter Plastrik, Madeleine Taylor, and John Cleveland, *Connecting to Change the World: Harnessing the Power of Networks for Social Impact* (Washington, DC: Island Press, 2014).

Brian J. Robertson, *Holacracy: The New Management System for a Rapidly Changing World* (New York: Henry Holt, 2015).

Marina Sitrin, ed., *Horizontalism: Voices of Popular Power in Argentina* (Oakland, CA: AK Press, 2006).

Spark Policy Institute and ORS Impact, *When Collective Impact Has an Impact: A Cross-Site Study of 25 Collective Impact Initiatives*, 2018. http://sparkpolicy.com/wp-content/uploads/2018/02/CI-Study-Report_February-2018.pdf.

Steve Waddell, *Global Action Networks: Creating Our Future Together* (New York: Palgrave Macmillan, 2011).

Videos

Argentina: Hope in Hard Times

"Something extraordinary happened in Argentina after the economic collapse [2001]. With times so difficult people could have turned on each other in fear and desperation but instead they turned to each other in mutual support.... Ordinary people took it upon themselves to make their country look more like their dreams." From cover of the DVD *Argentina: Hope in Hard Times*, a must-see documentary.[167] The video refers to the birth and achievements of so-called Argentine Horizontalism.[168]

The Take

To have an idea of what a process of a *toma* involves, see the compelling documentary *The Take* from director Avi Lewis and writer Naomi Klein.[169] It follows day by day the story of 30 Buenos Aires auto-parts workers putting to use their idle factory and seeking legal recognition. The movie is a real-life thriller following a process that is fluid and far from easy.[170]

Zapatista

This documentary follows the emergence of a self-organizing movement that celebrates and affirms the cultural independence of indigenous communities in southern Mexico, and their subordination of the political process to their cultural identity.[171] In 1996 the Zapatista National Liberation Army (EZLN) fought against the North American Free Trade Agreement. Sustainable development and cultural identity stood against the erosion

---

[167] http://www.bullfrogfilms.com/catalog/arg.html.
[168] See also https://luigimorelli.wordpress.com/2009/06/14/argentinas-horizontalism/.
[169] http://www.thetake.org/.
[170] See https://luigimorelli.wordpress.com/2009/06/19/argentina-horizontalism-ideas-for-a-new-economy/.
[171] https://www.kanopy.com/product/zapatista.

of sovereignty and the race to the bottom line enshrined in the globalist political agenda and NAFTA.

Trainings and Resources

Buurtzorg International:
https://www.buurtzorg.com/collaboration/

Collective Impact trainings:
http://www.collectiveimpact.com/page.php?num=460

Holacracy trainings:
https://www.holacracy.org/events/view-all

Network Impact: http://www.networkimpact.org/

Networking Action: https://networkingaction.net/

Network Weaver: https://networkweaver.com/events/

In Conclusion

Giving Birth to a New Social Culture

When you set out for Ithaka
ask that your way be long,
full of adventure, full of instruction. . . .

Ithaka gave you the marvelous journey.
Without her you wouldn't have set out.
She has nothing left to give you now.

And if you find her poor, Ithaka won't have fooled you.
Wise as you will have become, so full of experience,
you'll have understood by then what these Ithakas mean.

Constantine P. Cavafy

WE ARRIVE AT THE END of this exploration. The three paradigms we have explored all form radical departures from business as usual. We can call them three separate paradigms or else see them as three parts of the articulation of a new culture, when we define culture as something more than a set of values, no matter how great these could be. Indeed a new culture establishes and enlivens new values, but it is something more than the values themselves.

We have approached culture as a series of paradigms that set out in contrast to the existing predicament. Everything we have been exploring put together forms the stepping stones of a new culture, a new way of seeing the human being, one that moves away from dualism and determinism to something more. Let's put this on hold for now, until we review the three propositions one by one, and acquire a larger perspective.

Reviewing the Whole

In Chapter 2 we looked at length of the shift from a bipolar society to a tripolar one, from a logic of confrontation to one of dialogue, no matter how vigorous this may be at first. We can approach this stance from a purely pragmatic angle, but need not stop there. We can move from a purely functional stance to a place in which we reach that form of social thinking that transcends and includes, one that sees beyond either sets of seeming opposites, one that is not content to intellectually engage with just one side of a polarity. We gave Martin Luther King Jr's Hegelianism as an example of that.

MLK saw what society presents as two terms of an impelling choice as nothing more than thesis and antithesis. He saw no reason to stop there, when he knew that the synthesis transcends and includes the terms of the polarity-thesis and antithesis. This is in effect a thinking of both/and that contrasts with the either/or thinking that the modern mind knows almost exclusively. We have a choice: with effort we can shift from one to the other; from what is easier and familiar in ourselves to what is more productive and ultimately closer to reality but requires a creative effort. To this effort follows the possibility of unleashing the imagination beyond the ordinary prescribed formulas of the ideologies of the twentieth century and their present legacy.

In Chapter 3 we looked at what it means to meet the whole human being. We started from the experiential premise acknowledging that we are beings of head, heart, and hands. It is only when we meet as such full human beings that we can recognize each other's full humanity and transcend what opposes one group of stakeholders to another. This implies a shift that can be articulated in a variety of ways. When we embrace the social practices such as those of social technology, we realize that we do not live in a social world of cause and effect, of wrong views against right views, nor of saints and villains, no matter how nuanced and subtle this discourse may become in academic terms. It seems closer to reality to argue that we live in webs of relationships in which we weave patterns and dynamics. Those may collectively help us or hinder us, affirm life or stifle it. Since they are dynamics and patterns in which we are all involved, and which we all tend to perpetuate, we can only move forward and transform them with a systemic approach. This is what has been called the multi-stakeholder approach. And the change that needs to happen at this level is one of deep, inner felt attitudes. What I say here in the pages of a book may seem so easy as to sound trite; applying it to real life and making it one's own is much harder. Let us look at the finished product, if we can call it such.

To one who truly believes that he cannot demonize his fellow human beings, social issues need to be tackled with the largest possible variety of stakeholders. Instead of fearing adverse reactions (an old way of thinking), we will be welcoming missing perspectives. Instead of desiring to "win" against the opposition, we can ask ourselves in which way we can best hear each other and build upon each other's perspectives. Instead of priding ourselves of having stuck to the same ideas for all of our lives, we would welcome the changes we can experience in ourselves in truly hearing somebody else's perspective. Instead of prevailing, we will look forward to creating a new reality that has not been previously envisioned; in fact, one that nobody could have conceived of previously.

In Chapter 4 we looked at new ways of overcoming the social structures of the past. Hierarchies are the most obvious, but "bottomocracies," even though rare, can be just as insidious. We called this the paradigm of emergence, which occurs when something old starts crumbling and new forms emerge that cannot be predicted from the past, even though they will carry some metamorphosed elements of it in new forms. It's the paradigm of encouraging and nurturing what naturally emerges, what wants to self-organize. In Sociocracy the two forms (top down and bottom up) are kept in check. In Holacracy there is no such a need because a form has arisen that is not the opposite of top down or bottom up, but something of an emergent nature, something completely new. We can recognize something of the top down but in a refined/sublimated fashion: the deeply entrepreneurial and leaderful spirit that Holacracy promotes. And we can recognize something of the bottom up in how the form privileges the whole and leaves little room for power plays and ego. We have seen the contrast between the familiar tree structure and the nested circles. That's the most eloquent illustration of departure from the old.

What is done in one organization can be carried further at the level of networks of organizations, in that delicate dance of balancing all sorts of tensions so that the many can work for the common good by minimizing competition, duplication, gaps, and redundancies. Furthermore, we can bring the many to act with agility at a variety of scales simultaneously, at undertaking initiative where new possibilities emerge, at promoting the entrepreneurial spirit and the awareness of the common good throughout the system.

Building a New Culture

All of the above paradigms conjugate the reality of both/and instead of either/or. They integrate and transcend two seemingly opposite poles in front of which we most often feel compelled to choose. And this is where we need to challenge ourselves for deeper understanding. The paradigm of both/and does not oppose the old paradigm of either/or. Otherwise it would be another either/or ideological position such as "We stand for both/and, therefore we oppose either/or." Since the idea of opposing is so ingrained, what would change look like from an either/or stance?

Let's go back to the subtitle of this book: *changing ourselves as we impact the world*. The old paradigm is that of the spectator. Incremental change or reform need not involve us in the first person. Here we are simply talking of changing something in the world. We devise a strategy of change, we coordinate our efforts, and we apply it. The world changes without our needing to change.

In the new paradigm we are positing that the greatest change in the world comes from the greatest changes a number of us can achieve in ourselves. Mind you, these changes happen in ourselves as we act and bring change in the world. This is a paradigm of participatory consciousness, no longer the detached stance of the spectator consciousness, which has been natural to the zeitgeist of our time up to now.

Let us try to picture what participatory consciousness will imply. Changing ourselves as we change the world means allowing ourselves to be touched by the pain of what we are part of that we want to transform.

In wrestling with that pain and participating in the change, we become aware of the beauty of looking at the world in a new way, even in the midst of pain, not to mention the impact we can generate and see from acting in new ways. As this grows we can carry in ourselves two perfectly opposite feelings constructively vying within ourselves, to which we could give two voices. Voice 1 could mourn all of the misery and ugliness that touches us and impels us to seek change by allowing ourselves to be impacted. Voice 2 would emerge after some practice. It could grow in us with the realization of how much we can achieve when we think differently and act together from new places within ourselves. We will more and more be part of that reality we want to construct, of islands of beauty, even if these were in the midst of seas of dreariness. We will be nourished by what we can learn from living within and experimenting from the new paradigms. Straddling the edges of paradigms on a regular basis is also what allows us to understand that we are never part of one without being part of the other. We are really part of both/and. Over time the pain, hurt, anger, and rage will lessen; the beauty and joy of what we want to build and who we want to become will increase. Voice 1 will recede; voice 2 will sing with a louder voice. But both will continue to live side by side in a creative tension.

The above sum of the parts is another both/and. The three paradigms put together spell out what it takes to create a new culture, not just some new or better values. It is truly a cultural shift that defines a new way of being human: from a spectator consciousness to a participatory consciousness. Obviously it is a path that needs to be walked, not a platform that can be broadcast or a slogan that can be shouted. It is slow work that will take time and patience.

The culture-building aspect of the paradigms deserves closer scrutiny. What we have explored corresponds to the discovery of human, universal archetypes derived from extended observation. Together they contribute to redefining what it means to be human and to be an individual in our time. This universal cultural aspect of the paradigms does not derive from either dogma or tradition. These are entirely new propositions for renewing culture that can be applied anywhere in the world. And it should be added that these universal aspects of what it means to be human do not stand in contrast or opposition to the various local aspects of culture.

This book has explored the difference between political and cultural change. Cultural change takes longer to build up and requires that deep inner shift that is not necessary in political change. However, a simple look at history can prove that cultural change is much more long lasting than political change. In *Legends and Stories for a Compassionate America* I explored the tidal change generated on the Eastern seaboard by the Haudenosaunee Confederacy; its genesis is estimated to the fifteenth century, and its beneficial impacts were lessened only because of European disruption. Closer to us, no movement has been as impactful on American values as the civil rights movement, a deeply culture-shaping movement, as I have argued here and more extensively in the same book.

Which One Is Your Strength?

I will argue that each of us naturally has something we can do best, one of the three paradigms in which we can find ourselves at home, one that we are most naturally attracted to. That is often the best place to start from: recognizing our natural strength and inclination, cultivating and deepening it.

Simply ask yourself: Which paradigm do I already know, or which one speaks most to me? And when you have determined which one it is, try to imagine what would be your "course of study" look like. In this I would include for example books, a variety of approaches, workshops leading to practice, learning journeys to the places of greatest interest, and conversations with people who have expertise.

In addition to the above, you can ask yourself: Which other paradigm will I explore next? Which one do I feel reticent about? How can I lessen the distance to this paradigm, knowing that I will not be exploring it in depth any time soon? How can I prepare myself for another round of transformation? How can I lay the groundwork for collaborating with those who are familiar with the paradigms I know least?

Expanding Our Horizons by Embracing
the Three Paradigms

In the fieldwork leading to the writing of this book, I have offered a slide presentation that illustrated how change in the food system could be approached from three different perspectives. From this firsthand experience I detected the following phenomena. The public with whom I discussed these matters could either primarily recognize the social imaginations on one hand, social processes on the other, or a combination of these. When I looked further afield, I could see that social processes form a bridge between social imaginations and social forms. We have seen this in the previous chapters.

On one side, when we recognize the importance of the three sectors from a purely practical perspective, change can only happen if we can convene a variety of stakeholders from the three sectors through very carefully structured interventions requiring generative conversations.

On the other hand, people working from the perspective of new social forms—Sociocracy, Holacracy and Buurtzorg are the examples we met— necessarily encounter the question of adopting new social processes that favor self-organizing and emergence.

This book predicates that of course it is difficult to see the panorama of the three paradigms, let alone acquire a degree of proficiency and mastery in each one of them, but bringing them together is a necessity if we want to accelerate social change.

Conjugating the Three Paradigms for
More Effective Social Change

Now that we are coming to the end of the exploration, I want to tentatively share what has emerged for me in the course of the four months of on the road exploration. There is something organic about the articulation of the three paradigms. They show their faces in between the lines of what is said, and when this happens, they can be invited consciously, potentizing the conversation. We have seen in the previous chapters that each one of them implies a transition from an either/or to a both/and zeitgeist. And, when

I look at them, I see that they build up the whole of a new panorama for achieving social change.

In the first instance we are talking about multi-sector order of reality. And when we push this reality to its logical conclusion, we are entering a new realm of social ideas. We are moving from a reality of dualism and opposition of the number two (business versus government) to one of dialogue and balance of the number three (business, government, and civil society). Unlike the ideologies of the past, this is an organic, encompassing thinking that transcends the spectator consciousness that can fashion ideas oftentimes regardless of their grounding in reality. If it is truly organic, living thinking, then we have those that we can call *social imaginations*. They are not recipes for action; rather, they are springboards for freeing the imagination in the direction of unprecedented action. A better understanding of reality offers much more than ideology or theory can formulate, but it needs to be approached differently. It has to be worked through and digested more thoroughly, and it only works within a given context: social change in the United States is different from change in the United Kingdom, in the East Coast different from the West Coast.

In the second instance we are talking about new ways of relating and collaborating. Here we are overcoming the adversarial stances that find their most explicit manifestation in radical polarization, of which the United States presents one of the most obvious examples in the present. Being immersed in that reality requires from each one of us quite an effort to humanize those who are at the other end of a spectrum, most of all the political, but also the religious and cultural. The multi-stakeholder level of reality offers us the opportunity to change enemy pictures, to change the way we feel about other people, and to establish new relationships. Social technology has most of all to do with *social processes*. The old social processes of opposition can be replaced with the differentiation and integration of all meaningful and willing stakeholders. Majority/minority dynamics can give way to supermajorities.

Our social reality needs to be conceived more organically. The way we relate to social actors needs to move towards greater inclusion and fuller participation through social processes designed toward the meeting of the whole person. So what is left?

The reality of emergence offers us the possibility of moving away from old forms and structures toward new ones. The old is crumbling and a new reality is *emerging* that we can only very partially surmise from what we know of the past. Sociocracy, Holacracy, Buurtzorg, Horizontalism, socially generative networks—all of these speak about new *social forms*.

The stance of waiting for change to come through the existing structures can be overcome by taking initiative immediately. We do not need to wait for a new president, for a new political majority, for our organization to change to dare to take action. Jos de Blok did not need to wait for the health system to change in the Netherlands when he decided to start Buurtzorg; Precision Nutrition is bringing about a shift of great dimension in food habits; Vermont Farm to Plate, Energy Action Network in Vermont, and RE-AMP are affecting change without waiting for political permission. This means we can all step into the reality of new social forms. It certainly does take courage.

The above is a natural progression. Once we conceive of social reality differently—through a qualitatively different kind of thinking—and once we relate to all social actors in a qualitatively different way, it is only natural to expect that qualitatively different social forms will emerge. Social imaginations, social processes, and social forms are part of a natural sequence leading from vision to action.

The most common way of seeing social reality at present derives from a theory of change that explicitly or implicitly reconnects with either of socialistic or capitalistic models, or mixes and matches of the two. We are saying that the greatest possibility for change derives from none of the above, from thinking organically and deliberately outside of the box; from thinking out of the past to thinking out of the future.

The most common way to manifest change at the social level happens through the political process. It requires moving from being a minority to acquiring a majority. We are saying here that this model was necessary and appropriate until the present. We can now start to think about working with large areas of consensus and with supermajorities.

All social organizational models up until the present have been hierarchical or equalitarian. This exploration has shown that they are two sides of the same coin. The way out of hierarchical trees is not an equalitarian,

229

flat organization that rests on the same logic, though at the other end of the spectrum. The way out lies in liberating energy towards self-organization, mimicking natural systems in which there is both autonomy of the part and subordination to the whole: nested circles instead of trees.

Each of the three ways of looking at the world is a whole. But that doesn't mean that each, taken purely on its own, cannot be one-sided.

Listening to the Future

This book has not discovered anything new. It has simply gathered strands that are of great promise for the social future. We are presently immersed in irreversible processes of dissolution and destruction. This would seem enough reason to give up. However, what has the capacity to subvert reality as we know it (a paradigm) can also reverse what appears irreversible. It can do this, not by restoring the past, but by moving into new evolutionary stages. To this we have given the name of *emergence*. The three paradigms nurture the dissolution of the old and the emergence of the new.

In conclusion, this book has been an exploration, just a primer. The greatest gift it has offered the author, which in turn I want to offer to the reader, is that of showing us that at the eleventh hour, we have all we need to turn the corner. All the tools that we need already exist, and we have explored some of them. This doesn't mean that change is easy. The resources in each chapter and your own curiosity will direct you to what you specifically need in your field of interest and action.

And not just that. Everything you need in order to accelerate change is also what can enable you to operate from a place of greater creativity and presence. It will allow you to embody change to a greater extent than has been possible so far from an evolutionary standpoint. May you fully be the visionary and change agent you wish to be! May the end of this journey be the beginning of many others.

Bibliography

Atlee, Tom. *Empowering Public Wisdom: A Practical Vision of Citizen-Led Politics.* Berkeley, CA: Evolver Editions, 2012.

Brown, Juanita and David Isaacs. *The World Café: Shaping Our Futures through Conversations That Matter.* San Francisco: Berrett-Koehler Publishers, 2005.

Buck, John and Villines, Sharon. *We the People: Consenting to a Deeper Democracy.* Washington DC: Sociocracy Info, 2007.

Cooperrider, David L., Whitney, Diana and Stavros, Jacqueline M. *Appreciative Inquiry Handbook for Leaders of Change,* Second Edition. San Francisco: Berrett-Koehler Publishers, 2008.

Dressler, Larry. *Consensus Through Conversation: How to Achieve High-Commitment Decisions.* San Francisco: Berrett-Koehler Publishers, 2006.

Fallow, James. The Atlantic, May 2018 issue, "Americans don't realize how fast the country is moving toward becoming a better version of itself". See https://www.theatlantic.com/magazine/archive/2018/05/reinventing-america/556856/

Friedman, Thomas L., July 3, 2018. "Where American Politics Can Still Work: From the Bottom Up Civic coalitions are succeeding at revitalizing old towns where governmental efforts have failed." See https://www.openpolitics.com/links/where-american-politics-can-still-work-from-the-bottom-up/

Graeber, David. *Enacting the Impossible: On Consensus Decision-making* in The Occupied Wall Street Journal, Saturday October 22, 2011.

Groh, Trauger and McFadden, Steven. *Farms of Tomorrow Revisited: Community Supported Farms—Farm Supported Communities*. San Francisco: Biodynamic Farming Association, 2000.

Henderson, Elizabeth and Van En, Robyn. *Sharing the Harvest: A Citizen's Guide to Community Supported Agriculture*, revised and expanded version. White River Junction, VT: Chelsea Green Publishing Company, 2007.

Holley, June. *An Introduction to Network Weaving*. Athens, OH.: Network Weaver Publishing, 2013.

Holman, Peggy. *Engaging Emergence: Cultivating Leadership for Complex Times*. San Francisco: Berrett-Koehler Publishers, 2010.

Holman, Peggy, Devane, Tom and Cady, Steven. *The Change Handbook: The Definitive Resource on Today's Best Methods for Enlarging Whole Systems*. San Francisco: Berrett-Koehler Publishers, 2007.

Jaworski, Joseph, Flowers, Betty Sue editor. *Synchronicity, the Inner Path of Leadership*. San Francisco: Berrett-Koehler Publishers, 1996.

Jenkins Jon C. and Jenkins, Maureen R. *The Social Process Triangles*. Toronto: Canadian Institute of Cultural Affairs: 1997, out of print.

Kunkler, Tracy. *The Path Forward is Under Our Feet*, Dec 30, 2016; see https://www.circleforward.us/2016/12/30/the-path-forward-is-under-our-feet/

Laloux, Frederic. *Reinventing Organizations*, illustrated version. USA/UK: Nelson Parker, 2016.

Lamb, Gary. *Wellsprings of the Spirit; Free Human Beings as the Source of Social Renewal*. Association of Waldorf Schools of North America, 2007.

Large, Martin. *Common Wealth for a Free, Equal, Mutual and Sustainable Society*. Stroud, UK: Hawthorn Press, 2010.

Meter, Ken. *Building Community Food Webs*. Washington, Covelo: Island Press, 2021.

Meter Ken and Phillips Goldenberg, Megan. *Commodity system creates persistent losses*, Organic Broadcaster, Volume 27 | Number 2, Midwest Organic & Sustainable Education Service, March | April 2019. See https://mosesorganic. org/wp-content/uploads/2019/03/MOSES-Broadcaster27.2-for-web.pdf

Mintzberg, Henry. *Rebalancing Society: Radical Renewal Beyond Left, Right and Center*. San Francisco: Berrett-Koehler Publishers, 2015.

Morelli, Luigi

- *A Revolution of Hope: Spirituality, Cultural Renewal and Social Change.* Victoria B.C., Canada: Trafford, 2009.
- *Legends and Stories for a Compassionate America.* Bloomington, IN: Open Books Editions of Berrett Koehlers/iUniverse, 2014.
- *Visions for a Compassionate America.* Bloomington, IN: Open Books Editions of Berrett Koehlers/iUniverse, 2015.

Oates, Stephen B. *Let the Trumpet Sound: A Life of Martin Luther King.* NY: Harper Collins Publishers, 1982.

Owen, Harrison. *Open Space Technology: A User's* Guide. San Francisco: Berrett Koehlers Publishers, 2008.

Perlas, Nicanor:

- *Associative Economics: Responding to the Challenge of Elite Globalization.* Quezon city, Philippines: Center for Alternative Development Initiatives, out of print.
- *Shaping Globalization: Civil Society, Cultural Power and Threefolding.* Forest Row, UK: Temple Lodge, 2019.

Plastrik, Peter, Taylor, Madeleine and Cleveland, John. *Connecting to Change the World: Harnessing the Power of Networks for Social Impact.* Washington DC: Island Press, 2014.

Pollan, Michael. *The Omnivore's Dilemma: A Natural History of Four Meals.* New York: The Penguin Press, 2006.

Rau, Ted J. and Koch-Gonzalez, Jerry. *Many Voices One Song: Shared Power with Sociocracy.* Amherst, MA: Sociocracy for All, 2018.

Rush, Cynthia R. "Cartels' Soy Revolution Kills Argentine Farming," *Executive Intelligence Review*, November 19, 2004. See: https://larouchepub.com/other/2004/3145soy_argentina.html

Scharmer, Otto. *Theory U: Leading from the Emerging Future; The Social Technology of Presencing.* Cambridge, MA.: Society for Organizational Learning, 2007.

Schroeder, Nathan. *How it came about, what it means, how it works and everything else you need to know about Occupy Wall Street*, in The Nation of September 29, 2011: https://www.thenation.com/article/occupy-wall-street-faq/

Senge, Peter. *The Necessary Revolution: Working Together to Create a Sustainable World.* New York: Broadway Books, 2010.

Senge, Peter, Scharmer, Otto, Jaworski, Joseph and Flowers, Betty Sue. *Presence: Exploring Profound Change in People, Organizations and Society.* New York: Doubleday, 2004.

Sitrin, Marina.

- *Horizontalism: Voices of Popular Power in Argentina.* Oakland, CA: AK Press, 2006.
- Ruptures in imagination: Horizontalism, autogestion and affective politics in Argentina in Policy and Practice, a Development Education Review, Issue 5, Autumn 2007: https://www.developmenteducationreview.com/issue/issue-5/ruptures-imagination-horizontalism-autogestion-and-affective-politics-argentina

Stanfield, R. Brian.

- *The Courage to Lead: Transform Self, Transform Society.* Canadian Institute of Cultural Affairs: Toronto, 2000.
- *The Art of Focused Conversation: 100 Ways to Access Group Wisdom in the Workplace.* Gabriola Island, Canada: New Society Publishers, 2000.

Waddell, Steve:

- *Societal Learning and Change: How Governments, Business and Civil Society are Creating Solutions to Complex Multi-Stakeholder Problems.* Sheffield, UK: Greenleaf Publishing, 2005.
- *Global Action Networks: Creating Our Future Together.* New York: Palgrave Macmillan, 2011.

Weisbord, Marvin and Janoff, Sandra:

- *Don't Just Do Something, Stand There; Ten Principles for Leading Meetings That Matter,* San Francisco, CA: Berrett-Koehler Publishers Inc., 2007.
- *Future Search: An Action Guide to Finding Common Ground in Organizations and Communities,* second edition, San Francisco: Berrett-Koehler Publishers, 2000.

Weisman, Alan. *Gaviotas: A Village to Reinvent the World.* White River Junction, VT: Chelsea Green Publishing Company, 1998.

Wheatley, Margaret J. *Leadership and the New Science: Discovering Order in a Chaotic World.* San Francisco: Berrett-Koehler Publishers, 1999.

Online Documents

Chapter 1

Food Systems

http://buschberghof.de/wirtschaftsgemeinschaft/solidarische-landwirtschaft/.

https://luigimorelli.wordpress.com/2019/05/05/systems-thinking-at-the-state-level-relish-rhody-a-food-strategy-for-rhode-island-the-steps/.

https://foodsolutionsne.org/new-england-food-vision

Vermont Farm to Plate

"VT Farm to Plate 2016 Annual Report": https://www.vtfarmtoplate.com/ uploads/Farm%20to%20Plate%202016%20Annual%20Report_FINAL.pdf? utm_source=Copy+of+Vermont+Food+System+News%253A+January+ 2017&utm_campaign=January+Farm+to+Plate+Newsletter&utm_ medium=email

"Gathering the Herd: a Vermont Meat Processing Case Study", Carrie Abels, 2017: https://www.vtfarmtoplate.com/assets/activities/files/F2P%20 Meat%20Processing%20Case%20Study_FINAL%206.20.17-1.pdf

"VT Farm to Plate Energy Success Stories": https://www.vtfarmtoplate.com/ resources/farm-to-plate-energy-success-stories-released

"Cookie Royalty: How Liz Lovely used royalty financing to grow a pace that made sense": https://www.vtfarmtoplate.com/assets/resource/files/ Financing%20Case%20Studies_Liz%20Lovely_June%202015.pdf;

"Complex Dough: How Bread and Butter farm worked with a patchwork quilt of funding sources to keep land conserved for agriculture": https://www. vtfarmtoplate.com/assets/resource/files/Financing%20Case%20Studies_ Bread%20and%20Butter%20Farm_FEB%202015.pdf; Seeding the Future with

"Convertible Debt: How High Mowing Organic Seeds used convertible debt to plan wisely for its future and keep fueling its growth": https://www. vtfarmtoplate.com/assets/resource/files/Financing%20Case%20Studies_ High%20Mowing%20Organic%20Seeds_Sep%202014.pdf

https://www.dudleyneighbors.org/ for general information; https://www. yesmagazine.org/economy/2015/09/17/land-trusts-offer-houses-low-income-people-can-afford-and-a-stepping-stone-to-lasting-wealth/

Dwyer, Lee. "Mapping Impact: An Analysis of the Dudley Street Neighborhood Initiative Land Trust." Masters Thesis. MIT Department of Urban Studies and Planning, 2015: https://www.dsni.org/for-researchers

Chapter 2

"How Martin Luther King, Jr. Used Nietzsche, Hegel & Kant to Overturn Segregation in America": http://www.openculture.com/2015/02/how-martin-luther-king-jr-used-hegel-to-overturn-segregation-in-america.html

Chapter 3

Vogt, Eric E., Brown, Juanita and Isaacs, David. *The Art of Powerful Questions: Catalyzing Insight, Innovation, and Action,* 2003. See https://umanitoba.ca/admin/human_resources/change/media/the-art-of-powerful-questions.pdf

"The Global Compact Leaders Summit United Nations Headquarters 24 June 2004, Final Report": from https://appreciativeinquiry.champlain.edu/wp-content/uploads/2016/01/UN-Global-Compact-Appreciative-Inquiry-Summit_rep_fin.pdf

The Ten Principles of the UN Global Compact: https://www.unglobalcompact.org/what-is-gc/mission/principles

"Why the UN Global Compact is a CSR commitment that works": https://resources.ecovadis.com/news-press/why-the-un-global-compact-is-a-csr-commitment-that-works

Finn Voldtofte, 2005, "Introduction to Magic in the Middle" (part five): http://www.theworldcafe.com/tag/magic-in-the-middle/

Conversation Café: http://www.conversationcafe.org/

Chapter 4

Sarah Lozanova, "What Can a School Teach Us about Organizational Agility?": https://www.triplepundit.com/story/2014/what-can-school-teach-us-about-organizational-agility/41261

Sarah Lozanova, "How This Residential Care Home Bumped Employee Engagement Into Overdrive": http://www.triplepundit.com/2014/07/residential-care-home-sees-jump-employee-engagement-dynamic-governance/

The Buurtzorg Story video by Ard Leferink at https://wiki.businessagility.institute/w/CaseStudies:The_Buurtzorg_Story (April 2018)

About Buurtzorg Web: https://www.buurtzorg.com/innovation/buurtzorg-web/

"New hope for Argentina in the recovered factory movement", Oliver Balch, The Guardian, March 12, 2013: https://www.theguardian.com/sustainable-business/argentina-recovered-factory-movement

"Occupy Buenos Aires: the workers' movement that transformed a city, and inspired the world", Matt Kennard and Ana Caistor-Arendar, The Guardian, March 10, 2016: https://www.theguardian.com/cities/2016/mar/10/occupy-buenos-aires-argentina-workers-cooperative-movement

"History of Holacracy; The Discovery of an Evolutionary Algorithm", Brian Robertson, July 28, 2014: https://blog.holacracy.org/history-of-holacracy-c7a8489f8eca,

Why practice Holacracy? https://www.holacracy.org/what-is-holacracy

Manifesto for Agile Software Development at https://agilemanifesto.org/

Pepijn van de Kamp, April 2014, "Holacracy – A Radical Approach to Organizational Design": https://www.researchgate.net/publication/264977984_Holacracy_-_A_Radical_Approach_to_Organizational_Design/link/53fa346a0cf27c365ceed4fe/download

Holacracy Success Stories: *Precision Nutrition*: https://www.holacracy.org/precision-nutrition/

Karsten Heuer, Y2Y conservation senior advisor, on 20 years of Y2Y progress: https://www.youtube.com/watch?v=eqHinMdejEc

Harvey Locke presents "From Yellowstone to Yukon" at the Buffalo Bill Center of the West, Cody, Wyoming: https://www.youtube.com/watch?v=1mDnkTxOy8E

Heather McLeod Grant, Fall 2010, "Transformer: How to build a network to change a system A Case Study of the RE-AMP Energy Network": https://www.reamp.org/wp-content/uploads/2014/01/Monitor-Institute-RE-AMP-Case-Study.pdf

"Case Study: RE-AMP and Midwest Energy News: Communication Strategies that Fast Track Policy Change": https://www.slideshare.net/mediaimpactfunders/tce-casestudy-reampfnlonline

The Appalachian Center for Economic Networks (ACEnet) Mission and History: https://acenetworks.org/about/mission-history/

"When Collective Impact has an Impact: A Cross-Site Study of 25 Collective Impact Initiatives", a collaborative effort between Spark Policy Institute of Denver, CO and ORS Impact of Seattle, WA, 2018: http://sparkpolicy.com/collective-impact-impact-cross-site-study-25-collective-impact-initiatives/

Emily Tow Jackson, "Reforming New York State's juvenile justice system", January 27, 2014: https://www.fsg.org/blog/return-investment-new-york-state-juvenile-justice-reform

Documentaries

The Man Who Stopped the Desert, directed by Mark Dodd: https://www.imdb.com/title/tt1694580/?ref_=nv_sr_srsg_0

Ethiopia Rising: Red Terror to Green Revolution, directed by Mark Dodd: https://www.imdb.com/title/tt5089398/?ref_=nm_flmg_cin_2

Taking Root: The Vision of Wangari Maathai, directed by Lisa Merton & Alan Dater: https://takingrootfilm.com/

Argentina: Hope in Hard Times, directed by Mark Dworkin and Melissa Young: http://www.bullfrogfilms.com/catalog/arg.html

The Take, directed by Avi Lewis: http://www.thetake.org/

Printed in the United States
by Baker & Taylor Publisher Services